THE HERCULEAN HERO

THE RAPE OF DEIANIRA

Detail of a painting by Antonio Pollaiuolo

THE
HERCULEAN
HERO

*in Marlowe, Chapman, Shakespeare
and Dryden*

by

Eugene M. Waith

New York: Columbia University Press
London: Chatto & Windus
1962

COPYRIGHT © 1962
EUGENE M. WAITH
LIBRARY OF CONGRESS CATALOG CARD NUMBER: 62-7592
PRINTED IN GREAT BRITAIN

For M.D.W.

CONTENTS

ILLUSTRATIONS

The design on the title page is a conjectural drawing of
the signboard of the Globe Theatre, reported to have,
as Malone said, "a figure of Hercules supporting the
Globe, under which was written *Totus mundus agit
histrionem.*"

ACKNOWLEDGEMENTS

AN author's indebtedness to other authors whose work has informed and stimulated him and to friends who have given help of many sorts can never be fully acknowledged. I have indicated in the notes the books and articles to which I am most specifically indebted. Here I want to express my gratitude for the personal assistance upon which I have depended heavily. Among my colleagues at Yale I am especially indebted to Bernard Knox of the Classics Department, who read my first chapter in rough draft and again in final form and gave me invaluable suggestions; to Clarence Mendell, who gave me the benefit of his comprehensive knowledge of Seneca; to Charles Seymour of the History of Art Department, whose detailed criticism of my second chapter enabled me to rewrite it entirely; to Talbot Donaldson and Louis Martz, who read the complete manuscript and, by their friendly but penetrating criticism, helped me to see it as a whole. At a later stage, Clifford Leech of the University of Durham was most generous and helpful with his comments on both style and substance, and S. F. Johnson of Columbia University put me greatly in his debt by his encouragement and criticism. I am grateful to Erwin Panofsky for answering at length some queries I addressed to him.

I was given every possible assistance by the staff of the Yale Library—in particular by Miss Marjorie Wynne, the Librarian of the Rare Book Room. Leon Nemoy, a Research Associate of the library, very kindly checked my transcriptions of Biblical glosses in Chapter II. It is a pleasure to record my gratitude to my English publishers for their courtesy and helpfulness throughout.

My thanks are due to the University of Chicago Press for permission to quote from two plays in *The Complete Greek Tragedies*, edited by David Grene and Richmond Lattimore: Sophocles' *The Women of Trachis*, translated by Michael Jameson (Copyright 1957 by the University of Chicago), and Euripides' *Heracles*, translated by William Arrowsmith (Copyright by the University of Chicago, 1956); to the Harvard University Press and the Loeb Classical Library for permission to quote from *Seneca's Tragedies*, edited and translated by F. J. Miller; and to the following publishers for permission to quote from the works listed after their names: the Clarendon Press: B. Jowett's translation of *The Dialogues of Plato* and W. P. Ker's edition of *Essays of John Dryden*; Wayne State University Press: Allan H. Gilbert's *Literary Criticism: Plato to Dryden*; Methuen and Co.: U. M. Ellis-Fermor's edition of Marlowe's *Tamburlaine*; Routledge and Kegan Paul: T. M. Parrott's edition of *The Tragedies of George Chapman*; The Modern Language Association of America: Phyllis B. Bartlett's edition of *The Poems of George Chapman*; Ginn and Co.: G. L. Kittredge's edition of *The Complete Works of Shakespeare*; and Scott, Foresman and Co.: G. R. Noyes's edition of *Selected Dramas* by Dryden.

I am grateful to the galleries and museums which have given me permission to reproduce the illustrations in this book and to Charles Scribner's Sons for permission to use on the title page the conjectural drawing of the sign-board of the Globe Theatre printed on page 50 of Irwin Smith's *Shakespeare's Globe Playhouse* (New York, 1959).

Introduction

THIS is primarily a study of seven English plays. Each asserts its individuality—lives its own life—and most of this book is devoted to a consideration of the seven separate entities. It is also a study of a particular kind of hero, once popular, now less so and often misunderstood. Before he appeared on the stage he was celebrated in epic, and his most recent avatars are probably to be found in nineteenth-century fiction. Though I do not attempt a history of the type, a continuous concern with this kind of hero unites the discussions of individual plays.

The seven plays are Marlowe's *Tamburlaine*, Chapman's *Bussy D'Ambois*, Shakespeare's *Antony and Cleopatra* and *Coriolanus*, and Dryden's *The Conquest of Granada*, *Aureng-Zebe* and *All for Love*. The critical reputations of all of them have fluctuated widely, and only one is rated very high today; yet I believe that all of them can be shown to have great merit as plays and, more generally, as works of art. These merits have often been obscured by a misunderstanding of the protagonist. It is possible to speak of "the protagonist" because, although the heroes of these seven plays are far from being identical, they resemble each other so closely that they can be considered as so many versions of the hero to whom I have already referred. To study the nature of this hero is to get at the central problems of interpretation posed by the plays.

There is no great difficulty in pointing out what sort of man this hero is. He is a warrior of great stature who is guilty of striking departures from the morality of the society in which he lives. The problem is what to think of him. What values does he represent? What is the meaning of his disregard for certain moral conventions? Ultimately, what attitude is expressed in the play towards him, towards the values he represents, and towards society? A great deal of attention has been given to these questions, for it is axiomatic that the author's attitude towards his material is a major part of the meaning of any piece of writing. In a play this attitude is projected in the presentation of each character, so as to evoke a comparable attitude on the part of the audience. To miss these indications of attitude is to risk going far astray in interpretation. Unfortunately, the attitudes critics have found in the plays under consideration range over a wide gamut: the plays justify the values of society, showing the hero to be deeply flawed (a kind of interpretation which can readily be based on the Aristotelian concept of hamartia); they justify the hero, showing society to be wrong; the hero is wrong, but the playwright has such sympathy for him that he is willing to be of the devil's party. In the hands of the critics who furnish these answers the questions sometimes become detached from the plays, and we are invited to consider what a given author would have thought of the hero as an actual person or how the author himself acted in regard to moral conventions. While the answers to such questions may be relevant to the plays, they are apt to mislead us, since there is no guarantee that the author's customary attitudes and beliefs will be carried over into the imaginative world he creates. We are on much safer ground if we seek assistance from the author's response to comparable figures in literature or his awareness of certain literary conventions. The existence of a traditional way of regarding such a hero in literature can help greatly in deciding between the answers that have been given or in finding new ones, for however original an artist may be, he works in relation to the conventions of his medium. Familiarity with the conventions may open the critic's eyes to the meanings they had in the lifetime of the author. A range of values may be suggested for the hero and his situation in society, as one may find in a dictionary a range of meanings for a word. In this study I draw constantly upon traditional depictions of the hero and upon a few other literary conventions in an effort to make clearer the attitudes towards the hero expressed in these plays.

The conventions of genre provide partial answers to some of the questions I have referred to. To say that an author's attitude is or is not the one usually adopted towards an epic hero or a tragic hero immediately narrows the range of possibilities. This is particularly true of writing in the Renaissance, when the theory of genres was well established. With regard to the heroes of these plays, therefore, it is significant that they move in a territory shared by two genres, epic and tragedy.

Dryden is explicit in the essay "Of Heroic Plays" about modelling Almanzor after the heroes of epic, and the protagonists of the earlier plays are also closely akin to epic heroes. Hercules, as he appears in four classical tragedies, provides an instructive analogy which I discuss in the first chapter. Before he was made into a tragic hero his legendary feats had been celebrated in epic form, and the attitude adopted towards him by these dramatists owes something to both genres. It is not that found in some of the better known tragedies, such as *Agamemnon*, or *Oedipus the King*, or *Antigone*, nor is it precisely that of the *Iliad*, the *Odyssey*, or the *Aeneid*, though having much closer affinities with the first of these than with the second or third. Generically speaking, the Hercules plays correspond closely to the plays with which I am mainly concerned.

In the effort to understand these plays Hercules is an especially useful figure because of the particular heroic characteristics assigned to him by myth. Though for reasons which I discuss in the first two chapters he was for many Greeks and Romans and for many men of the Renaissance the hero of heroes, he was also an extreme example of character traits which were often deplored in later ages. Such reverence for a hero whose distinctive traits might be expected to repel more than attract suggests a way of looking at a Tamburlaine or an Almanzor. A number of striking allusions show that the English playwrights I discuss were aware of resemblances between their heroes and Hercules, though there is no indication that any one depiction of him served them as a model. On the basis of such resemblances I refer to the protagonists of these plays as Herculean heroes.

Although my object is to illuminate these seven plays rather than to rewrite the history of heroic drama or propose a special theory of tragedy, certain beliefs about the relationship between tragedy and the heroic inevitably underlie such a study as this. Some of them had best be left to emerge from the discussion of particular plays, but others should perhaps be stated frankly at the outset. I do not exclude from the category of tragedy the "heroic play", whether we mean by that term what Dryden meant, referring to the drama of his time, or whether we also mean some of the predecessors of those Restoration plays. I believe that the concept of the heroic was so integral a part of the concept of the tragic throughout the periods I am treating, that there were very few tragedies which were not to some extent heroic. As Cedric Whitman says, "Much has been written about the tragic character, but it has not perhaps been sufficiently noticed that the tragic character is first the heroic character; it is so, at least in origin, and it remains consistently so in Sophocles."[1] It remains so whenever tragedies portray men "better" or "greater" than ourselves, as it was usually assumed, down to the end of the seventeenth century, that they should do. Many years ago, William Macneile Dixon wrote that tragedy "leans upon our native attachment to the heroic",[2] and more recently Peter Alexander has sustained a very similar thesis.[3] The heroic looks always towards some wonderful possibility in man, and this is a theme to which tragedy has continually returned even in its sternest depictions of failure. Richard B. Sewall says:

> Ideally, tragedy reveals simultaneously, in one complete action, man's total possibilities and his most grievous limitations—all that he should and can do as creator of good, all that he does or fails to do or cannot do as creature of fate, chance, or his own evil nature. Actually, no tragedy can tell the whole truth. All tragedies to this extent only approximate Tragedy, and the stress on one side or the other of the paradox of man differs from one tragedy to another.[4]

It is more usual today to think of the portrayal of human limitations as the distinctive feature of tragedy and consequently to feel that the heroic play lacks a dimension essential to tragedy, but this is to overlook an element frequently present in both heroic poems and heroic plays. A keen awareness of limitations is often to be found in the epic (the *Iliad* is a good example) and in the plays which most clearly imitate it. I think it must be concluded that if one puts formal considerations aside for the moment and considers only "tragic vision" and "heroic vision", one finds a considerable area of shared concerns. However, a distinction may be drawn on the basis of stress. The more heavily it falls on "total possibilities", the more heroic is the vision, and hence tragedies in which this stress is very marked are truly heroic tragedies, whereas those in which the stress falls mainly on "grievous limitations" are the least heroic of tragedies. All of the tragedies which I shall discuss are heroic, according to this distinction, but to varying degrees the stress on limitation is also felt. In referring to these different stresses I use the terms "heroic potential" and "tragic limitation" without implying that either one belongs exclusively to one genre or the other.

I believe that the Herculean hero not only is a legitimate kind of tragic hero, but furnishes the most striking example of an attitude which some recent critics consider an important part of tragedy. To quote Sewall once more:

> The tragic vision impels the man of action to fight against his destiny, kick against the pricks, and state his case before God or his fellows. It impels the artist, in his fictions, toward what Jaspers calls "boundary situations", man at the limits of his sovereignty—Job on the ash-heap, Prometheus on the crag, Oedipus in his moment of self-discovery, Lear on the heath, Ahab on his lonely quarter-deck.[5]

No hero fights harder against his destiny or tries more desperately to extend the limits of his sovereignty than does the Herculean hero.

Nevertheless, I do not present the Herculean hero as the typical protagonist of tragedy nor even of heroic tragedy. He differs almost as much from Corneille's Horace or Rodrigue as from Shakespeare's Hamlet or Lear. Hercules and his successors comprise a distinct type whose characteristics are analysed in the opening chapters. Consequently, although my discussion of the plays in which this hero appears will presumably have some bearing on other tragedies and on the general problems of tragedy and heroic already referred to, it is aimed primarily at a special variety of tragic experience produced when the Herculean hero is portrayed.

I

Demigod

Think you there was or might be such a man
As this I dreamt of?
                    Gentle madam, no.

THE hero of mythology belongs to the realm of the semi-
divine, the wonderful, the mysterious. Though he is a man,
he is so far removed from the ordinary that the generic classifica-
tion hardly contains him. His origins may lie in religious ritual;
his life is imbued with meanings only half understood. His
exploits are strange mixtures of beneficence and crime, of
fabulous quests and shameful betrayals, of triumph over wicked
enemies and insensate slaughter of the innocent, yet the career
is always a testimony to the greatness of a man who is almost a
god—a greatness which has less to do with goodness as it is
usually understood than with the transforming energy of the
divine spark. This is not to say that tales about the hero excuse
his moral defects, but rather that they point to a special
morality. What matters most is something difficult to define,
which pushes the hero to the outermost reaches of the human
and even beyond. To the Greeks this quality, which makes the
hero a dream-image of what a man might be, was *areté*, the
ideal of the nobility, the *aristoi*. The Romans called it *virtus*,
a word related to both *vir* and *vis*, "man" and "energy".

In his chapter on areté Werner Jaeger writes, "There is no
complete equivalent for the word areté in modern English: its
oldest meaning is a combination of proud and courtly morality
with warlike valour."[1] Courage in battle is the basis of this
ancient ideal and remains central to it even when it is later
broadened to include nobility of mind. The desire for honour,
even carried to the point where we might brand it as un-
justifiable pride, is as Jaeger points out, "an essential concomitant".[2]

Hercules, the performer of legendary feats of strength, the
warrior whom only the gods could vanquish, embodies these
essentially heroic characteristics and something else as well.

HERCULES AND THE HIND

Statue from Pompei

Sir Kenneth Clark, in discussing the frieze of the Mausoleum, applies the useful term "moral energy" to the warrior heroes:

> We feel in every line of these purposeful bodies a capacity for endurance and self-sacrifice for which the word moral is not inappropriate. Of this the Greeks themselves were, of course, perfectly conscious; and it was as an embodiment of moral energy, triumphing through physical means, that they created the myth of Herakles.[3]

The virtue of these heroes is in their force. Quite naturally, Hercules is their prototype. In him the force is almost divine.

Although Hercules has often been thought of as *the hero*, the embodiment of what is quintessentially heroic, his career is not a paradigm of the career of all heroes. It reveals a strength and fierceness which relate him more closely to the Achilles who refuses to be reconciled with the Greeks, for example, or the Ajax who commits suicide to defend his heroic reputation than to the Odysseus who wins out through cunning or the Aeneas who sacrifices himself to the great purpose of founding Rome. Certain of the great warrior heroes, then, are more "Herculean" than others, but Hercules differs (in important ways) from even those who resemble him most closely. "This is no Achilles," says R. C. Jebb, emphasizing the differences, "no image of that chivalry which Aeolian legend had delineated and Ionian poetry adorned . . . he has never known such tears as came into the eyes of the young Achaean warrior, when the aged king of Troy, kneeling at his feet, kissed the hand that had slain Hector."[4] Hercules, the Dorian hero, is a more primitive embodiment of areté than Achilles. He is incapable, as Jebb suggests, of the scene with Priam, and is even more rigorous, more god-like, in his wrath. In Hercules the core of primitive strength, never completely transmuted by the refining power of more civilized ideals, is touched with the strangeness and mystery which belong to a demigod.

The outlines of the figure of this particular hero are to be sought first in the many stories of Hercules recorded by the classical mythographers and poets, and next in four classical plays which, because of their dramatic form, are more directly relevant to the seventeenth-century plays which will occupy

B

the foreground of this study. The present chapter deals with these earlier versions of Hercules. Renaissance modifications of this classical figure are presented in the following chapter.

Much has been written about the origins of the myth, its meaning, and the successive layers of development by which both myth and meaning grew. The famous twelve labours performed for Eurystheus make a coherent body of legend which may preserve the kernel of the original Dorian conception.[5] In these stories the hero, naked except for his lion-skin, and armed with the simplest of weapons, his club, or sometimes his bow, overcomes giants and monsters, and fearlessly penetrates even the domain of the gods of the underworld, whence he leads the conquered Cerberus away. These are "tall tales" of a fabulous strong-man, but they are obviously more than that: they present a concept of the heroic—of "moral energy". Whether they signify the supremacy of Dorian man in Argolis or of man in the universe, they clearly tell of a wonderful force inherent in the human body, capable of conquering this world and even of defying the world beyond. Terrible as are the manifestations of this force, there is no doubt that its effects are beneficial to mankind.

Both in classical times and later, these stories were sometimes interpreted allegorically as triumphs of man's higher nature over bestiality and evil. The story of Hercules and Antaeus, which eventually became attached to the stories of the labours, seems to invite such an interpretation. The hero wrestles with the giant son of Gaia (the earth), who regains his strength whenever he touches the ground. To defeat him, Hercules holds him in the air until he is weak. In this instance the hero's *virtus* can readily be seen as a noble force which is superior to mere earthly power. The Sophist, Prodicus, with a teacher's compulsion to make the lesson of the labours quite clear, told a purely allegorical story of how Hercules as a young man came to a place where two paths branched off, one leading up a steep hill, the other into a pleasant glade. At the dividing point two fair women met him, one modest and sober, urging him to take the steep path; the other meretriciously seductive, using her arts to attract him to the other path.[6] The hero, of course, chose Areté rather than Hedoné.

Around the central Dorian core of the twelve labours are

grouped many other stories of Hercules, deriving apparently from Boeotia, Thessaly and elsewhere. A number of them bear on his special relationship to the gods. The story of his begetting is one—Zeus's seduction of Alcmena, by impersonating her husband, Amphitryon. The wrath of the jealous Hera pursues Hercules to his death. This motif is present in the twelve labours, too, for it is Hera who makes Hercules serve Eurystheus, but a far more dreadful example of her wrath is the madness she sends to make him kill his children and, in Euripides' version, his wife, Megara, as well. Only after his death, when Zeus has translated him to the heavens, does Hera allow herself to become reconciled. Where exceptional human potentiality is stressed in the twelve labours, here divine favour or divine wrath are what determine the hero's career. In all later treatments of Hercules one or the other of these complementary views of his situation is emphasized.

Though Hercules is shown chiefly as warrior and champion, he also has his amorous adventures. Perhaps the only real love-story is that of the beautiful youth, Hylas, whose loss Hercules mourns. But there are many women in his life: the fifty daughters of Thespius, whom he enjoys (some say in one night) in his youth; Megara, whom he marries and later kills in his madness; Omphale, whom he is forced to serve as a slave because of his murder of Iphitus; Hesione, whom he rescues from a monster; Deianira, whom he marries and also saves from the centaur, Nessus; and Iole, the captive who arouses Deianira's fatal jealousy. Although there are no romantic attachments in the stories of Hercules' relationships with these women, the incidents involving Megara and those involving Deianira have an extraordinary importance. The story of Megara and the madness of Hercules is, as we have seen, the crucial example of the wrath of Hera. The jealousy of Deianira is part of one of the most famous of all the stories—the suffering of Hercules in the shirt, or poisoned robe, of Nessus, and his death on the flaming pyre on Mount Oeta. It is a story which can be told either to assert the limits beyond which even the greatest of men cannot go, or, by emphasizing Hercules' ultimate reward, to demonstrate the transcendence of the hero. Wilamowitz juxtaposes the human and the divine elements in the nature of Hercules in a romantic epigram, characteristic of his style and of his sympathetic perception of the meaning of the myth: "Mensch gewesen, Gott geworden; Mühen erduldet, Himmel erworben."[7]

The stories of the madness and death of the hero became the subjects of two Greek tragedies, later reworked by Seneca. Sophocles treated the death of Heracles[8] in *The Women of Trachis* and Euripides, the madness in *Heracles*. Both plays are remarkable and remarkably neglected.

The Women of Trachis[9] is a powerful dramatic presentation of the ironic fulfilment of a heroic career and the horrible disparity between justice and event. As Jameson points out, "the play begins with his wife's anxiety over Heracles' last labors, which will mean the 'end' (*telos*) for him and for her, in all its ambiguity . . .".[10] Waiting for his return, Deianira says, "Now he wins through to the end of all his labors" (l. 36), and she speaks to their son Hyllus of the prophecy that, having carried out his present task (the conquest of Oechalia), Heracles would either meet death or enjoy a happy life for the rest of his time (ll. 79-81). The puzzle, so typical of oracles, about what the end will be dominates the entire play. When Deianira again refers to the prophecy her very words are charged with double meaning. They may be translated: "He said that this was fated by the Gods to be the final limit of the labors of Heracles" (ll. 169-70 in Jameson's translation), or "Such, he said, was the doom ordained by the gods to be accomplished in the toils of Heracles" (Jebb's translation). The Greek supports both meanings: that the doom of death or a happy life merely marks the end of the labours or that it is to be accomplished in the labours, as if it were somehow inherent in them. At the end of the play, when Heracles realizes that Nessus, the centaur, gave Deianira the poison which is consuming him, he understands that his death was determined by an adventure long ago, and the meaning of another prophecy then becomes clear: that his death would be caused by "someone dead". There is a terrible logic in the working out of the prophecies but no justice for the slayer of giants and monsters. Looking at his tortured body, one might be moved to ask with Kent, "Is this the promised end?"

This emphasis on the unexpected horror of the end may in part explain a troublesome peculiarity in the structure of the

play. Only in the last quarter of it does Heracles appear; up to
that time Deianira is the dominant figure. Because of these
proportions, and for other reasons which will presently emerge,
the play has sometimes been taken as the tragedy of Deianira
or as a double tragedy.[11] However, the long delay of Heracles'
appearance—a delay filled with eager questions about his
activities, with answers containing both false and true information, and with mounting anticipation of the "promised end"—
undoubtedly heightens the dramatic effect of the part of the
play in which he is present. There is scarcely a moment when
he is not the topic of conversation. The end of his labours is the
end to which the play always points.

In Deianira Sophocles has created a most appealing figure.
She is the first speaker, and her opening words reveal the pathos
of her situation:

> It was long ago that someone first said:
> You cannot know a man's life before the man
> has died, then only can you call it good or bad.
> But I know mine before I've come to Death's house
> and I can tell that mine is heavy and sorrowful.

She recalls her fear that she might be the bride of the river-god,
Acheloüs, and her joy when Heracles came to fight him. But
then, as the wife of Heracles, her life became a continual anxiety.
The pathos of her situation as an ordinary mortal married to a
hero is convincingly imagined in this opening speech and in
subsequent dialogues between Deianira and the Nurse, Hyllus,
and the Chorus. It is deepened in her conversations with the
Messenger and Lichas about the captive Oechalian women
who are sent ahead of Heracles. Sophocles obtains the maximum
dramatic effect from her pity for these women, and particularly
for Iole, for as Deianira asks questions about them she is first
told only half-truths about them but finally the whole truth that
Iole is her husband's mistress, for whose sake the conquest of
Oechalia was undertaken. Deianira's discovery of a greater un-
happiness than any she has known before carries out the
ominous suggestion of her first words and prefigures the yet
more terrible discovery of the fatal power of Nessus' charm,
which brings the career of Heracles to its unexpected end. After
suppressing her jealousy of Iole, she has dipped a robe in the

blood of the centaur, believing his promise that it will act as a love-charm to bring back her husband's affection. Then after sending the robe to Heracles, she has seen some wool soaked with the blood burst into flame when exposed to the sun. Her fears are almost immediately confirmed by an account of Heracles' suffering in the poisoned robe, and she determines on suicide. The pattern of her discovery of ever deeper sorrow fuses here with the larger pattern of the end of the labours of Heracles. Though Deianira is an appealing and moving character, what gives significance and emotional power to her story is her relationship to Heracles. Separation from this greatest of men is a torment; the knowledge that she has killed him is unbearable. Instead of turning sympathy and attention away from Heracles, she focuses both upon him. No character could more effectively portray his unique worth.

The praise of Heracles so often reiterated by Deianira, the Chorus and other characters does not eclipse the actions which are discreditable to him, notably the murder of Iphitus and the affair with Iole. Iphitus is an innocent victim of Heracles' desire for revenge against Eurytus, the father of Iphitus, and Heracles takes advantage of him when he is not on guard. Zeus punishes him by making him serve Omphale. The consuming passion for Iole leads to the destruction of Oechalia and (what touches us much more) the insult to Deianira. To these two serious counts against Heracles another is added in the account of his reception of the poisoned robe. Lichas, the bearer of the robe, is dashed to death, another innocent victim of the hero's wrath. The surprising thing is that the hero is hardly blamed for any of these actions, though all of them are recognized as discreditable in themselves. Lichas partly defends the murder of Iphitus by saying that the gods themselves would not have objected if it had been carried out openly; Heracles' infatuation for Iole is largely blamed on Aphrodite, even by Deianira; the story of Lichas' death, though told by Hyllus with circumstantial detail, is only part of the story of the suffering of Heracles. In each case the fault is recognized but passed by as if it had no real importance in the evaluation of the hero. The last instance is the most striking, for the point to Hyllus' narration is the concluding indictment of Deianira, already sick with fear for what she may have done:

Mother, this is what you have planned and done to my father,
and you are caught. For this, Justice who punishes
and the Fury will requite you. If it is right
for a son, I curse you, and it *is* right, since you
have given me the right by killing the best of all men
on earth, such as you shall never see again.   (ll. 807-12)

The horror is not what Heracles has done to Iphitus, Lichas, or
Deianira, but what has been done to him. There is never any
suggestion that his suffering is a punishment for misdeeds.[12]

Before Heracles enters, the already familiar character of the
mythical hero has thus been reaffirmed: a wonderful and, in
some respects, terrible man—"the best of all men on earth".
These reminders of heroic greatness are essential to the force
of the peripeteia and perhaps also to the very acceptance of the
man whom Sophocles finally brings before the eyes of the
spectators. The hero is carried on to the stage in a litter. When
he awakes from the sleep into which he has fallen, he at first
ignores the sympathetic lamentations of those around him and
speaks, as if alone, to himself and to Zeus, insistently protesting
the magnitude and the injustice of his suffering. Gruesome
description of the corrosive poison is mixed with reminiscences
of the heroic exploits and with bitter complaints that "a woman,
a female, in no way like a man" (l. 1062) should have reduced
him to a pathetic creature, "sobbing like a girl" (l. 1072). The
hero's feelings are not only violent but totally unconcealed. To
an audience accustomed to more restraint they may seem
almost indecent, and yet they are both psychologically credible
and artistically appropriate. Everything about this hero is
shown as larger than life and his response to every situation is
immediate and direct. To the Chorus there is nothing discreditable in Heracles' behaviour:

My friends, I hear and shudder at the king's misfortunes—
so great a man, hounded by such suffering.   (ll. 1044-5)

O unhappy Greece, I can see how great
a mourning you shall have if you lose this man.   (ll. 1112-13)

If it is difficult for a modern sensibility to accept Heracles'
colossal complaints, it is even more difficult to accept his lack

of consideration for Deianira and Hyllus. Once he has understood from Hyllus that the guile of Nessus was responsible for
Deianira's unwitting act and that she has killed herself out of
remorse, Heracles seems to put her entirely out of his mind.
With a composure very different from his recent mood he proceeds to make plans for his death. He exacts two promises from
his son. One is to construct a funeral pyre on Mount Oeta, place
his body on it, and ignite the pyre. Most reluctantly Hyllus
agrees to carry his father and arrange for the pyre but not to
build and ignite it with his own hands, for that would be
murder. Heracles is satisfied and grateful, but there is one more
"small favour". Hyllus is to marry Iole, whom he blames for
his mother's suicide and his father's imminent death. He resists
until Heracles makes obedience a test of filial piety. Then he
agrees.

To many critics the hero who can act in this way is gross,
brutal, self-centred, and untragic.[13] There is not the slightest
indication of such a judgment in the play. The hero's disregard
for others is a striking feature of his isolation and of his stature.
There is no question of his reciprocating the feelings others have
for him. His self-absorption is a concomitant of the primitive
areté which makes obligations to others secondary to the hero's
devotion to his own integrity. That he is concerned for Iole's
welfare is a whim which even his son may not question. The
major concern of Heracles at the end is a death suitable to his
greatness. Hyllus, who has the last speech, is so far from
reproaching his father that he expresses only dismay that the
gods permit such suffering:

> Raise him, my helpers. From you let me have
> much compassion now for what I do.
> You see how little compassion the Gods
> have shown in all that's happened; they
> who are called our fathers, who begot us,
> can look on such suffering.
> No one can foresee what is to come.
> What is here now is pitiful for us
> and shameful for the Gods;
> but of all men it is hardest for him
> who is the victim of this disaster.
> [*Hyllus turns to the leader of the Chorus.*

Maiden, come from the house with us.[14]
You have seen a terrible death
and agonies, many and strange, and there is
nothing here which is not Zeus.

These last words of the play restate the major theme of ironic fulfilment with a bold emphasis on injustice. It has often been remarked that nothing is said of the apotheosis which is to follow, unless, as Bowra suggests,[15] Heracles' specific directions for the funeral pyre are intended to remind the audience that the hero will rise from the flames. Even if this is the case, it is no more than a hint, and the impression left by the end of the play is one of horrible finality. It seems, in fact, to be the recognition of an end, rather than of a promised reward, which brings about the change in Heracles' behaviour. He has been raging until he hears that the blood of Nessus has been the instrument of his undoing. Then, suddenly, he understands the true meaning of the prophecies:

Woe, woe is me! This is my miserable end.
Lost! I am lost! I see the light no longer.
Ah! now I know the doom that is upon me.
(ll. 1143-5)

Understanding brings neither remorse nor a radically altered view of himself but a calm detachment which enables him to accept this end as a limit foreordained. Fortitude returns as he faces what is clearly now the final exploit, endurance of death. Having obtained the promises of Hyllus, he says:

The true
respite from suffering is this—my final end.   (ll. 1255-6)

Come then, O my tough soul,
before this sickness is stirred again,
set a steel bit in my mouth,
hold back the shriek, and make an end
of this unwanted, welcome task.   (ll. 1259-63)

By omitting specific reference to the apotheosis to follow, the play seems to balance tragic limitation against heroic potential. A marvel has terminated, and wonder that such greatness could exist in a man mixes with bitterness that even he must die. As Achilles says:

> For not even the strength of Herakles fled away from destruction,
> although he was dearest of all to lord Zeus, son of Kronos,
> but his fate beat him under, and the wearisome anger of Hera.[16]

The hero of this tragedy is, without any doubt, very different from most tragic heroes. He is almost god-like in valour and strength; his suffering, his rages, and his pride are so vast that they are difficult to comprehend. And, as Bowra says, "Heracles cannot be judged by humanitarian standards."[17] His injuries to others and his infringements of society's moral codes are incidental to a career whose end is an undiluted tragedy for society. If he is not in the ordinary sense of the word a sympathetic character, he inspires in the other characters extraordinary love and loyalty, and becomes almost an object of veneration.

The hero of Euripides' *Heracles* is made thoroughly sympathetic. In this respect, as in many others, the two tragedies differ importantly, but in one respect they are remarkably alike. Both of them obtain their major effect from the contrast between the seemingly invincible hero of the twelve labours and a man almost broken by suffering, who nevertheless finds strength to endure. Instead of the physical suffering in the poisoned robe, Euripides' play presents the mental suffering of Heracles when he discovers the crimes he has committed in his madness, but the cause of the suffering is as external in one case as the other. Both tragedies depict a universe hostile to the greatest of men.

Where Sophocles consigns the portrayal of the victorious hero to the reminiscences of other characters—mainly of Deianira, Euripides brings him on the stage with a maximum of theatrical effectiveness. The situation is carefully prepared. The opening of the play, occurring just before the return of Heracles from Hades with Cerberus, shows how much he is needed by his family and by Thebes; for Lycus, who has seized power, is that emblem of evil, the ruthless tyrant. To eliminate any threat to his position he now plans to put to death Amphitryon, Megara, and the children of Heracles. He exults over his helpless victims, reminding them of the power he holds and ridiculing the mere physical strength of the man who "made his reputation fighting beasts" (l. 158).[18] Heracles, who is now gone for good, was in any case no true warrior, since he fought with his hands and with a bow instead of with spear and shield. In spite of Amphitryon's defence of his son's weapon, the power of Heracles seems to be a thing of the past. The chorus, after extolling one by one the famous labours, says: "To your hands your house still turns, and you are gone!" (ll. 434-5). At this moment the hero appears and adds one more to the long list of benefactions given by the chorus: he kills Lycus and thus becomes an agent of justice and divine retribution, a scourge of tyrants.

Euripides lays great stress on the externality of the means by which the great forces of Heracles are perverted. Iris appears on the stage with Madness, who is to execute the will of Hera by goading Heracles to crime. Hera's motives are shown to be jealousy and fear: "For the gods are nothing, and men prevail, if this one man escape" (ll. 841-2). Even Madness, the daughter of Night, is depicted as rebelling against the role she is to play, and offering a defence of Heracles in order to prevent Hera from making a mistake. Inevitably, she is silenced by Iris and obliged to perform her task. Through this episode Heracles is shown as the victim of divine malevolence and a kind of champion of man against the gods. If there is some ambiguity in the words which end *The Women of Trachis*: "There is nothing here which is not Zeus"—some suggestion that all may in some mysterious way be right in spite of seeming so wrong—there is none in Euripides' depiction of the malice of Hera. An innocent hero is made to murder his children and his wife, supposing that he is attacking the family of his tormentor, Eurystheus. The irony is compounded. Madness comes upon him just after he has saved his family from the cruelty of Lycus, and after the Chorus, celebrating his victory, has proclaimed him the "better king . . . if justice still finds favor among the blessed gods" (ll. 809-14).

The central importance of Hera in the action contrasts oddly with Heracles' avowed disbelief in the gods. Towards the end of the play, when he is offered the consolation that the gods have also done dreadful things, he says:

> Ah, all this has no bearing on my grief;
> but I do not believe the gods commit
> adultery, or bind each other in chains.

> I never did believe it; I never shall;
> nor that one god is tyrant of the rest.
> If god is truly god, he is perfect,
> lacking nothing. These are poets' wretched lies.
>
> (ll. 1340-6)

William Arrowsmith interprets this seeming inconsistency as an important indication of the nature of the force represented by Hera:

> The consequences of Heracles' words for the play are,
> I suggest, this: that the story of Hera's action as
> dramatized is true enough, but the Hera who afflicts
> Heracles as she does thereby renounces any claim to the
> kind of divinity which Heracles asserts . . . [The play]
> converts her into a hovering symbol of all the unknown
> and unknowable forces which compel Heracles and men to
> suffer tragically and without cause or sense.[19]

Interpreted in this way, Heracles' words can be accepted without denying the greatness of the power brought to bear on the hero. We see the hero confronted by the terrible force of the irrational.

Greatness itself may be dangerous. This idea became tiresomely familiar in the Stoic *sententiae* of Seneca and his imitators and in the medieval portrayals of the wheel of fortune, but it was also Greek. Although it is easily confused with the condemnation of *hubris* or pride, the two ideas are distinct. In Euripides' tragedy it is especially clear that Heracles is not punished for presumption but because he is so much greater than the average man that Hera fears for the gods if he goes unchecked. Her acts are presented as defensive warfare. As G. M. A. Grube puts it, "In this world governed by powerful, ruthless, superhuman forces, greatness is dangerous in and by itself, without sin on the great one's part, except the sin of greatness."[20]

The latter part of the play is entirely concerned with Heracles' attitude towards his crime, towards himself and towards the gods. When Amphitryon has made clear to him what he has done, he at first determines upon suicide. The burden of persuading him to live falls chiefly upon Theseus, whom he has rescued from the underworld, and who has now

come to offer help to Heracles in his war against Lycus. Confronted with the horrible spectacle of Heracles' victims, he
decides instantly that this is the work of Hera, and turns to
counsel the hero. The advice he gives in the course of his
dialogue with Heracles could be put in the form of a syllogism:
endurance distinguishes the hero from ordinary men; you, as
the benefactor of mankind, are the very type of the hero; therefore you must endure rather than take your life. When the hero
has been persuaded by Theseus, he says,

> The man who cannot bear up under fate
> could never face the weapons of a man.
> I shall prevail against death.   (ll. 1349-51)

A crime has been committed. The real criminal is a goddess,
but the human agent must acknowledge his guilt and bear the
sorrow of knowing what he has done, even though no one
blames him for it. Endurance is emphasized here even more
than in the last moments of *The Women of Trachis*. The action
chosen by Euripides enables him to make an effective contrast
between the physical might through which Heracles' nobility
is expressed in the first part of the play and the inner fortitude
he musters at the end. The one great temptation to which he is
exposed is despair, and the core of his heroism is revealed when
he determines to stand up to whatever fate sends him.[21]

His reason for not committing suicide fits well with his dis-
claimer of belief in the gods of legend. Without denying a power
greater than himself—Hera or necessity—he makes his decision
on the basis of human considerations. He must endure his fate
if he is to be able to face "the weapons of a man", and he must
acknowledge the bonds of friendship for Theseus and of love
for his foster-father, Amphitryon.

In Euripides' play the hero is compellingly represented as a
human being—he is "reduced to his humanity", as Arrowsmith
puts it, "as the condition of the only heroism that counts"[22]—
but he remains a marvellously exceptional human being. The
point is made early in the play when Lycus tries unsuccessfully
to prove that Heracles is entirely ordinary. At the end it is
reiterated in the demonstration of his extraordinary courage in
facing the vast, hostile powers beyond his control or understanding, and the horrible consequences of his crime.[23]

Though it seems at first surprising that Hercules, the strong man, the warrior, the seducer, should have been a favourite with the Stoics, the attitudes reflected in these two plays (particularly those seen in Euripides) help to explain why this was so. The hero who returned victorious from the underworld to rescue his family and his city from a cruel tyrant had an obvious appeal to the Stoic, with his concern for universal order and the dignity of individual man.[24] So, for different but equally obvious reasons, did the hero who bravely endured the sufferings visited upon him by the gods or by fate. Finally, Hercules as benefactor of humanity was easily taken as a symbol for the Stoic's sense of obligation to society. A single sentence of Cicero's gives the kernel of the Stoic view. Refuting the Epicurean position from the Stoic point of view, Cicero asks, whether it is preferable to live in calm enjoyment of pleasure free from all pain and fear of pain or be a benefactor of the human race and bring safety to the distressed even at the cost of enduring the dolours [*aerumnas*, suggesting both pains and labours] of Hercules.[25] Seneca refers to Hercules several times in his *Moral Essays*. In *De Beneficiis* (I, xiii, 3) Hercules appears as the benefactor who conquered nothing for himself, but all for the public good.[26] In two essays his name is coupled with that of Cato, as in *De Constantia* (II, 2), where Cato is said to be a truer exemplar of the wise man than Hercules or Ulysses.[27] If the combination of names is startling, the explanation is immediately forthcoming. The Stoics, says Seneca, call these men wise because they were unconquered by struggles, were despisers of pleasure, and victors over all terrors. Though Cato is the supreme exemplar of this kind of wisdom, Hercules is shown to be a mythic embodiment of the qualities which Cato displayed as a truly human being. The difference Seneca points to is not one of type or degree but of mode of being. In *De Tranquillitate Animi* (XVI, 1-4), in a discussion of the sad fate of the good man who comes to a bad end, Cato appears along with Socrates, Rutilius, Pompey and Cicero. Hercules follows shortly. The important thing is the way these men died, says Seneca; we shouldn't weep for Hercules, burned alive, or for Regulus or Cato, for all of them, by sacrificing time made themselves eternal.[28] In this Stoic view the physical strength of Hercules is identified with moral strength as in the allegorical interpretations of the labours or in the story of Hercules at the crossroads. Hercules becomes the supreme example of greatness of soul, of steadfastness, of scorn of fate and circumstance, of self-sacrifice, and of aspiration for the highest. Hercules amid the flames of Mount Oeta returns to the purity of nature—to primal fire.[29]

The Stoic idealization of Hercules, which was to have a strong influence on the Renaissance, modifies the older concept without adding anything totally new. Hercules, as we have seen, had always been thought of as a benefactor of humanity, but the Stoics associate his benefactions with a degree of self-sacrifice which the stories of Hercules hardly seem to support. Again, the tendency to allegorize episodes from the hero's life was ancient, but the Stoics push this tendency to the point of paradox when they represent the wrathful and sometimes lustful Hercules as an emblem of mastery over the passions. In emphasizing his return to primal fire they go back to a very ancient part of the legend, but one which neither Sophocles nor Euripides had developed.

In Seneca's two Hercules plays[30] many of these Stoic views appear, though, as some scholars have pointed out,[31] the Stoicism of Seneca's drama is eclectic and fitful. *Hercules Furens* begins like Euripides' play, by which it was clearly influenced: praise of the great benefactions of Hercules alternates with lamentations over the state of a world dominated by the tyrant Lycus. Seneca gives a characteristically rhetorical presentation of Hercules' virtues in the dialogue of Lycus with Megara and Amphitryon. He adds considerably to Euripides' debate between Lycus and Amphitryon and prefaces it with a debate between Lycus and Megara, begun when the tyrant offers to marry her. These changes and additions form an excellent example of the sort of rhetorical elaboration inherent in the tradition represented by Seneca's father, the *rhetor*.[32] When the antagonist questions the divinity of Hercules' parentage and even the bravery of his deeds, Amphitryon replies with comparisons to Bacchus and Apollo, and with catalogues of some of the greatest exploits. In this way the heroism of Hercules is questioned more basically and at far greater length than in Euripides. It is the strategy of Lycus to show that he and Hercules are essentially similar as men whose strength brings them authority. If this is so, then Megara and Amphitryon have no reason to prefer Hercules to the man who now has the upper hand, and it might be added that the audience must then see Hercules as no more than an ambitious adventurer. Not that Seneca leaves room for even momentary doubt about how the question is to be resolved. Yet the question is of central importance, and the unhesitating loyalty of Megara and Amphitryon is an effective way of asserting the difference between the hero and the man whose ambition is merely quantitatively superior to that of the ordinary mortal. In this debate the separation of Hercules not only from Lycus but from all other men is given an almost schematic clarity, as if Seneca were developing the components of an idea present in Euripides.

Seneca draws fully upon his poetic resources to underscore the extraordinary superiority of his hero by associating him with the light, as to a lesser extent both Sophocles and Euripides had done. The Chorus, at its first entry, gives a description of the morning light driving away the pale stars of the night, and Megara's first speech is an invocation to her husband to burst forth, dispelling the shadows (of the underworld, and figuratively, of unhappy Thebes). There are many allusions to his descent into the world of darkness, where, according to Megara, he has gone in order to ascend into the heavens.[33] Hercules' first words when he returns to the upper world are a prayer to Apollo as the "lord of kindly light" (l. 592), and Theseus' lengthy description of Hades in Act III, a set-piece which has often been censured, is a rhetorical elaboration of the dark side of the contrast. The association of Hercules with light gains by one's knowledge of the flames on Mount Oeta from which his spirit will finally ascend to become a star. Though this story is not treated in *Hercules Furens* it is ingeniously anticipated in the opening description of dawn, where the chorus depicts the sun rising over "Oeta's ridge". When madness comes upon Hercules it appears to him as a darkness at noon: "medium diem cinxere tenebrae" (ll. 939-40), and the bitter irony of the end of the play is expressed in his longing for the infernal shades as a place to hide from the world's knowledge of his crimes.

The cosmic significance of Hercules and his disinterested motives are shown in his prayers after the slaying of Lycus. Amphitryon tells him to pray that his tasks be ended. He replies:

HERCULES AND ANTAEUS
Bronze by Antonio Pollaiuolo

Myself will I frame prayers worthy of Jupiter and me: May
heaven abide in its own place, and earth and sea; may the eternal
stars hold on their way unhindered; may deep peace brood upon
the nations; may the harmless country's toil employ all iron, and
may swords lie hid; may no raging tempest stir up the sea, no
fires leap forth from angered Jove, no river, fed by winter's snows,
sweep away the uptorn fields. Let poisons cease to be. Let no
destructive herb swell with harmful juice. May savage and cruel
tyrants rule no more. If earth is still to produce any wickedness,
let her make haste, and if she is preparing any monster, let it be
mine.   (ll. 926-39)

Immediately after this speech his madness begins. This is the
monster he has to meet. In Seneca as in Euripides the criminal
truly responsible for the murder of Megara and the children
is Juno, who fears the power of Hercules. Seneca brings her
onstage as prologue to announce her terrible plan *in propria
persona*, and prepare in this way for the onset of the madness.
When it comes it is not personified but portrayed realistically
as a change in the mental processes of the hero. He imagines
that some of the monsters he has slain are restored to life in the
heavens, and soon he is planning to storm the heavens himself,
in case Jove forgets his promise to deify Hercules. Seeing his
sons, he imagines them to be the children of Lycus, seizes one
of them, and drags him from the stage. Amphitryon then
watches his offstage action and describes the murder of the
children and of Megara, whom Hercules thinks to be Juno.
Thus some of what is reported by the Messenger in Euripides
occurs onstage and the rest is reported as it occurs, punctuated
by the offstage voices of the participants.[34] The greater
immediacy achieved by this treatment makes the crime of
Hercules more shocking and thus heightens the paradox that
one who can be guilty of such repellent cruelty can also be the
great benefactor of the first scenes and the devoted son of the
final scene.

In Seneca's depiction of his hero there is a suggestion that in
some sense he wills his own destruction. Megara, arguing with
Lycus, makes the point that the servitude of Hercules to
Eurystheus and the labours he is compelled to perform are
essential to the manifestation of his heroic valour, just as his
descent to Hades is part of his ascent to the heavens. When

c

Lycus is conquered he asks, in a passage already quoted, for more criminals to punish or monsters to encounter. Even in his madness he consistently pursues the same goal, saying that if the earth and the underworld can provide no more antagonists he must try the heavens. To attain the star promised him by Jupiter he will challenge the wrath of Juno by storming Olympus. Whether sane or mad, Hercules seems almost to embrace his opposing fate, as if by this embrace to overpower another Antaeus. The ironical outcome is, in this sense alone, the logical consequence of his will.

The theme of aspiration has to wait for *Hercules Oetaeus* for full development, but it is already present here, treated with a characteristic Stoic mixture of approval and disapproval. The Stoic's moral acrophobia is well known because it gave ready support to Christian humility and was therefore absorbed into the mainstream of Christian philosophy. The opening chorus of *Hercules Furens* is full of praise of the quiet, humble life and fear of ambition. But the other side of the coin is the almost boundless hope for what the man of great spirit may accomplish. In the midst of an epistle which praises the great soul's preference for "mediocria", Seneca writes:

> No man of exalted gifts is pleased with that which is low and mean; the vision of great achievement summons him and uplifts him. Just as the flame springs straight into the air and cannot be cabined or kept down any more than it can repose in quiet, so our soul is always in motion, and the more ardent it is, the greater its motion and activity.[35]

Taken out of context, these words seem like a prosy anticipation of Marlowe's Tamburlaine. In a similar way the heroic potential of Hercules is glorified by Seneca in a play which depicts his tragic downfall. The case is even more extreme than that of the moral epistle, for the great soul of Hercules does not prefer "mediocria". Its restless motion and aspiration, which come close to hubris even in the first part of the play, do not become blameworthy until the madness sent by Juno has pushed them to a desire to storm Olympus. Even this is perhaps more folly than impiety. In spite of the seeming emphasis on "mediocritas", which is in part a practical awareness of danger, Seneca's Stoic view allows more scope for aspiration than the view of either Sophocles or Euripides.

In spite of this change of emphasis, however, Seneca follows Euripides in "reducing" his hero "to his humanity". The ultimate test of his strength is, once more, to face the knowledge of his murders and go on living. Theseus advises him to meet adversity with all of his accustomed courage (ll. 1272-7). Though he finally agrees to do so, Hercules is more bent on suicide than Euripides' hero, and the final persuasion is not the argument of Theseus but the threat of Amphitryon to commit suicide also. Some of the strength of Hercules at the end of Euripides' play is sacrificed to Seneca's more violent contrast between the hero's madness and his filial piety.

Hercules Oetaeus is, even by Senecan standards, a monster of a play. It is by far the longest of the tragedies, and in the loving fullness of its presentation of the hero, it becomes tiresomely repetitious. However, it is not by any means a complete failure. Seneca's reworking of *The Women of Trachis* achieves a remarkable unity and concentration, and it succeeds in projecting, partly by means of its repetitions, a clearly defined interpretation of Hercules.

The dramatic portrait which finally emerges is made up of five different portraits, one superimposed upon another. They are: Hercules the benefactor, the lustful Hercules, Hercules transformed by suffering, Hercules the model of Stoic endurance, and Hercules the god. The play opens, unlike *The Women of Trachis*, with a long speech by Hercules, in which is presented the first of these portraits—a self-portrait. With all the self-absorption apparent in other depictions of him, Hercules recounts his exploits, associating himself with the gods as the scourge of "perjured kings" and "cruel tyrants" and the champion of world order.

"My courage, more relentless than Juno's self, has urged me on" (ll. 62-3). The motive for his heroism is within him. And now he seeks as his reward the admission to the heavens which Jupiter has promised him. The immortal longings thus revealed constitute a highly ironic introduction to the Oetaean Hercules, for they plant the suggestion that in a way he cannot understand he is willing the end to which he will come through horrible suffering. Both the aspiration and the self-destruction hinted at in *Hercules Furens* are more fully developed here.

As a prelude to the next portrait Iole and her companions

describe the fearsome hero who conquered Oechalia, killed her father, and took her captive—"the angry Hercules". Then Deianira in a jealous rage presents the lustful Hercules at full length, depicting the captor of Iole as an adventurer who has no just claim to his reputation as a hero: ". . . unrestrained excess is called heroic" (ll. 421-2). Like Lycus in *Hercules Furens* and very unlike the Deianira of Sophocles, she plays the part of the prosecuting attorney, explaining all the supposedly heroic accomplishments as the products of an extravagant sexual passion. When her anger is spent, however, she admits to the Nurse that she still loves Hercules. The admission leads to the next episode, the sending of the fatal "love charm".

As in *The Women of Trachis*, it is Hyllus who reports to his mother the effects of the poisoned robe. In his description we first see the suffering Hercules, startlingly transformed from the confident hero of the first portrait. Driven to exasperation by pain and by the thought that so insignificant a person as the herald Lichas should have been responsible for his downfall, he hurls Lichas to his death. After Deianira has left, followed by Hyllus, the suffering Hercules is presented in person. Having discovered that the poison was sent by Deianira, he is even more bitter than before, and descriptions of his excruciating agony alternate with complaints that Jupiter has allowed him to be destroyed by so unworthy an antagonist. To the Chorus this is an entirely proper heroic sentiment: "Seest thou how virtue, conscious of its fame, shrinks not from Lethe's stream? He grieves not at death but blushes for its cause . . ." (ll. 1207-9). But though the Hercules of these speeches is like himself in longing for an enemy worthy to test his metal, he is most unlike himself in his strident complaints of the pain he is undergoing. The Chorus comments, "What may not suffering overcome?" (l. 1279). Seneca emphasizes this change by bringing Alcmena to counsel restraint and try to restore his heroic self-mastery.

As Deianira's lustful Hercules is contrasted with Hercules the benefactor, so this suffering Hercules serves as a foil for the next portrait, the supreme example of endurance. The change is made in an instant when Hercules hears that Nessus, rather than Deianira, was responsible for the poisoned robe. "We complain no more," he says (l. 1479), and as in *The Women of Trachis*, makes his last demands of Hyllus. Instead of showing

the reactions of Hyllus to these demands, however, Seneca moves
on to the full development of his theme of endurance in the
account given by Philoctetes of the death of Hercules. The hero
is depicted upon his funeral pyre, accepting the pains of both
the poison and the flames with the serenity recommended in
every Stoic treatise. Philoctetes describes Alcmena, wildly
lamenting, and Hercules urging her to restrain her grief. Their
roles of complaint and endurance have been exactly reversed
with true Senecan pointedness. Philoctetes' account as a whole
is a *locus classicus* of Stoic fortitude, as the following brief excerpt
shows:

> Midst scorching heat and threat'ning flames, unmoved, unshaken,
> to neither side turning his tortured limbs, he encourages, advises,
> is active still, though all aflame.   (ll. 1740-3)

"Accepting" does not fully convey the quality of Hercules'
endurance in the scene described by Philoctetes. The fortitude
displayed here is as active as any that Hercules has shown in his
heroic labours. The flame of his valour faces the flames of the
poison and the funeral pyre, so that the hero rather burns than
is burned. The suggestion is given in the three words, "urere
ardentem putes" (l. 1744). Not only concurring in his fate, he
seems to will it from the moment he recognizes the fatal bequest
of Nessus as the fulfilment of a prophecy. He identifies his will
with cosmic order—again flame with flame, the primal element
in nature—and thus transcends his mere humanity.

Seneca's dependence on poetic description in this fourth and
most important of the portraits is conspicuous. If the play is to
be produced in the theatre, a report of the action is necessary
here because of the impossibility of performing it on the stage,
but even if the play is to be read, the extraordinary greatness
of the hero is a marvel which only the suggestiveness of poetic
image can convey. The very essence of such a protagonist is
almost inevitably relegated to description, to narrative rather
than purely dramatic passages.

For the final portrait, an outgrowth of the preceding one,
Seneca returns to dramatic means, though the end of the play
is more a tableau than an ordinary scene. As a preparation for
the portrayal of Hercules as god, Alcmena is again brought in.
As in the account of Philoctetes, she is grieving bitterly, and

now laments for the death of her son are mingled with recollec-
tions of him as benefactor. She makes a formal lament for her
son's death, including in it a eulogy of his famous exploits,
described here for the fourth time in the play. Then, as if her
words had been an evocation, the voice of Hercules is heard
from above, offering his mother comfort, and soon his form
appears briefly in the heavens. This manifestation of the god
Hercules completes the portrayal of the hero. The many
suggestions of transcendence in the portrait of the enduring
Hercules are made explicit in his two final speeches, as he
proclaims the triumph of his divine nature, separated now from
his body and made eternal among the stars. The chief meaning
of this metamorphosis is made clear in his words and in those
of the chorus: that valour, the chief heroic virtue, does not die.
"Virtus in astra tendit, in mortem timor," he says (l. 1971),
and the Chorus: "Vivunt fortes" (l. 1984). The ending insists
more unequivocally than any of the other treatments of
Hercules considered so far that the immortality of the hero is
somewhat more than his undying fame: he is himself half a
god.[36]

In spite of the differences between these plays and between
the possible interpretations of any of them, the Hercules who
appears in all four of them is basically the same character. He
is a warrior whose extraordinary strength is matched by his
valour and fortitude. His self-assurance and self-centredness
amount to inordinate pride, but are not treated as hamartia.
Though his savage anger is at times almost brutal, he is capable
of great devotion, is dedicated to a heroic ideal, and is regarded
as a benefactor of humanity. In him areté is pushed to the
ultimate degree; yet, in defiance of justice, he is rewarded with
extraordinary suffering. His ability to endure it is the final
proof of his heroism. Excessive in everything, his aspirations
extend even beyond the bounds of the earth, and there is
always something in his nature of the god or demigod; yet the
plays set an awareness of human limitation against this vision
of infinite heroic potential. In the Stoic Hercules both aspiration
and endurance are given a value which throws the final emphasis
upon transcendence rather than limitation. In every version,
this is a hero who, more even than other heroes, evokes the
response of wonder.

Heroic Man

A man so good, that only would uphold
Man in his native noblesse . . .

THOUGH the gods and heroes of classical antiquity, as
Jean Seznec has shown, had not disappeared from either
literature or art during the Middle Ages, their depiction had
undergone extraordinary modifications.[1] In literature the
process of allegory, carried even further than in classical times,
had completed their transformation into abstractions or types
of the great figures in the Bible. Hercules in a poem by Bishop
Theodulph is virtue; elsewhere he is seen as Samson, David and
even Christ. Artists at the same time, unfamiliar with the
classical tradition, portrayed the gods and heroes as medieval
knights or, still more oddly, gave them Oriental clothes
borrowed from the sky-maps of Arabian astronomers. Hercules
appears with turban and scimitar. "We can speak of a Renaissance," writes Seznec, "from the day Hercules resumed
his athletic breadth of shoulder, his club, and his lion's skin."[2]

1. Renaissance Interpretations of the Myth

When the Renaissance restored to Hercules his concrete
particularity as hero, however, it did not take away from him
the symbolic value so strongly fortified by medieval typology
and allegory. His association with the Old Testament heroes
and with Christ lasted throughout the period. Milton assigns
to the chorus of *Samson Agonistes* a comparison of Samson with
Hercules, and in *Paradise Regained* he compares Christ's struggle
with Satan to that of Hercules with Antaeus.[3] Furthermore, even
in his pagan shape Hercules continued to suggest an abstract
general virtue. An important early stage in the development of
Renaissance treatments of Hercules is marked by Coluccio
Salutati's *De Laboribus Herculis*, written in the last years of the
fourteenth century. Salutati's editor, B. L. Ullman, points to
the combination of medieval allegorizing and Renaissance

admiration of the classical authors.[4] Salutati is concerned to get at the true story by a painstaking comparison of the ancient accounts. One notices also that in giving the allegorical significance of each labour Salutati seems to be building up the picture of a perfect man, such as he says (p. 175) poets have seen in Hercules.

In the middle of the sixteenth century appeared the great compendia of information about classical information, Natalis Conti's *Mythologiae* (1551) and Vincenzo Cartari's *Imagini de i Dei degli Antichi* (1556). Here, in the midst of the most diverse explanations and interpretations of the myth of Hercules, the allegorical tendency frequently reasserts itself. Conti and Cartari both explain that the victories over monsters and tyrants may be understood as the triumphs of the mind over all sorts of vice. But perhaps the most striking examples of allegorical interpretation combined with the classical image of Hercules are those in a still later work, the *Iconologia* of Cesare Ripa (1593). Here Hercules is an emblem of valour (p. 635),[5] of virtue of mind and body (p. 674), of heroic virtue (three times, p. 673), and of unqualified virtue (p. 673). In one emblem he leans, nude, upon his club—nude because virtue does not seek riches but immortality, glory and honour. In another he lifts up the club with his right hand to slay a dragon, while he carries the lion skin over his left arm. Ripa explains that virtue demands the subduing of concupiscence, represented by the dragon; that the lion skin means generosity and strength of mind; and that the club is reason. He reminds his readers that Hercules as a youth chose the path of virtue rather than pleasure.

There is a tradition, then, at least as old as the Sophist Prodicus, running through the Stoics and the writers of the Middle Ages, and current throughout the sixteenth century, which rather surprisingly makes Hercules, the rough warrior-hero, into a model of reasonable control and moderation. Moderation of anger, moderation of avarice, and scorn of pleasure are given to him by Ripa in the form of three apples of the Hesperides, which he holds in his hand. This is a very proper Hercules from any point of view, and a hero especially easy for Christian thought to adopt. But in spite of allegorical interpretation the stories of Hercules continue to suggest

terrifying excesses as well as superb self-mastery. Even Seneca's
Hercules Oetaeus achieves control of himself only at the end.
In the Renaissance, whenever the myth is treated in any detail,
the significance of its hero extends beyond such labels as Ripa
gives him, and one sometimes has the impression that a somewhat subversive meaning asserts itself under cover of the
respectable official interpretation. However, this may be
Hercules is not all moderation even in the hands of a determined
allegorizer like Salutati. In *De Laboribus Herculis* he is presented
as a pattern of self-control, to be sure, but he rises so far above
the common degree of human virtue that he arrives at a kind of
excess which can be called heroic or divine virtue, the exact
antithesis of bestiality.[6] From here it is only a step to saying that
the greatness of such a hero removes him from the usual moral
judgments.

In discussing this extraordinary virtue Salutati almost para-
phrases Aristotle, who refers to a heroic or superhuman virtue
which is the opposite of bestiality; he quotes Priam's praise of
the god-like bravery of Hector.[7] It is scarcely a definition, but it
associates this greatness with whatever differentiates man from
the beast and approaches him to the gods. What Aristotle says
about *megalopsychia*, or magnanimity, also bears on the greatness
of the hero:

> . . . What we mean by a great-souled or superior man is one who
> claims, and is entitled to claim, high consideration from his
> fellows. . . . We see, then, that the superior man, while in the
> extent of his claim going to an extreme, still, by claiming no more
> than his due, is justified and so avoids both extremes, coming as
> he does between those who claim too much and those who claim
> too little—between the vain or conceited and the poor-spirited.[8]

Only in a very special sense is this virtue a mean. It is justifiable
pride, and hence, from a Christian point of view, closely related
to the most dangerous of all excesses. The meaning of Hercules
in the Renaissance approaches a paradox when it includes both
justifiable pride and reason subduing passion.

It is not surprising that the hero whom poets, as Salutati said
(p. 175), wished to present as "vir perfectissimus", and who put
his gifts to such spectacular use, appealed to the Italian
humanists, for the so-called "*studia humanitatis*", the studies of

literature, history and moral philosophy, had the practical end
of developing "a desirable type of human being".[9] To Florentine
scholars at the opening of the fifteenth century this appeal
would have been especially strong. Florence was engaged in a
mortal struggle to preserve her freedom from the encroachment
of Milan; Hercules was a slayer of tyrants as well as monsters.
He was a natural symbol for the active life for which even these
dedicated students were expressing a preference.[10] To the
Platonists of Ficino's famous "academy",[11] a half-century later,
Hercules was again a figure of absorbing interest, despite their
dominant concern with the life of the mind. The emphasis placed
by this group of men upon human dignity and aspiration is well
known. In Ficino's *Platonic Theology* (1474), as Paul Kristeller
points out, the soul of man is given a central position in creation
—"the center of nature, the middle term of all things . . . the
bond and juncture of the universe".[12] Giving the "argumentum"
of Plato's *Laches*, Ficino uses Hercules to illustrate the point that
fortitude is preferable to temperance: while temperance keeps
us from becoming beasts, fortitude may transport us to the
estate of all-conquering gods. Mainly because of this virtue, he
says, antiquity numbered Hercules among the gods, to whose
realm he mounted after conquering the earth.[13] In the *Oration
on the Dignity of Man* (c. 1486) Ficino's pupil, Pico della
Mirandola, has some rhapsodic passages on human potentiality.
For him man is most worthy of wonder of anything in the world
because of his freedom to become what he wishes. He has the
power to degenerate to the status of the brute or to be "reborn
into the higher forms, which are divine". If man wishes to
transcend the limits imposed upon the rest of nature, he has only
to will it. "And if, happy in the lot of no created thing, he with-
draws into the center of his own unity, his spirit, made one with
God, in the solitary darkness of God, who is set above all things,
shall surpass them all. Who would not admire this our
chameleon?"[14]

Another member of the circle, Ficino's teacher, Cristoforo
Landino, uses Hercules in the dialogue *De vita activa et contemplativa* of his *Disputationes* (or *Quaestiones*) *Camaldulenses* (1475).
Lorenzo de' Medici, the proponent of the active life, replying
to Leon Battista Alberti's praise of the contemplative life, is
made to say: "Hercules was wise. But not wise for himself;

rather, his wisdom served almost all men. For in his wanderings over the greater part of the world, he destroyed horrendous wild beasts, vanquished pernicious and savage monsters, chastised the most cruel tyrants."[15] Lorenzo's comment on Hercules comes between his praise of Frederick of Urbino (to whom Landino's dialogue is dedicated) and of St Paul—a contemporary and a Biblical example of such active wisdom. The debate ends when Alberti agrees that although the goals of life must be determined by contemplation, the wisdom thus gained must be put into practice and made active. Hercules himself, Lorenzo's example, is both wise and active.

In this interpretation of Hercules two other contraries also seem to meet. Hercules is both the great individual and the selfless benefactor. He is pitted against a cruel world, whose monsters he is obliged to combat, yet in fighting for himself he also saves the world. Though the typologists made his bene-factions into an analogue of the sacrifice of Christ, the myth more readily supports a concept of heroism in which the heroic act is first of all a vindication of individual integrity. Renaissance depictions of Hercules often seem, like Landino's, to stress un-selfishness and glorious individuality almost equally, with the implication, perhaps, that the two need not conflict in an ideal world.

When Machiavelli, somewhat earlier in the century, writes about the "personal ability", or *virtù*, of the prince who must learn "how to be not good",[16] he is not speaking of an ideal world. This Machiavellian *virtù*, which openly challenges con-ventional morality (though to be sure in the interest of main-taining order in the state) is only superficially like the *virtus heroica* ascribed to Hercules. It is advocated from an entirely practical viewpoint as a kind of behaviour which will lead, as Hiram Haydn has said, not to happiness or salvation, but to success.[17] Machiavelli's advice is grounded in a realistic appraisal of human nature, totally unlike the hopeful view of the Florentine Platonists. He is concerned with the self-preservation of both individuals and states, and recommends the use of whatever gifts man has, including those which he shares with the beasts. There is no question of rising to a *virtus* which is the antithesis of bestiality. It is much more a matter of recognizing and exploiting the beast in man.

A serious problem posed to such writers as Landino by the advocacy of a Herculean pattern of behaviour was the prominence of anger in the make-up of that hero.[18] If it was somewhat paradoxical in the pagan world that the friend of mankind should appear characteristically in the guise of a fighter, wreaking vengeance on his enemies, it was even more so in the Christian world. Anger was, of course, a dangerous sin, and if Hercules was to stand for an ideal sort of human behaviour, his anger had to be justified. In another dialogue, *De vera nobilitate* (*c.* 1475), Landino deals with precisely this question. He interprets the slaying of the Nemean lion as the overcoming of anger, which "so perturbs the mind that it totally extinguishes the light of reason".[19] However, he makes much of the fact that Hercules keeps and wears the skin of the lion in later encounters, for this is a sort of derivative of anger which the brave man uses in fighting injustice. Landino reminds us that there is a kind of anger which is approved of by the Peripatetics and also by Christians, and he quotes from St Paul (Ephesians iv. 26) "Be ye angry and sin not: let not the sun go down upon your wrath." He explains that the meaning is that wrath must be kept within bounds, but that righteous indignation is praiseworthy. Instead of extinguishing the light of reason, it serves to put an edge to fortitude as flint sharpens a sword.

The first phrase of the verse from *Ephesians* is a quotation by St Paul of Psalms iv. 4.[20] In Vulgate Bibles published shortly after Landino's time the glosses on both passages neatly demonstrate the orthodoxy of his distinction. In one (1504), a gloss on Psalms iv. 4 tells us that anger is of two kinds: a sinful anger, which puts out the light of the eye, and a zealous anger (*ira per zelum*), which lights up the eye, troubling it for a time like a collyrium, in order to make it clearer afterwards.[21] In another (1493), a gloss on Ephesians iv. 26 also speaks of *ira per zelum*, which is not contrary to nature but opposed to natural sin. The commentator warns that it is easy to exceed a reasonable limit when angry, and cites a story (told by Diogenes Laertius) that Plato turned over a slave to someone else for punishment, lest in his anger he exceed this limit.[22] Thomas Aquinas uses this term, *ira per zelum*, for a praiseworthy anger which is in accordance with right reason. He quotes Gregory the Great as saying that *ira per zelum* troubles the eye of reason whereas sinful anger

blinds it.[23] It is important to remember that the terrible rage of
Hercules, vanquishing monsters and chastising tyrants, or
suffering in his poisoned robe, could have the meaning of that
justifiable anger which is not opposed to reason and which the
great man requires in his struggle with a corrupt world. It is
evidence of greatness.

2. *Virtus Heroica* Visualized

The fierceness and energy of heroic virtue are most vividly
realized in the works of Antonio Pollaiuolo, where they are apt
to shock a twentieth-century observer unless he is aware of the
meaning of this belligerent activity for the Renaissance.
Pollaiuolo, a close friend of Ficino,[24] treated the myth of
Hercules in several works. In his statue of *Hercules and Antaeus*
the straining body of Hercules, his bulging muscles and con-
torted face, focus attention so sharply on his physical effort that
one does not instantly think of the statue as embodying an ideal
of heroic accomplishment. Similarly, Pollaiuolo's miniatures of
Hercules and Antaeus and *Hercules Slaying the Hydra*, replicas of
lost paintings,[25] convey a keen awareness of the potentialities
of the human body without suggesting much to the twentieth-
century observer about Biblical analogues or the latent divinity
of the hero. In *Hercules Slaying the Hydra* the hero's uplifted arm
and the extension of his entire body, accentuated by flying
drapery, impart to the canvas the feeling of swift and powerful
motion, while the face, surmounted by the head of Hercules'
lion skin, expresses intent ferocity. In another painting by
Pollaiuolo, the *Rape of Deianira*, the impression of vehement
activity is accentuated by every possible device. The river
across which Nessus is carrying Deianira looks peaceful enough
in its distant meanders in the background, but in the foreground
it rages over partly concealed stones; the centaur springs forward, his forepaws in mid air, while at the same time he twists
his human torso to the side, so as to embrace Deianira; with her
arms flung out, she seems to be trying to leap off the centaur's
back in an effort to escape from his arms; in the right foreground,
closest to the observer, the body of Hercules is strained to the
utmost in the bending of his bow. The face is drawn into a
scowl as the hero takes aim, and every muscle seems to con-

tribute to the effort which will in a moment dispatch the swift and deadly arrow. None of Pollaiuolo's Hercules scenes is more dramatically alive.[26]

The sheer physicality of all these male nudes by Pollaiuolo is clear evidence of the passionate interest at this period in the accurate portrayal of the human body. Vasari, in the next century, continually testifies to this interest and attributes great advances in this field to the exact knowledge Pollaiuolo gained by dissecting bodies. As a study of the musculature of the male body his *Battle of the Ten Nude Men* apparently fascinated and greatly influenced his contemporaries. The search for perfection in form, in this case the form of the male body, is inherent in all the Renaissance depictions of nude warriors, whether they are presented as Hercules, Samson, David, or without a name. One might say that inevitably the purpose of conveying some concept such as heroic energy is matched by an artistic purpose such as the accurate imitation of a form in nature, but in this case the artistic purpose also implies a philosophical concept. Vasari says that a fine style is to be achieved by copying "the most beautiful things, and by combining the finest members, whether hands, heads, bodies, or legs, to produce a perfect figure" (II, 151). These nude warriors, then, whose straining muscles convey the fierceness of their struggle, are versions of the "perfect figure" of a man. That he is shown in combat is not only a way to display his muscles but also to present him in a characteristically male activity, a perfection of masculinity. An idea about men, an attitude toward men, is implied. Perfection is defined as what is most characteristic, not as what ought to be. Heroic energy is not merely the physical representation of virtue but also the fulfilment of a potentiality seen in the male body.

Pollaiuolo's studies of Hercules are interesting not only as evidence in themselves of a certain concept of the heroic but also because of the artist's connection with the Florentine Platonists.[27] It is tempting to see in them direct reflections of the philosophy of man put forward by Ficino, Pico, Landino. The latter's interpretation of the meaning of the hero's lion-skin could almost serve as a commentary on the painting of *Hercules Slaying the Hydra*, where Hercules wears the lion-skin as he vents his just wrath on the monster. Landino's discussion of the

wisdom of Hercules is also relevant; for here he is wisely
vanquishing a "pernicious and savage monster".[28]

Vasari's comments on the companion picture, *Hercules and
Antaeus*, reveal an interpretation of heroic energy akin to
Landino's. His attitude is suggested by the remarkable similarity
between his descriptions of that painting and of Pollaiuolo's
St Michael and the Dragon. Of the first he says:

> . . . a very fine figure, with a splendid representation of the force
> of the hero, the muscles and nerves being all braced for the effort,
> while the grinding of the teeth and the attitude of the head accord
> with the tensions of the other members.

Of the second:

> St Michael is boldly confronting the serpent, grinding his teeth
> and frowning, so that he actually seems to have come down from
> heaven for the purpose of wreaking the vengeance of God upon
> the pride of Lucifer.[29]

What in one painting expresses "the force of the hero", expresses
the wreaking of divine vengeance in the other, and Vasari may
well have been conscious of the similarity which he seems to
suggest between the hero and the saint. It is no more far-fetched
than Landino's quotation of Scripture in his discussion of the
Nemean lion. To both of them heroic energy is almost
divine.

Dürer's engraving, *Der Hercules*, though in many ways very
different from the figures we have been considering, may be
related to them through the influence which Pollaiuolo seems
to have had on him, and may also exemplify an anger which
defends the cause of reason and is justifiable in either Christian
or Platonic terms. The engraving presents another corporal
epiphany of heroic energy, the more remarkable for the fact
that the subject, according to Panofsky's interpretation, is the
hero's least physical exploit, his choice between virtue and
pleasure.

As Panofsky points out, "Before Dürer, this allegory—conspicuously absent from medieval imagery but much in favor
with the artists of the Renaissance—had been represented in
very undramatic fashion. Hercules was shown between the two
personifications who were characterized by their appearance

and by scenic background rather than by their actions; they addressed themselves exclusively to the hero, paying no attention to each other."[30] In contrast to such depictions, the Dürer engraving is all action. Virtue, with an upraised club, prepares to strike Pleasure, who lifts her arm to protect herself as she sits in the lap of a satyr. Hercules, instead of listening passively to the rival claims of the two women, stands aggressively in the foreground, his feet planted far apart, both hands grasping his club, which he holds horizontally at the level of his head, as if to indicate that he will settle the dispute himself. "Without as yet participating in the fight he is . . . a 'supporting witness' of Virtue."[31] The nude figure of the hero is seen from the back, its muscular strength emphasized by minute attention to anatomical detail. Panofsky believes that Dürer modelled it on a drawing called *The Abduction*, in which he copied a now lost composition by Pollaiuolo.[32] Moral choice in *Der Hercules* is presented as heroic action, and heroism is again shown in the figure of a nude male fighter.

The most lasting impression made by these Hercules figures is of extraordinary power. It is the power of *virtus heroica*, exercised in the struggle for a noble ideal, and hence it may be called "moral energy", in the special sense of Sir Kenneth Clark's term, but like the wrath of God, it is also terrible in some of its manifestations. It is a distinctly human power, however, its divine analogues serving mainly to stress the wonderful potential which such philosophers as Pico della Mirandola saw in man. It is the power of the active man, called upon to shape the world in which he lives.

For various reasons, some of which have been mentioned, Hercules seized upon the Renaissance imagination. As he was in origin in some sense *the hero*, so he was again in this later manifestation. Yet in both cases he was a distinguishable type rather than the sum of all heroic traits. The later manifestation was truly a "renaissance" of the type which Sophocles, Euripides and Seneca had presented, whether or not these dramatic portrayals were directly influential on the writers and artists discussed in this chapter. The hero whose extraordinary power is so memorably delineated by Pollaiuolo and Dürer is essentially the proud, fierce, aspiring warrior of classical times.

DER HERCULES

Engraving by Albrecht Dürer

3. Admiration for Hercules

Sixteenth-century poetics tended to encourage the depiction of this type of hero in literature, not only because of the lively interest in classical mythology but also because one of the major concerns of several of the Italian critics was the ability of the poet to arouse admiration, in its root sense of "wonder".[33] As I remarked at the end of the first chapter, Hercules, even more than other heroes, evokes the response of wonder.

The special appeal of mythology to Renaissance poets is related to the persistent vogue of allegorical interpretation. If learned readers looked well beneath the surface for the meanings of the old tales and legends, it was partly because they believed that the poet should conceal his special insights from the rude gaze of the many. Boccaccio, in his *Life of Dante*, says that poetry is like Holy Scripture in revealing its mystery to the wise but protecting the simple from more than they can or should comprehend.[34] In *De Genealogia Deorum* (1472) he says it is the poet's office to protect "matters truly solemn and memorable" and "remove them from the gaze of the irreverent that they cheapen not by too common familiarity".[35] A myth, offering many possibilities for concealment, was therefore promising material for a poet and a perfect example of one operation of poetry. It was the right way to convey truth to the right people. Conti explains on the first page of his *Mythologiae* that the fables of the Greeks were an occult way of philosophizing, learnt from the Egyptians.[36]

Boccaccio gives a curious example of the power of poetry in the course of his discussion of its obscurity. The poets, he says, used their fictions to confirm the power of princes by portraying them as the offspring of the gods.[37] One may speculate that this attitude toward the writing of poetry had some connection with such paintings as Paolo Uccello's Sir John Hawkwood (c. 1432) and its companion piece, Andrea del Castagno's Niccolò da Tolentino, where men are depicted as statues. Reality is placed at one further remove from the spectator, and the subject of the painting is shown as already ennobled by the shaping process of art and hence by his kinship to other great men of the past, honoured by statues raised in their memories. In a somewhat similar way, the poet who associates his hero with Hercules or

D

Achilles shows him, momentarily at least, in a pre-existing heroic form, as if already part of a great tradition. At the same time, the poet puts an important part of his meaning in code. It will only be understood by a reader familiar with mythology and with the further truths which it conceals.

A few pronouncements by Antonio Minturno will illustrate the critical concern with admiration. Minturno's *De Poeta* (1559) was one of the ambitious treatises inspired by the rediscovery of Aristotle's *Poetics* and written, as William K. Wimsatt has said, "in the manner of what Aristotle's notes might be thought to represent".[38] Starting with the general problem of poetry, Minturno moves on to the particular problems of the various genres. He pronounces flatly that no one is to be called a poet who does not excite admiration. To do so is not an alternative to the teaching, pleasing, and moving which Minturno, like most of his contemporaries, expects of the poet; it is an additional effect, characteristic of poetry, and not necessarily produced by oratory, which also teaches, pleases, and moves (p. 106).[39] Admiration is in part caused by excellence of contrivance—the mastery of the poet's craft, and may thus be produced by all sorts of poetry, but Minturno speaks most of the admiration caused by tragic and epic poetry. Referring to tragedy in terms which obviously echo Aristotle, he writes that, "To be admired are those things which either compel pity or excite terror, and more fully those things which, though they follow as a consequence, happen contrary to hope or expectation" (p. 180). Here and elsewhere Minturno lays the greatest stress on the ability of poetry to arouse wonder by means of surprise, though of course it is the poet's task to make the surprising turn seem to follow logically. The supernatural takes on great importance for Minturno as it was to do much later for Dryden. Ovid's *Metamorphoses* are given as examples of stories which are justifiable as poetry because they are "admirable", even though contrary to human experience (p. 155).

An important source of admiration is the greatness of the events depicted, whether they are terrifying or pitiable. He cites the "dire and horrible death of Hippolytus, Hercules' shocking and terrible insanity, the pitiful exile of Oedipus". There is nothing "small or moderate" about this kind of poetry; it is "magnificent" and "brilliant", treating the most illustrious persons and the greatest actions—the deeds of heroes (p. 179). The logic of this emphasis upon heroic action leads Minturno to rate the epic even above tragedy, for the heroic exploits recounted by Homer and Virgil constitute the fountain from which "every variety of poetry flowed" (p. 105).[40] Narrative poetry can do fuller justice to some of these exploits, such as Achilles' pursuit of the fleeing Hector, or Aeneas' pursuit of Turnus, which arouse wonder in the reader, where the same events on the stage might produce laughter.[41] For Minturno the deeds of warrior heroes are ideally suited to produce admiration, the most characteristic effect of poetry.

Other Italian critics, such as Giraldi Cinthio, Castelvetro and Robortello, could be cited on the importance of admiration and its connection with heroic action, but for the student of English literature Sidney is more directly relevant. Not only does he speak of tragedy as "stirring the affects of admiration and commiseration", but he states that "moving is of a higher degree than teaching". The moving to which he refers is very closely related to admiration; in fact Minturno himself implies a connection between the two.[42] None of the Italian critics shows more plainly than does Sidney how heroic poetry moves its readers: "For as the image of each action stirreth and instructeth the mind, so the lofty image of such worthies [as Achilles, Aeneas, etc.] most inflameth the mind with desire to be worthy, and informs with counsel how to be worthy."[43] In another passage Sidney writes, ". . . as virtue is the most excellent resting place for all worldly learning to make his end of, so poetry, being the most familiar to teach it, and most princely to move towards it, in the most excellent work is the most excellent workman" (p. 430).

As one reads Minturno or Sidney on the effect of poetry, one notices how they warm to the subject of its powerful "moving". Their diction reveals their attitudes. "Concitat", "permovet vehementer", "excitat admirationem", says Minturno; and Sidney: "most inflameth the mind", "most princely to move towards it". One becomes aware that for these critics, as much later for Carlyle, the poet himself has much in common with the hero, and poetry is a sort of heroic enterprise. If the poet is to be valued as an active, compelling champion of virtue—a "supporting witness", as Panofsky calls Dürer's Hercules—then it is natural that heroic poetry should seem to be the most essentially poetic, and therefore that despite Aristotle's preference for tragedy, the epic should be the best of all genres in the eyes of these critics. The frequent choice of heroic deeds as the theme of poetry is made to appear inevitable.

The taste for heroic deeds in poetry is obviously related to the preference for an active life reflected in Landino's dialogue, *De vita activa et contemplativa*. Sentiments very similar to those of the Florentine scholars had also been expressed in England in the sixteenth century. In Thomas Starkey's *A Dialogue Between Reginald Pole and Thomas Lupset* (*c.* 1535), for instance, Lupset is made to argue, much as Lorenzo de' Medici does, that "the perfection of man standeth not in bare knowledge and learning without application of it to any use or profit of other; but the very perfection of man's mind resteth in the use and exercise of all virtues and honesty. . . ."[44] Sidney's contemporary, Gabriel Harvey, wrote numerous marginal notes revealing his admiration for great warriors and other active men. "Quicquid est in Deo, est Deus; Quicquid est in Viro, sit Virtus, et vis," he wrote in one place (p. 148)[45]; "A Lusty Boddy: & a Brave Mind: ye mighty dooers in ye world. Heroical valour, nothing else" (p. 156); "Who would not rather be on[e] of ye Nine Worthyes: then on[e] of ye Seaven Wise masters?" (p. 151). Sidney recommends the portrayal of the kind of hero who excites Harvey's imagination.

Thomas Heywood, in his *Apology for Actors*,[46] demonstrates the tonic effect of dramatic performances with the story that Hercules was moved to perform his labours by a show of "the worthy and memorable acts of his father *Jupiter*". Heywood goes on to say that Theseus was then inspired by Hercules, Achilles by Theseus, Alexander by Achilles, and Julius Caesar by Alexander. In each case the "hawty and magnanimous attempts" inspired by the actions of a predecessor inspired in turn the admiration of successors. And for Heywood the mere description of such actions is nothing compared to their portrayal on the stage "to moove the spirits of the beholder to admiration". He gives a rhapsodic account of the effect produced by the most admirable of contemporary stage heroes. They are all warrior heroes, and the most moving of all is Hercules:

... to see a souldier shap'd like a souldier, walke, speake, act like a souldier: to see a *Hector* all besmered in blood, trampling upon the bulkes of Kinges. A *Troylus* returning from the field in the sight of his father *Priam*, as if man and horse even from the steeds rough fetlockes to the plume in the champions helmet had bene together plunged into a purple Ocean: To see a *Pompey* ride in triumph, then a *Cesar* conquer that *Pompey*: labouring *Hanniball* alive, hewing his passage through the Alpes. To see as I have seene, *Hercules* in his owne shape hunting the Boare, knocking downe the Bull, taming the Hart, fighting with Hydra, murdering *Gerion*, slaughtring *Diomed*, wounding the *Stimphalides*, killing the Centaurs, pashing the Lion, squeezing the Dragon, dragging *Cerberus* in Chaynes, and lastly, on his high Pyramides writing *Nil ultra*, Oh these were sights to make an *Alexander*.[47]

"Admiration", as some of the preceding quotations may have suggested, covered a range of responses from awe to astonishment. The very imprecision of the term may have been responsible for producing one important modification of the Herculean hero—his incorporation in romance; for admiration in the sense of astonishment at apparent impossibilities was the obvious response to the extraordinary doings in romance. The high value placed on admiration not only encouraged the depiction of the Herculean hero such as we have already seen him but provided an argument for introducing romance elements into the story of such a hero. In the well-known critical debate over the place of romance in the hierarchy of poetry the defenders of romance could point to its special power to arouse admiration.[48] Giraldi Cinthio, one of the foremost defenders of the romance, shows the importance of the marvellous in a discussion of verisimilitude in poetry. He cites Boiardo, Ariosto, Homer, Virgil and Ovid to show that what happens in a poem need not be historically true, and recalls that Aristotle placed a high value on feigning. He continues:

There is nothing marvelous in that which happens often or naturally, but there is in what appears impossible and yet is assumed to have happened if not in truth at least in fiction, such as the changes of men into trees, of ships into nymphs, of branches into ships, the union of the gods with men, and other such things which, though they are false and impossible, are still so accepted by custom that a composition cannot be pleasing in which these fables do not appear. And perhaps the poet is called poet for this more than for any other reason, for this name of poet signifies nothing other than maker. And not because of his verses but chiefly through his subjects he is called a poet, in so far as these subjects are made and feigned by him in such a way that they are fit and suitable for poetry.[49]

The material of romance lends itself especially well to poetic enterprise, according to this view.

Another point in favour of the romance was the illustriousness of the knights and ladies by whom it was peopled. Even Minturno, who will not admit Ariosto into the company of Homer and Virgil, agrees that the romance is "an imitation of great and illustrious actions that are worthy of epic poetry".[50] The prowess—one might even say the areté—of many a chivalric knight reveals his kinship with the heroes of antiquity. Minturno's chief objection to the romance is a formal one: it lacks unity; but he sees no reason why the material of romance cannot be made into heroic poetry if it is properly handled.

When the material of romance was introduced into the heroic there was, of course, a vast increase in the importance of women and of the theme of love. As a result, even the Herculean hero, who had a warrior's low regard for women, came to be portrayed as a lover also. In some cases love remained peripheral to his main concerns, but in others it came to be valued with, or even identified with, his areté. Though the distinguishing features of the type were not radically altered, the Herculean hero was given an added complexity when his love as well as his valour became an object of admiration.

Among the critics who discuss the portrayal of the hero, Tasso is particularly useful in showing what is praiseworthy about the great warrior. In his essay "Della virtù eroica e della carità" he distinguishes between moral virtue, which consists in a mean between extremes, and heroic virtue, which is "I know not what greatness, and an excess, so to speak, of virtue" (p. 173).[51] He supports his argument with references to both Plato and Aristotle, associating heroic virtue closely with understanding and with magnanimity. As the chief joy of the magnanimous man is honour, he says that the hero rejoices chiefly in glory (p. 175). His essay emphasizes the inclusiveness of this sort of virtue, in which every virtue is represented; yet Tasso concludes that it is more active than contemplative (p. 176).

The accent comes inevitably on the active hero in Tasso's *Discourses on the Heroic Poem*. Both tragedy and epic, he says, have a concern with "great affairs", though this concern is manifested in quite different ways in the two genres. "In tragedy it appears in an unexpected and sudden change of fortune, and in the greatness of the happenings that produce pity and terror, but the splendid action of the heroic poem is founded on lofty military virtue and on a magnanimous resolution to die, on piety, on religion, and on actions in which these virtues are resplendent, which are in harmony with the nature of the epic and not fitting in a tragedy."[52] Here and elsewhere it is apparent that Tasso finds a place in the epic for heroes who are not warriors as well as for those who are, but his comments on the virtues common to both reveal an attitude which is particularly interesting in connection with the Herculean hero. Continuing his distinction between epic and tragedy, he points out that whereas tragedy requires "persons neither good nor wicked, but of a middle sort", epic "requires the highest degree of virtue; therefore the persons are heroic as their virtue is. In Aeneas is found the excellence of piety, in Achilles that of military courage, in Ulysses that of prudence. And if sometimes the tragic and the epic poet both take the same person as their subject, he is considered diversely by them and from different points of view. The epic writer considers in Hercules, Theseus, Agamemnon, Ajax and Pyrrhus their valor and ability in arms; the tragedian is concerned with them in so far as they have fallen into infelicity through some error" (p. 484[4]). In this account the epic hero epitomizes "the highest degree of virtue", an Achilles no less than an Aeneas or a Ulysses. It is not absolutely clear whether Hercules and the others are also to be thought of as having this degree of virtue, or whether, since tragedy may also use them, they occupy an intermediate position on the moral scale. What is clear is that when they are presented in the epic, the emphasis is not to fall upon moral failings and their sad consequences, but upon "valor and ability in arms".

In another passage of the *Discourses* Tasso speaks of the

essential nobility of the action of the epic and the necessity to "excite wonder". The best example from antiquity is the noble action of the *Aeneid*, but modern subjects are also possible, such as the liberation of Italy from the Goths or "those enterprises for the confirmation of the Christian faith or for the exaltation of the Church and the Empire that were fortunately and gloriously accomplished. These actions in themselves win over the souls of the readers and produce expectation and marvelous pleasure, and when the art of an able poet is added there is nothing they cannot accomplish in our souls" (pp. 487-9). Like Minturno and Sidney, he emphasizes the power of poetry, and especially of that poetry which presents the power of heroic man.

In *Jerusalem Delivered* Tasso showed how the material of the crusades and, to a certain extent, the material of medieval romance could be used in the writing of an epic. The critical controversy which ensued is famous.[53] In the course of justifying the romantic episodes and asserting the unity of the poem, Tasso wrote the *Allegory of Jerusalem Delivered*, in which he related the characterization of his three heroes, Goffredo, Rinaldo and Tancredi, to certain elements in the nature of man. Goffredo, the leader of the crusade, represents the understanding, and is hence the type of contemplative man. Both Rinaldo and Tancredi are types of active man. Tancredi, whose "fault was love" (I, 45)[54], represents the concupiscible power of the soul, though of all the princes in Goffredo's army only Rinaldo exceeds him in prowess. Rinaldo, the "Star of this spheare, the dimond of this ring" (I, 58), represents the irascible power of the soul. What Tasso has to say of Rinaldo's relationship to Goffredo seems almost to be a summary of the Renaissance attitudes toward the Herculean hero. For this reason I shall quote at some length.

In this section of the Allegory Tasso is dealing with some of the major episodes of his poem: Rinaldo's slaying of his fellow-crusader, Gernando, his subsequent estrangement from Goffredo, his capture by the enchantress, Armida (the more brilliant prototype of Spenser's Acrasia), his release and reconciliation to Goffredo, and his victory over the spirits of the enchanted wood, the prelude to the final victory of the crusaders.

Godfrey which holdeth the principall place in this storie, is no other in the Allegorie but the *Understanding*, which is signified in many places of the *Poeme* as in that verse,

> *By thee the counsell given is, by thee the scepter rul'd.*

And more plainly in that other:

> *Thy soule is of the campe both minde and life.*

And *Life* is added, bicause in the powers more noble, the lesse noble are contained: therefore *Rinaldo*, which in action is in the second degree of honour, ought also to be placed in the Allegorie in the answerable degree: but what this power of the mind, holding the second degree of dignitie is, shall be nowe manifested. The *Irefull* vertue[55] is that, which amongst all the powers of the minde. is lesse estranged from the nobility of the soule, insomuch that *Plato* (doubting) seeketh whether it differeth from reason or no. And such is it in the minde, as the chieftaine in an assemblie of souldiours[56]: for as of these the office is to obey their princes, which do give directions and commandements to fight against their enimies: so is it the dutie of the irefull, warlike, and soveraigne part of the minde, to be armed with reason against concupiscence, and with that vehemencie and fiercenes (which is proper unto it) to resist and drive awaie whatsoever impediment to felicitie. But when it doth not obey Reason, but suffers it selfe to be carried of her owne violence, it falleth out, that is fighteth not against concupiscence, but by concupiscence, like a dogge that biteth not the theeves, but the cattle committed to his keeping. This violent, fierce, and unbridled furie, as it can not be fully noted by one *man of warre*, is nevertheless principally signified by *Rinaldo*, where it is said of him, that being

> *—A right warrelike knight*
> *Did scorne by reasons rule to fight.*

Wherein (whilest fighting against *Gernando*, he did passe the bounds of civill revenge, and whilest he served *Armida*) may be noted unto us, *Anger*, not governed by reason: whilest hee disinchanteth the wood, entreth the citie, breaketh the enimies array, *Anger*, directed by reason. His return and reconciliation to *Godfrey*, noteth *Obedience*, causing the *Irefull* power to yeelde to the *Reasonable*. In these Reconciliations two things are signified, first, *Godfrey* with civill moderation is acknowledged to be superiour to *Rinaldo*, teaching us, that Reason commandeth Anger, not imperiously, but curteouslie and civillie: . . . Secondly, that as the reasonable part ought not (for heerein the Stoiks were very much deceived) to exclude the *Irefull* from actions, nor *usurpe* the offices thereof, for this usurpation shoulde bee against nature and justice, but it ought to make her her companion and handmaid: So ought not *Godfrey* to attempt the adventure of the wood himselfe, thereby arrogating to himselfe the other offices belonging to *Reinaldo*. Lesse skill should then be shewed, and lesse regard had to the profite, which the Poet, as subjected to policie, ought to have for his aime, if it had been fained, that by *Godfrey* onlie, all was wrought, which was necessarie for the conquering of Jerusalem. Neither is there contrarietie or difference from that which hath been said, in putting downe *Rinaldo* and *Godfrey* for that figure of the *Reasonable* and of the *Irefull* vertue, which *Hugo* speakes of in his dreame, wheras he compareth the one to the Head, the other to the *right Hand* of the army, bicause the *Head* (if we believe *Plato*) is the seat of Reason, and the *right Hand*, if it be not the seat of wrath, it is at least her most principall instrument.   (Sig A4$^{r\&v}$.)

Rinaldo is the active man, the powerful and successful warrior, a man susceptible to love, but less so than other men. Inspired by a great cause, to which he devotes his energies, he is second only to the representative of that cause, and essential to its success. There are times when he rebels against any control or limitation, but in the end he accepts them. Although the incidents of Rinaldo's career are not modelled on the myth of Hercules, the distinguishing traits of his character are those which were associated with Hercules in classical times and in the Renaissance. In this sense Rinaldo is an excellent example of a Herculean hero.

As a person of extraordinary virtue, he belongs, by Tasso's distinction, in epic, and Tasso's point of view is exactly what he says it should be in epic, as opposed to tragedy, for he emphasizes valour rather than the unfortunate consequences of error. Rinaldo can be blamed for not keeping his anger within reasonable bounds, and his affair with Armida is a further sign of his lack of control, yet this excessiveness scarcely affects the estimate of his virtue. Achilles is conceived in a similar way; he is in many respects the model for Rinaldo.

Despite Tasso's distinction, however, tragedy too may emphasize virtue more than moral failing. In the tragedies examined in the first chapter Hercules is presented from this point of view, and so are the heroes of the tragedies we are about to consider. In these later tragedies the influence of epic is often felt, not only in this matter of point of view but in structure and style as well. At the end of the period with which we shall be concerned the drama deliberately seeks for epic dimensions, as if they were needed for the portrayal of so admirable a hero.

3

Marlowe

His looks do menace heaven and dare the gods,
His fiery eyes are fixed upon the earth,
As if he now devis'd some stratagem,
Or meant to pierce Avernas' darksome vaults
To pull the triple headed dog from hell.

THE brilliance of the heroic image Marlowe created in *Tamburlaine* has proved to be both attractive and blinding. The glittering verse, the sound of trumpets, the movement of armies across the stage, seem to have concealed more than they have revealed of one essential part of the play's meaning, the author's attitude towards his hero. The question of whether this extravagantly unconventional protagonist is presented with approval or disapproval has received answers so various and contradictory that a reader of the criticism might easily conclude that the play contains no sure indications of attitude—that Tamburlaine is whatever his audience makes of him. However, one point on which all critics agree is that Marlowe had a well-defined attitude towards his hero. It is worth seeking again even at the cost of another reconsideration of a play which has been much discussed.

The spectacular circumstances of Marlowe's life have figured in the interpretation of his plays from his own times down to ours, for if he was an atheist, a homosexual, a spy, a scoffer and a quarreller, it seems more than a coincidence that he chose for principal characters an atheistical warrior, a scholar who sold his soul to the devil, a homosexual king, a Machiavellian schemer. An older group of critics emphasized what might be called the brighter side of Marlowe's unconventionality by interpreting Tamburlaine's boundless ambition as a joyous assertion of Marlowe's Renaissance paganism—a celebration of human worth in general and of his own aspirations in particular.[1] To more recent critics this sort of interpretation has seemed to rest upon a romanticized view of the Renaissance. Hence a somewhat grimmer picture has been drawn of a

Tamburlaine who is the mirror image of a resolute defier of convention, remarkably "advanced" in his freedom of thought, but pathologically attracted by cruelty, and characterized, as one critic has put it, by "abnormal nervous energy" and "unco-ordinated personality factors".[2]

The difficulties which attend upon such identifications of Marlowe and Tamburlaine may be illustrated from the most impressive of these studies, Paul H. Kocher's *Christopher Marlowe*. Looking at the play for the light it may throw on the mind and character of Marlowe, Kocher finds that Part I is dominated by two religious conceptions: one, that the law of nature commands Tamburlaine and others to seek regal power; the other, that in his conquest Tamburlaine is acting as the scourge of God. Though the first conception is thoroughly anti-Christian, the second is, of course, perfectly compatible with Christianity, so that Kocher is faced with a conflict in Marlowe's thought as he understands it. He asks whether these ideas may not be harmonized "by simply amputating the Christian appendages" but concludes that even then some inconsistency remains.[3] In considering the character of Calyphas, Tambur-laine's cowardly son in Part II, Kocher finds that in certain scenes the boy is made ridiculous but that in the first scene of Act IV his mockery of the warrior code of conduct is "a personal outburst by the dramatist". Kocher speculates that Marlowe was "thoroughly satiated and weary with excess" by this time but that Calyphas' mockery "cannot have been any part of Marlowe's plan for the drama".[4] The dangers of this method of interpretation are obvious. Although it would be naive to expect perfect consistency of an Elizabethan play, it is an act of critical desperation to discount or "amputate" whatever does not fit with a predetermined picture of Marlowe's opinions, or to explain all discordant elements as lapses and unpremeditated changes in the artist's plans. Such an interpretation takes the opinions of Marlowe as reported by his contemporaries, Thomas Kyd, Richard Baines, and others, as fixed points of reference and, rather than explain any contradictory ideas which appear in the play, explains them away. Whether or not Marlowe held the opinions ascribed to him (a matter which has never been established beyond doubt), the attitudes expressed in *Tamburlaine* should be determined by a careful weighing of all the evidence given in the play. The knowledge of Marlowe's reputation hinders almost as much as it helps such a process.

Unfortunately, the refusal to identify Marlowe with his hero by no means solves the problem of interpretation. The crucial problem remains: is Tamburlaine presented with approval or disapproval? As J. C. Maxwell says, "No one can ever have doubted that Marlowe displays in a high degree the imaginative sympathy with his hero which is required for successful dramatic presentation,"[5] but sympathy does not mean approval, and even the critics who agree on Marlowe's objectivity in creating Tamburlaine differ as to the attitude the play presents. It has been said that Marlowe makes his hero both physically and morally more admirable than he appears in the sources,[6] but it has also been suggested that Part II, where the sources provide much less of the action, shows a progressive disenchantment with the hero.[7] The two parts of the play together have been read as a chronicle of the Renaissance discovery that human nature cut off from its divine source is not emancipated but impoverished,[8] or even as an indictment of Tamburlaine from a conservative Renaissance point of view, and hence "one of the most grandly moral spectacles in the whole realm of English drama."[9] Roy Battenhouse, from whose study these last words are quoted, sees Tamburlaine's death as the divine punishment such as a "scourge of God" was inevitably given, once his mission had been accomplished.

There could scarcely be greater diversity of opinion, yet through it all runs a discernible pattern. The critics who believe that Marlowe approves of Tamburlaine either try to show that he passes over his hero's disagreeable qualities to emphasize others (such as the aspiration for knowledge and beauty) or believe that Marlowe, as a rebel against the morality of his time, approves of Tamburlaine's cruelty, pride, atheism and ruthless exercise of power. Those who believe that Marlowe disapproves of Tamburlaine assume that such behaviour must be recognized as bad, and that Marlowe's frank portrayal of it indicates his moral condemnation. Neither group of critics suggests the possibility that Tamburlaine's faults might be an integral part of a kind of heroic nature familiar to Marlowe and his audience and unlikely to offend anyone but "precise" churchmen or the poet's enemies. It is possible, of course, that

Marlowe's attitude toward his hero shifts from scene to scene, or from Part I to Part II, but it seems to me more likely that his concept of heroic character is sufficiently complex to include what appear to be contradictory elements and that his attitude, going beyond simple approval or disapproval, remains constant.

Hercules, as he appears in Sophocles, Euripides, and above all Seneca, is revitalized in Tamburlaine. No one of the older plays was used as a model, but Hercules was often in Marlowe's mind as he wrote.[10] Several allusions in the play make this fact indisputable, and, as Mario Praz pointed out many years ago, there are striking resemblances between Tamburlaine and Hercules Oetaeus.[11] However, it is finally less important to decide whether Marlowe was deliberately fashioning a Herculean hero than to remember that the traditional depictions of Hercules, especially those from Rome and Renaissance Italy, were thoroughly familiar to him. It is not surprising that Tamburlaine, who had already been used by Louis Le Roy and others as a symbol of the physical and intellectual vigour of the Renaissance,[12] should suggest the Greek hero to him. I believe that his attitude towards Tamburlaine, as expressed in the play, is very similar to the attitudes found in some of the portrayals of Hercules discussed in the previous two chapters. The images created by Seneca and Pollaiuolo can be of great assistance to the spectator of the twentieth century, partially cut off from the traditions in which Marlowe wrote; for they prepare the eye to discern the outlines of Marlowe's heroic figure.

The figure is vast. The very structure of the play conveys this impression, for the succession of scenes—some of them might almost be called tableaux—stretching over great expanses of time and space, presents the man in terms of the places he makes his and the time which at the last he fails to conquer. It is no accident that we always remember the effect of Marlowe's resounding geography, for earthly kingdoms are the emblems of Tamburlaine's aspirations. At the end of his life he calls for a map, on which he traces with infinite nostalgia his entire career and points to all the remaining riches which death will keep him from:

And shall I die, and this unconquered? (Part II, V. 3, 150).[13]

To be a world-conqueror in the various senses which the play gives to the term is the essence of Tamburlaine's character. That this insight is conveyed in part by the sprawling structure of the play is an important advantage to weigh against some of the obvious disadvantages of such a structure in the theatre. Although complication and even conflict in its fullest sense are almost missing, each successive episode contributes something to the dominant idea—the definition of a hero. There is a forward movement of the play in unfolding not only the narrative but the full picture of the hero. When the play is well acted and directed, it has ample theatrical life, no matter how much the form is indebted to epic.

The first view we have of Tamburlaine is a kind of trans-formation scene. It is preceded by the brief, and basically snobbish descriptions given at the court of Mycetes, the ludicrously incompetent king of Persia, to whom Tamburlaine is a marauding fox,[14] a "sturdy Scythian thief", and the leader of a "Tartarian rout" (I, 1, 31, 36, 71). The Tamburlaine who walks on the stage dressed as a shepherd and leading Zenocrate captive has some of the outward appearance suggested by these descriptions, and the earlier impression of social inferiority is conveyed in the words of Zenocrate,who at first takes him for the shepherd he seems to be (I, 2, 8). However, his words and actions reveal a strikingly different man: he boasts like a genuine hero if not a gentleman, and exchanges his shepherd's weeds for complete armour and curtle-axe. Before our eyes he assumes the outward appearance which matches his warrior's spirit.

Tamburlaine is a proud and noble king at heart, yet his Scythian-shepherd origins give a clue to the absolute difference between him and the world's other kings. His is the intrinsic kingliness of the hero, associated with the ideal of freedom, whereas other kings are presented as oppressors, the products of a corrupt system. The garb of the Scythian shepherd, even though he discards it, relates Tamburlaine to the simpler world of an earlier, mythical time. The king he becomes carries with him into a decadent world something of this primitive simplicity. Like his successors, Chapman's Bussy and Dryden's Almanzor, he is an early edition of the "noble savage".

Thus far Tamburlaine appears as a hero in the classic mode, but when he tells Zenocrate that her person "is more worth to

Tamburlaine / Than the possession of the Persian crown"
(ll. 90-1), the influence of the romance tradition is apparent.
In fact, for the moment it seems that the "concupiscible power"
of his soul dominates the "irascible power", though the subsequent action shows that this is not true. Tamburlaine's love,
expressed in the poetry of the famous speech beginning "Dis-
dains Zenocrate to live with me?" (ll. 82-105), further distinguishes him from his rival warriors. Their pride and their
ambition are not accompanied by the imagination which
informs his promises to Zenocrate:

> With milk-white harts upon an ivory sled
> Thou shalt be drawn amidst the frozen pools,
> And scale the icy mountains' lofty tops,
> Which with thy beauty will be soon resolv'd.
>
> (ll. 98-101)

The cold fire of this speech is the first testimony of Tamburlaine's imaginative scope and of the paradoxes of his nature;
the icy mountain tops are the first memorable image of his
aspiration.

The arrival of Theridamas with the Persian forces provides
for another surprising revelation of the hero. We have just seen
him in the guise of a lover; we now see him as an orator, overcoming Theridamas with words. Marlowe insists on the unexpectedness of these aspects of the hero. "What now? in love?"
says Techelles (l. 106), and, when Tamburlaine asks whether
he should "play the orator", replies disdainfully that "cowards
and faint-hearted runaways / Look for orations" (ll. 130-1). In
defiance of this advice, Tamburlaine delivers his brilliantly
successful oration, winning from Theridamas the tribute that
even Hermes could not use "persuasions more pathetical"
(l. 210). Yet, surprising as this eloquence is to Tamburlaine's
followers, it is not alien to the Renaissance concept of the
Herculean hero. Cartari specifically reminds his readers that
Hercules, like Mercury, whom he has just discussed, has been
called a patron of eloquence. It is, so to speak, perfectly proper
to present a Herculean hero as orator.

Tamburlaine begins his oration with a complimentary picture
of Theridamas, but soon turns to himself with the famous boast,
"I hold the Fates bound fast in iron chains", and the com-

E

parisons of himself to Jove. The effect of the speech is double, for though it displays the hero as orator, it also presents, by means of eloquence, his self-portrait as conqueror of the world and even as demigod. Such self-praise might be taken as Marlowe's way of portraying a man who will say anything to get ahead or of pointing to the ironical contrast between a man's pride and his accomplishment, but one of the puzzling features of *Tamburlaine* is that the hero's actions also show him in the guise of a demigod, and only his death proves that he does not control the fates. Even death is not presented unequivocally as defeat. Tamburlaine's extravagant boasts, like those of Hercules, are largely made good, so that he and his followers become the amazement of the world. In Usumcasane's words, "These are the men that all the world admires."

Before Tamburlaine unleashes his persuasive forces Theridamas comments on his appearance in words which emphasize the importance of visual impressions in this play:

> Tamburlaine! A Scythian shepherd so embellished
> With nature's pride and richest furniture!
> His looks do menace heaven and dare the gods,
> His fiery eyes are fixed upon the earth,
> As if he now devis'd some stratagem,
> Or meant to pierce Avernas' darksome vaults
> To pull the triple headed dog from hell.   (I, 2, 154-60)

Again we have the transformation of the Scythian shepherd into a noble warrior, but here even the armour appears as part of nature's endowment of the hero. The eyes fixed on the earth are the symbolic equivalent of one of Tamburlaine's best-known speeches, in which he makes an earthly crown the ultimate felicity, but this fixation on the earth is accompanied by looks which menace heaven and also suggest a Herculean conquest of hell. The description is perfect, though to use it when the character described stands before the audience is to risk a ludicrous incongruity.[15] Marlowe depends on unhesitating acceptance of the verbal picture.

Marlowe's heavy dependence on description is again illustrated in the next scene, when Menaphon gives Cosroe an even fuller account of Tamburlaine's looks than we have had from Theridamas. In this speech the hero's body is made

symbolic of his character. He is tall like his desire; his shoulders
might bear up the sky like Atlas; his complexion reveals his
thirst for sovereignty; he has curls like Achilles; and his
arms and hands betoken "valour and excess of strength" (II,
1, 7-30).

One of Tamburlaine's most important traits, his infinite
aspiration, receives its first major treatment in a much discussed speech in the second act about the "thirst of reign and
sweetness of a crown" (II, 7, 12-29). Menaphon's encomium of
Tamburlaine's physical beauty provides a clue to the understanding of this passage. Just as his body seems beautiful not
simply in itself but in that it expresses his character, so Tamburlaine extols the "sweet fruition of an earthly crown" not because
anything the earth has to offer has final value for him, but
because domination of the earth represents the fulfilment of his
mission—the fulfilment of himself. The speech is about the
infinite aspiration taught us by nature and the never-ending
activity to which the soul goads us. "The sweet fruition of an
earthly crown" is indeed bathos, as it has often been called,
unless the earthly crown means something rather special in this
play.

There is a good deal of evidence that it does. In an earlier
scene Usumcasane says, "To be a king, is half to be a god", and
Theridamas replies, "A god is not so glorious as a king" (II, 5,
56-7). Tamburlaine never puts it quite thus, for it is clear that
like Hercules he already considers himself partly divine, yet
kingship is obviously glorious to him. The "course of crowns"
which he and his followers eat in Act IV, Scene 4, is the visual
equivalent of the constant references to sovereignty. The earth
itself is despicable—inert—the negation of heroic energy, as
appears in the speech of Theridamas immediately following the
lines about the earthly crown:

> For he is gross and like the massy earth
> That moves not upwards, nor by princely deeds
> Doth mean to soar above the highest sort.   (II, 7, 31-3)

but ruling the earth is not an end in itself. It is a manifestation
of the will to "soar above the highest sort". When Tamburlaine
seizes his first crown, the crown of Persia, he makes the act
symbolic of his will:

> Though Mars himself, the angry god of arms,
> And all the earthly potentates conspire
> To dispossess me of this diadem,
> Yet will I wear it in despite of them . . .   (II, 7, 58-61)

His contempt for earthly potentates and the assertion of his will combine in his conception of himself as the scourge of God, a conception which he shares with Hercules (III, 3, 41-54).[16] He is the avenger, nemesis to the mighty of the world, contemptuous demonstrator of the absurdity of their claims, liberator of captives. He is not so much the instrument as the embodiment of a divine purpose. His serene confidence that his will is seconded by destiny gives him the magnificence of the hero who transcends the merely human. The activities of such a hero are always confined to the earth, though always pointing, in some sense, to a goal beyond. Thus Seneca's Hercules Oetaeus, while rejoicing in his earthly deeds, never forgets that he is destined to become a star. Toward the end of Part II Tamburlaine begins to speak of an otherworldly goal,[17] but even before this time the thrones and crowns of the world stand for something which though *in* the earth is yet not *of* it. Their importance to Tamburlaine lies in taking them away from tyrants like Bajazeth, for whom they have intrinsic value. Tamburlaine's last instructions to his son are to sway the throne in such a way as to curb the haughty spirits of the captive kings (Part II, V, 3, 234-41). An earthly crown represents the sweet fruition of his purpose in being.

Tamburlaine's moving description of the aspiration for sovereignty has the utmost value in the play in presenting his double attitude towards the earth. And as he both seeks and despises earthly glory, he both claims and defies the power of the gods. "Jove himself" will protect him (I, 2, 179); not even Mars will force him to give up the crown of Persia (II, 7, 58-61). He does not belong entirely to either earth or heaven. Though he has distinctly human characteristics, both good and bad, he has something of the magnificence and the incomprehensibility of a deity.

Tamburlaine speaks of Mars as "the angry god of war", and the words might serve as self-description, for when he is angry the awe that his looks inspire is almost that of a mortal for a god.

Agydas, when Tamburlaine has passed, "looking wrathfully" at him, expresses a typical reaction:

> Betrayed by fortune and suspicious love,
> Threatened with frowning wrath and jealousy,
> Surpris'd with fear of hideous revenge,
> I stand aghast; but most astonied
> To see his choler shut in secret thoughts,
> And wrapt in silence of his angry soul.
> Upon his brows was pourtrayed ugly death,
> And in his eyes the fury of his heart,
> That shine as comets, menacing revenge,
> And casts a pale complexion on his cheeks.
>
> (III, 2, 66-75)

Later a messenger speaks of "The frowning looks of fiery Tamburlaine, / That with his terror and imperious eyes / Commands the hearts of his associates" (IV, 1, 13-15), and the Governor of Damascus calls him "this man, or rather god of war" (V, 1, 1). Anger is the passion most frequently displayed in his looks, his words, and the red or black colours of his tents.

Not only is he a man of wrath, as the Herculean hero characteristically is; he is also fiercely cruel. This trait of character receives a continually increasing emphasis; it is strikingly demonstrated in Tamburlaine's treatment of Bajazeth. In Scene 2 of Act IV the defeated emperor is brought on in his cage, from which he is removed to serve as Tamburlaine's foot-stool. But Scene 4 is even more spectacular. Tamburlaine, dressed in scarlet to signify his wrath towards the besieged city of Damascus, banquets with his followers while the starving Bajazeth in his cage is insulted and given scraps of food on the point of his conqueror's sword. In the midst of these proceedings Tamburlaine refuses Zenocrate's plea that he raise the siege and make a truce with her father, the Soldan of Egypt. In the last act of Part I we see Tamburlaine order the death of the virgins of Damascus, who have been sent to beg for mercy after the black colours have already indicated Tamburlaine's decision to destroy the obstinate city. With inhuman logic he points out that it is now too late and that they "know my customs are as peremptory / As wrathful planets, death, or destiny" (V, 2, 64-5). At the end he says that his honour—that personal honour which is the basis of the hero's *areté*—"consists in shedding blood / When men presume to manage arms with him" (V, 2, 415-16). Tamburlaine's is a cosmic extension of the cruelty Achilles shows to Hector or Hercules to the innocent Lichas. Though it is a repellent trait, it is entirely consistent with the rest of the character. Instead of passing over it, Marlowe insists on it. One need not assume, however, that Marlowe himself loved cruelty nor, on the other hand, that he is depicting here a tragic flaw. It is an important part of the picture, a manifestation of Tamburlaine's "ireful Virtue", to use Tasso's phrase, and one of the chief occasions for wonder. One may disapprove and yet, in that special sense, admire.

Marlowe's method of constructing his dramatic portrait is essentially dialectical. Not only is love balanced against hate, cruelty against honour, but these and other traits are constantly brought out against a background of parallels or contrasts. Tamburlaine is contrasted with other monarchs and with Zenocrate. In the last act an entire city is his antagonist. Throughout the play his followers are like variations on the Tamburlaine theme, imitating his ferocity and zest for conquest, but incapable of his grandeur. The first three monarchs with whom the hero is contrasted are the foolish Mycetes, his brother, Cosroe, and the emperor Bajazeth. Mycetes is a grossly comic foil in his inability to act or speak well, to control others or himself. In the opening speech of the play he deplores his own insufficiency to express his rage, "For it requires a great and thundering speech" (I, 1, 1-3), a thing Tamburlaine can always provide.

In a low-comedy scene in the first act, he comes alone on to the battlefield, the picture of cowardice, looking for a place to hide his crown. This action in itself takes on great significance when we come, three scenes later, to Tamburlaine's praise of crowns. Mycetes curses the inventor of war and congratulates himself on the wisdom that permits him to escape its ill effects by hiding the crown which makes him a target. To put the censure of war and the praise of scheming wisdom in the mouth of such a character inclines the audience to see virtue in the hero's pursuit of war and in a kind of wisdom more closely allied to action.

The contrast with Cosroe is another matter. Patently

superior to his brother Mycetes, Cosroe appears to be an ordinarily competent warrior and ruler. In fact, his one crippling deficiency is his inability to recognize the extraordinary when he sees it in the person of Tamburlaine. His attempt to pat Tamburlaine on the head, and reward him for a job well done by giving him an important post in the kingdom, as any normal king might do, is as inept, given the nature of Tamburlaine, as the feckless gesturing of Mycetes. Cosroe is perfectly familiar with the rules of the game as it is generally played in the world, where the betrayal of a Mycetes is venial and competence has at least its modest reward. His cry of pain when Tamburlaine turns against him, "Barbarous and bloody Tamburlaine" (II, 7, 1), expresses the outrage of one who finds that the rules he has learned do not apply. Tamburlaine's strategy is so much more daring and his treachery so much more preposterous that they are beyond the imagination of Cosroe.

Bajazeth, Tamburlaine's third antagonist, is no mere moderately successful king. A proud and cruel tyrant, he rejoices in the sway of a vast empire. With his first words a new perspective opens up: "Great kings of Barbary, and my portly bassoes" (III, 1, 1). Here is a ruler served by kings. "We hear the Tartars and the eastern thieves, / Under the conduct of one Tamburlaine, / Presume a bickering with your emperor." The tone is superb. One notes the condescension of "one Tamburlaine" and the hauteur of "presume a bickering". He is assured ("You know our army is invincible"); he is used to command ("Hie thee, my basso . . . Tell him thy lord . . . Wills and commands, for say not I entreat"); and he is obeyed by thousands ("As many circumcised Turks we have, / And Warlike bands of Christians renied, / As hath the ocean or the Terrene sea / Small drops of water").

If Cosroe is a little more like Tamburlaine than is his foolish brother, Bajazeth is decidedly more so. He speaks of "the fury of my wrath" (III, 1, 30), and shows his cruelty by threatening to castrate Tamburlaine and confine him to the seraglio while his captains are made to draw the chariot of the empress. The famous (and to a modern reader ludicrous) exchange of insults between Zabina and Zenocrate reinforces the parallel. Yet Marlowe emphasizes the ease with which this mighty potentate is toppled from his throne. The stage directions tell the story:

"BAJAZETH *flies and he pursues him. The battle short and they enter.*
BAJAZETH *is overcome*" (III, 3, 211 ff.). This contrast brings out
what was suggested by the contrast with Cosroe, the truly
extraordinary nature of Tamburlaine. For Bajazeth is what
Mycetes would like to be but cannot be for lack of natural
aptitude. He is what Cosroe might become in time with a little
luck. As a sort of final term in a mathematical progression, he
presents the ultimate in monarchs, and in himself sums up the
others. That even he should fall so easily defines the limitations
of the species and sets Tamburlaine in a world apart. He is not
merely more angry, more cruel, more proud, more powerful.
Though sharing certain characteristics with his victims, he
embodies a force of a different order.

Zenocrate, by representing a scale of values far removed from
those of the warrior or the monarch, provides further insights
into Tamburlaine's character. Something has already been said
of his courtship of her in the first act, when, to the surprise of
Techelles, he shows that he is moved by love. The inclusion in
his nature of the capacity to love is a characteristic Renaissance
addition to the classical model of the Herculean hero. One
recalls that Tasso's Rinaldo, though chiefly representing the
"ireful virtue", is susceptible to the charms of Armida. Yet
Zenocrate is not an enchantress like Armida nor is Tamburlaine's love for her presented as a weakness.[18] Love, as opposed
to pure concupiscence, is a more important part of Tamburlaine
than of Rinaldo. As G. I. Duthie has pointed out, it modifies
considerably his warrior ideal,[19] leading him to spare the life
of the Soldan and "take truce with all the world" (V, 2, 467).

Marlowe leaves no doubt that the commitment to Zenocrate
is basic and lasting, but it is not allowed to dominate. Tamburlaine refuses Zenocrate's plea for Damascus, and when he also
refuses the Virgins of Damascus he says:

> I will not spare these proud Egyptians,
> Nor change my martial observations
> For all the wealth of Gihon's golden waves,
> Or for the love of Venus, would she leave
> The angry god of arms and lie with me. (V, 2, 58-62)

This clear evaluation of the claims of Venus as opposed to those
of Mars precedes by only a few lines the long soliloquy in which

he extols the beauty of Zenocrate. Here he admits that he is tempted to give in to Zenocrate, who has more power to move him than any of his enemies. By implication it is clear that this power is due to her beauty, which is so great that if the greatest poets attempted to capture it,

> Yet should there hover in their restless heads
> One thought, one grace, one wonder, at the least,
> Which into words no virtue can digest.   (V, 2, 108-10)

But on the verge, as it might seem, of capitulating to this softer side of his nature, he first reproves himself for these "thoughts effeminate and faint", and then presents beauty as the hand-maid of valour. This passage is a textual crux,[20] and its syntax is so treacherous that a close analysis of the meaning is nearly impossible, but I think it is fair to say that Tamburlaine's con-victions about the role of beauty are given in the lines:

> And every warrior that is rapt with love
> Of fame, of valour, and of victory,
> Must needs have beauty beat on his conceits . . .
>
> (V, 2, 117-19)

The conclusion of the speech looks forward to what beauty may inspire Tamburlaine to do, and it is as important a part of his mission as the scourging of tyrants. This is to show the world "for all my birth, / That virtue solely is the sum of glory, / And fashions men with true nobility" (V, 2, 125-7); that is, that the hero's goal is to be attained by an innate power which has nothing to do with the accidents of birth. To Theridamas, Techelles and Usumcasane he has said much the same thing, assuring them that they deserve their titles

> By valour and by magnanimity.
> Your births shall be no blemish to your fame;
> For virtue is the fount whence honour springs.
>
> (IV, 4, 129-31)

In several ways the power of love and beauty is subordinated to Tamburlaine's primary concerns. The encomium of Zeno-crate leads to the statement of beauty's function in the warrior's life and then to Tamburlaine's intention of demonstrating true nobility. Furthermore the entire soliloquy is carefully framed.

Before it begins, Tamburlaine orders a slaughter, and after his lines about true nobility he calls in a servant to ask whether Bajazeth has been fed. Tamburlaine's love for Zenocrate, extravagant as it is, is part of a rather delicately adjusted balance of forces.

Zenocrate is a pale character beside the best heroines of Shakespeare and Webster, but her attitude towards Tamburlaine is an important part of the meaning of the play. After her initial mistake—not wholly a mistake—of thinking he is just the Scythian shepherd he seems to be, her feelings towards him change rapidly. When she next appears she defends him to her companion, Agydas, who still sees Tamburlaine as a rough soldier. He asks:

> How can you fancy one that looks so fierce,
> Only disposed to martial stratagems?   (III, 2, 40-1)

Zenocrate replies by comparing his looks to the sun and his conversation to the Muses' song. When Tamburlaine enters he rewards each of them with behaviour suited to their conception of him: "*Tamburlaine goes to her, and takes her away lovingly by the hand, looking wrathfully on Agydas, and says nothing*" (III, 2, 65 ff.).

Zenocrate enters enthusiastically into the exchange of insults with Bajazeth and Zabina, but it is her speeches after the sack of Damascus and the suicides of Bajazeth and Zabina which truly reveal her attitude towards Tamburlaine. Sorrowing for the cruel deaths of the Virgins of Damascus, she asks:

> Ah, Tamburlaine, wert thou the cause of this,
> That term'st Zenocrate thy dearest love?
> Whose lives were dearer to Zenocrate
> Then her own life, or aught save thine own love.
>
> (V, 2, 273-6)

His cruelty is recognized for what it is without its impairing her love. Similarly, when she laments over the bodies of the emperor and empress, she acknowledges Tamburlaine's pride, but prays Jove and Mahomet to pardon him. This lament is a highly effective set-piece, whose formality gives it a special emphasis. Its theme, the vanity of earthly power, is resoundingly stated in the refrain, "Behold the Turk and his great emperess!" which occurs four times, varied the last time to "In this great Turk and hapless emperess!" (V, 2, 292, 295, 300, 306). But within the statement of theme there is a movement of thought as Zenocrate turns from the most general aspect of the fall of the mighty to what concerns her more nearly, its bearing on Tamburlaine. The orthodoxy of the moral she draws from this spectacle of death is conspicuous, and nowhere more so than in the central section:

> Ah, Tamburlaine, my love, sweet Tamburlaine,
> That fightst for sceptres and for slippery crowns,
> Behold the Turk and his great emperess!
> Thou that, in conduct of thy happy stars,
> Sleep'st every night with conquest on thy brows,
> And yet wouldst shun the wavering turns of war,
> In fear and feeling of the like distress,
> Behold the Turk and his great emperess!

The culmination of the speech is its prayer that Tamburlaine may be spared the consequences of "his contempt / Of earthly fortune and respect of pity" (V, 2, 302-3).

When Tamburlaine's enemies inveigh against his pride and presumption, their protests have a hollow ring, and Marlowe may seem to be laughing at the point of view they express. He is certainly not doing so when he puts criticism of the same faults in the mouth of Zenocrate. Through her an awareness of the standard judgment of Tamburlaine's "overreaching" is made without irony and made forcefully. Through her it is also made clear that such an awareness may be included in an unwavering devotion, just as Deianira's devotion can digest even the grave personal slight she suffers from Hercules. Zenocrate both presents the conventional view of hubris more convincingly than any other character, and shows the inadequacy of this view in judging Tamburlaine.

A contrast on a larger scale forms the final episode of Part I: Tamburlaine is pitted against the great city of Damascus. Since Zenocrate pleads for the city, this is an extension of the contrast between the hero and heroine. Since the city is ruled by Tamburlaine's enemies, it is the climax in the series of contrasts between him and the representatives of corrupt worldly power. His first three enemies are individuals of increasing stature, but the Governor of Damascus and his allies, the Soldan and

Arabia, are none of them imposing figures. Instead, the city of
Damascus becomes the collective antagonist, to which Tamburlaine opposes his personal will. Much more than the individual
monarchs of the first acts, the city seems to represent the point
of view of society, which Zenocrate also adopts when she
becomes the spokesman for conventional morality. When the
delegation of virgins asks the conqueror for mercy, the appeal
is in the name of the whole community:

> Pity our plights! O, pity poor Damascus!
> Pity old age . . .
> Pity the marriage bed . . .
> O, then, for these and such as we ourselves,
> For us, for infants, and for all our bloods,
> That never nourished thought against thy rule,
> Pity, O pity, sacred emperor,
> The prostrate service of this wretched town . . .
>
> (V, 2, 17-37)

Tamburlaine's refusal is based on the absolute primacy of his
will—of the execution of whatever he has vowed. He is as self-
absorbed as Hercules, whose devotion to his areté obliterates
any consideration for Deianira or Hyllus, in *The Women of
Trachis*. Homer portrays the hero's uncompromising adherence
to his own standard of conduct in the refusal of Achilles to fight.
In Book IX of the *Iliad*, when he is waited on by the delegation
of warriors, including his old tutor, Phoenix, heroic integrity
directly opposes obligation to others—to friends and allies in
war. The "conflict between personal integrity and social
obligation" was inherent in the story of the Wrath of Achilles,
according to Cedric Whitman, but Homer gave it special
importance, seeing it "as an insolubly tragic situation, the tragic
situation *par excellence*".[21] In the Renaissance it is not surprising
to find "social obligation" represented by the city, but in this
case it is an enemy city. Instead of being urged to fight for
friends Tamburlaine is urged to spare citizens whose only fault
is the acceptance of the rule of their foolish, and finally weak,
Governor. Hence the social obligation denied by Tamburlaine
is not that of supporting his friends' cause but of conforming to
an ideal of behaviour which places mercy above justice. The
code of Tamburlaine is a more primitive affair. His word once

given is as inflexible as destiny, and the imposition of his will upon Damascus is also the carrying out of a cosmic plan. To the demands of a segment of society he opposes a larger obligation to free the world from tyrants. Marlowe's setting him against Damascus reaffirms both his colossal individuality and his god-like superiority. The siege of this city is used to present the core of the problem of *virtus heroica*.

Marlowe puts far less emphasis upon the benefactions of his hero's career than was put upon the benefactions of Hercules; the punishment of the wicked is what Tamburlaine himself constantly reiterates. Nevertheless, the punishment of Damascus is balanced by the hero's generosity in sparing the Soldan. This is not a matter of just deserts. It is Tamburlaine's god-like caprice to spare Zenocrate's father. Because he does so the end of Part I suggests a positive achievement. Zenocrate's greeting of her "conquering love" is a mixture of wonder and gratitude, and even the vanquished Soldan joins in the general thanks-giving.

Whether Part II was planned from the first, as some have thought, or written in response to the "general welcomes Tamburlaine receiv'd", as the Prologue says, its general con-ception is strikingly similar to that of Part I. Its structure is again episodic, though the episodes are somewhat more tightly knit. The pattern is again a series of encounters between Tamburlaine and his enemies, leading at last to the one un-successful encounter—with death. To Mycetes, Cosroe and Bajazeth correspond the vaster alliance of Bajazeth's son Callapine and his allies. To the conflict between the factions in Persia corresponds the fight between Orcanes and Sigismund after a truce has been concluded. Here again, but even more circumstantially, we have the jealous struggles, the hypocrisies and the betrayals of conventional kings. Sigismund is a despic-able figure, Orcanes a rather sympathetic one—even more so than his structural counterpart, Cosroe. He is portrayed as a religious man, is given some fine lines on the deity, ". . . he that sits on high and never sleeps, / Nor in one place is circum-scriptible" (II, 2, 49-50), and, though born a pagan, acknow-ledges the power of Christ. That religion spares him none of the humiliations accorded to the enemies of Tamburlaine suggests that his religion, like his statecraft, is conventional. He is far

from being the worst of men or the worst of rulers, yet, like the
kings in Part I, he is given to boasting of his power and position
and making snobbish remarks about Tamburlaine's lowly
origin. It may be significant that he offers his partial allegiance
to Christ as a means of obtaining the victory over Sigismund,
who is a perjured Christian. This bargaining religion is the foil
to Tamburlaine's impious self-confidence.

Other elements of the pattern of Part I are also imitated here.
The siege of Damascus is matched by the siege of Babylon;
Bajazeth in his cage is matched by the conquered kings in
harness, to whom Tamburlaine shouts the famous "Holla, ye
pampered jades of Asia!" (IV, 3, 1), so often parodied. Tamburlaine in his chariot, actually whipping the half-naked kings who
draw him, is a powerful theatrical image. Preposterous as the
scene may be, it is satisfyingly right as a visual symbol of one of
the principal themes of the play. Part II develops the theme
more fully than Part I, giving it a prominent place in the dying
hero's instructions to his eldest son:

> So reign, my son; scourge and control these slaves,
> Guiding thy chariot with thy father's hand.
>
> .   .   .   .   .
>
> For, if thy body thrive not full of thoughts
> As pure and fiery as Phyteus' beams,
> The nature of these proud rebelling jades
> Will take occasion by the slenderest hair,
> And draw thee piecemeal, like Hippolytus . . .
>
> (V, 3, 228-9, 236-40)

Another theme developed in Part II is the cruelty of Tamburlaine. It is so prominent here that it may seem to mark a loss
of sympathy for the hero. Certainly the brutality to the conquered kings and to the Governor of Babylon, and above all
Tamburlaine's murder of his son, constitute more vivid and
more shocking examples than even the treatment of Bajazeth.
Yet one need not conclude that Marlowe has changed his mind
about his hero. All of these scenes may be understood as part
of a rhetorical amplification of a theme which is, after all, un-
mistakable in Part I. Furthermore these scenes serve to
emphasize other aspects of Tamburlaine's character indicated

in Part I. The portrait is not changed: its lines are more deeply incised.

The scenes presenting Calyphas, the cowardly son, are perhaps the most shocking of all, and may be used as examples of the amplified theme of cruelty in Part II. In the first of them (I, 4) Celebinus and Amyras, the two brave sons, win paternal approval by vying with each other in promises to scourge the world, while Calyphas is furiously rebuked for asking permission to stay with his mother while the rest are out conquering. As in all the scenes with the three sons, the patterning is obvious to the point of being crude, and the humour in the depiction of the girlish little boy not much to our taste. Nevertheless, the scene does more than show how hard-hearted Tamburlaine can be. For members of the audience who have not seen Part I it presents Tamburlaine's relationship to Zenocrate, and for the rest it restates that relationship in different terms. The scene opens with a loving speech to Zenocrate, who replies by asking Tamburlaine when he will give up war and live safe. It is this question which the scene answers by asserting the primacy of the irascible powers in Tamburlaine's nature. In spite of his love he identifies himself with "wrathful war", and as he looks at her, surrounded by their sons, suddenly thinks that his boys appear more "amorous" than "martial", and hence unworthy of him. Zenocrate defends them as having "their mother's looks" but "their conquering father's heart" (I, 4, 35-6), and it is then that they proclaim their intentions. Tamburlaine's rebuke to Calyphas is a statement of his creed, glorifying the "mind courageous and invincible" (I, 4, 73), and drawing a portrait of himself comparable to several in Part I:

> For he shall wear the crown of Persia
> Whose head hath deepest scars, whose breast most wounds,
> Which, being wroth, sends lightning from his eyes,
> And in the furrows of his frowning brows
> Harbours revenge, war, death and cruelty . . .   (I, 4, 74-8)

The furrowed brows belong to the angry demigod of Part I, and if the picture is somewhat grimmer, it is partly because of the hint that the demigod must suffer in the accomplishment of his mission.

The next scene with Calyphas (III, 2) takes place after the

death of Zenocrate, and like the former one, makes its contribution to the development of Tamburlaine's character. As the earlier scene began with the praise of Zenocrate, so this one begins with her funeral against the background of a conflagration betokening Tamburlaine's wrath. Again Calyphas is responsible for an unexpected note of levity when he makes an inane comment on the dangerousness of war just after his father has concluded stern instructions to his sons how to be "soldiers / And worthy sons of Tamburlaine the Great" (III, 2, 91-2). The consequence is not only a rebuke but a demonstration. Never having been wounded in all his wars, Tamburlaine cuts his own arm to show his sons how "to bear courageous minds" (III, 2, 143). Here his cruelty and anger are turned against himself, as perhaps they always are in some sense in the scenes with Calyphas.

The last of these scenes (IV, 1) is the most terrible and by far the most important, for Calyphas here prompts Tamburlaine to reveal himself more completely than ever before. In the first part of the scene the boy has played cards with an attendant while his brothers fought with their father to overcome the Turkish kings. He has scoffed at honour and, like Mycetes, praised the wisdom which keeps him safe (IV, 1, 49-50). When the victors return, Tamburlaine drags Calyphas out of the tent and, ignoring the pleas of his followers and of Amyras, stabs him to death. It is almost a ritual killing—the extirpation of an unworthy part of himself, as the accompanying speech makes clear:

> Here, Jove, receive his fainting soul again;
> A form not meet to give that subject essence
> Whose matter is the flesh of Tamburlaine,
> Wherein an incorporeal spirit moves,
> Made of the mould whereof thyself consists,
> Which makes me valiant, proud, ambitious,
> Ready to levy power against thy throne,
> That I might move the turning spheres of heaven;
> For earth and all this airy region
> Cannot contain the state of Tamburlaine.
>
>   (IV, 1, 111-20)

To interpret this murder as merely one further example of barbarous cruelty is to accept the judgment of Tamburlaine's

enemies. The cruelty is balanced against one of the most powerful statements of the spirituality of Tamburlaine. It is the
"incorporeal spirit" which makes him what he is, a hero akin
to the gods, and which, because it cannot bear to be other than
itself, pushes him to the execution of his cowardly son. As the
great aspiring speech of Part I obliges us to see an earthly crown
as the goal to which Tamburlaine's nature forces him, so this
speech and its accompanying action oblige us to accept cruelty
along with valour, pride and ambition as part of the spirit
which makes this man great. The soul of Calyphas, by contrast,
is associated with the "massy dregs of earth" (IV, 1, 123),
lacking both courage and wit, just as Theridamas described
the unaspiring mind as "gross and like the massy earth" (Part I,
II, 7, 31).

So far does Tamburlaine go in asserting his affinity to heaven
and contempt for earth, that for the first time he hints that
sovereignty of the earth may not be enough for him. It is an
idea which has an increasing appeal for him in the remainder
of the play. He makes another extreme statement in this scene
when his enemies protest the barbarity of his deed. "These
terrors and these tyrannies," he says, are part of his divine
mission,

> Nor am I made arch-monarch of the world,
> Crown'd and invested by the hand of Jove,
> For deeds of bounty or nobility . . .   (IV, 1, 150-2)

To be the terror of the world is his exclusive concern.

The emphasis on terror is consistent with the entire depiction
of his character. The denial of nobility is not. It is an extreme
statement which the emotions of the moment and dialectical
necessity push him to. Allowing for an element of exaggeration
in this speech, however, the scene as a whole, like the other
scenes with Calyphas, presents a Tamburlaine essentially like
the Tamburlaine of Part I, and not seen from any very different
point of view. As he grows older, as he encounters a little more
resistance, his character sets a little more firmly in its mould.
It remains what it has always been.

The death of Zenocrate is, as every critic has recognized, the
first real setback to Tamburlaine. In view of her association
with the city in Part I it is appropriate that Tamburlaine makes

F

a city suffer for her death by setting fire to it. His devotion to her and to the beauty she represents appears in the speech he makes at her deathbed (II, 4, 1-37), in his raging at her death, in the placing of her picture on his tent to inspire valour (III, 2, 36-42), and in his dying address to her coffin (V, 3, 224-7). As G. I. Duthie says, death is the great enemy in Part II, and his conquest of Zenocrate is in effect his first victory over Tamburlaine.[22] As he had to make some concessions to Zenocrate in Part I, so in Part II he has to come to terms with the necessity of death. The process begins with the death of Zenocrate, to which his first reaction is the desire for revenge. Not only does he burn the town where she died; he also orders Techelles to draw his sword and wound the earth (II, 4, 97). This prepares us somewhat for his later order, when death has laid siege to him, to "set black streamers in the firmament, / To signify the slaughter of the gods" (V, 3, 49-50). By keeping always with him the hearse containing her dead body he refuses wholly to accept her death as he now defies his own.

Only in the last scene of Act V does cosmic defiance give way to acceptance, and when this happens, Tamburlaine's defeat by death is partially transformed into a desired fulfilment. I have already mentioned his hint that the earth cannot contain him. It is followed by a suggestion that Jove, esteeming him "too good for earth" (IV, 3, 60), might make a star of him. Now he says:

> In vain I strive and rail against those powers
> That mean t'invest me in a higher throne,
> As much too high for this disdainful earth.   (V, 3, 120-2)

and finally:

> But sons, this subject, not of force enough
> To hold the fiery spirit it contains,
> Must part . . .   (V, 3, 168-70)

Like Hercules Oetaeus, he feels that his immortal part, that "incorporeal spirit" of which he spoke earlier, is now going to a realm more worthy of him, though imparting something of its power to the spirits of his two remaining sons, in whom he will continue to live. In these final moments we have what may be hinted at earlier in his self-wounding—a collaboration with death and fate in the destruction of his physical being. For the psychologist the drive towards self-destruction is latent in all heroic risks; it is the other side of the coin of self-assertion. Though Marlowe could never have put it this way, his insight may be essentially similar.

From the quotations already given it will be apparent that Tamburlaine's attitude toward the gods changes continually. He boasts of their favour or defies them to take away his conquests; likens himself to them, executes their will, waits for them to receive him into their domain, or threatens to conquer it. Tamburlaine's religious pronouncements, especially his blasphemies, have attracted a great deal of critical comment from his day to ours. Since Marlowe himself was accused of atheism, the key question has been whether or not Tamburlaine is a mouthpiece for his author. Some critics emphasize Tamburlaine's defiance of Mahomet and the burning of the Koran, but these episodes are surely no more significant than his "wounding" of the earth. As Kocher has pointed out (p. 89), his line, "The God that sits in heaven, if any god" (V, 1, 200) contains in its parenthetical comment more blasphemy for a Christian than does the whole incident of the Koran. Yet even this questioning of God's existence is only one of the changes of attitude just cited. To try to deduce Marlowe's religious position from these speeches is a hopeless undertaking, and to try to decide on the basis of the biographical evidence which of them Marlowe might endorse is risky and finally inconclusive. Somehow the relationship of these opinions to the rest of the play must be worked out. Either their inconsistency is due to carelessness (in this case carelessness of heroic proportions) or it has some bearing on the heroic character. Seneca's Hercules displays a similar variety of attitudes. In the earlier play he thanks the gods for their aid in his victory over the tyrant, Lycus, and offers to kill any further tyrants or monsters the earth may bring forth. Moments later, as his madness comes upon him, he says:

> To the lofty regions of the universe on high let me make my way, let me seek the skies; the stars are my father's promise. And what if he should not keep his word? Earth has not room for Hercules, and at length restores him unto heaven. See, the whole company of the gods of their own will summons me, and opens wide the door of heaven, with one alone forbidding. And wilt thou unbar

the sky and take me in? Or shall I carry off the doors of stubborn
heaven? Dost even doubt my power?   (*Hercules Furens*, ll. 958-65)

In the first lines of *Hercules Oetaeus* he again boasts of his activities
as a scourge of tyrants and complains that Jove still denies him
access to the heavens, hinting that the god may be afraid of him.
Later (ll. 1302-3) he almost condescends to Jove, remarking
that he might have stormed the heavens, but refrained because
Jove, after all, was his father. Greene could quite properly have
inveighed against "daring God out of heaven with that atheist
Hercules". At the end of *Hercules Oetaeus* the hero accepts his
fate with calm fortitude and even helps to destroy himself amidst
the flames. These changes in attitude are perhaps more easy to
understand in Hercules, since his relationship to the gods was in
effect a family affair. Tamburlaine is not the son of a god, but
his facile references to the gods, sometimes friendly, sometimes
hostile, may be interpreted as part of the heroic character of
which Hercules is the prototype. He has the assurance of a
demigod rather than the piety of a good man.

Such assurance, rather than repentance, breathes in the lines
in which Tamburlaine advises his son Amyras:

> Let not thy love exceed thine honour, son,
> Nor bar thy mind that magnanimity
> That nobly must admit necessity.
> Sit up, my boy, and with those silken reins
> Bridle the steeled stomachs of those jades.
>
> (V, 3, 199-203)

The advice to admit necessity[23] may reflect Tamburlaine's own
acceptance of his death, but in context it refers primarily to the
necessity for Amyras to take over Tamburlaine's throne. The
whole speech shows Tamburlaine's conviction of the rightness
of what he has done. The place of love is again made subordinate
to honour, the hero's chief concern. Magnanimity is stressed as
it is in Tamburlaine's advice to his followers to deserve their
crowns "by valour and magnanimity" (Part I, IV, 4, 129).
Even the bowing to fate is to be done nobly, as Tamburlaine
himself is now doing. Finally, the heroic enterprise of controlling
tyrants is to be continued. There is no retraction here, no
change in the basic character. He has come to terms with death,
but this is more a recovery than a reversal. He has spoken earlier

in the play of his old age and death, but, very humanly, has
rebelled when death struck at Zenocrate and then at himself.
Now he has regained calm with self-mastery.

Though the suffering of Tamburlaine is so prominent from
the death of Zenocrate to the end, retribution is not what is
stressed. The last scene of the play presents a glorification of the
hero approaching apotheosis. It opens with a formally patterned
lament, spoken by Theridamas, Techelles and Usumcasane, the
last section of which expresses the theme of the scene, Tamburlaine as benefactor:

> Blush, heaven, to lose the honour of thy name,
> To see thy footstool set upon thy head;
> And let no baseness in thy haughty breast
> Sustain a shame of such inexcellence,
> To see the devils mount in angels' thrones,
> And angels dive into the pools of hell.
> And, though they think their painful date is out,
> And that their power is puissant as Jove's,
> Which makes them manage arms against thy state,
> Yet make them feel the strength of Tamburlaine,
> Thy instrument and note of majesty,
> Is greater far than they can thus subdue;
> For if he die, thy glory is disgrac'd,
> Earth droops, and says that hell in heaven is plac'd.
>
> (V, 3, 28-41)

His sons live only in his life, and it is with the greatest reluctance
that Amyras mounts the throne at Tamburlaine's command.
When he speaks in doing so of his father's "anguish and his
burning agony" (V, 3, 209), he seems to imply that Tamburlaine's sufferings are the inevitable concomitants of his greatness and his service to humanity. It is he who pronounces the
final words:

> Meet heaven and earth, and here let all things end,
> For earth hath spent the pride of all her fruit,
> And heaven consum'd his choicest living fire!
> Let earth and heaven his timeless death deplore,
> For both their worths will equal him no more.
>
> (V, 3, 249-53)

Full of Herculean echoes, the lines form a perfect epitaph for
the hero, the product of earth and heaven.

Three times in this scene Tamburlaine adjures his son to control the captive kings and thus maintain order. He compares the task with Phaëton's:

> So reign, my son; scourge and control those slaves,
> Guiding thy chariot with thy father's hand.
> As precious is the charge thou undertak'st
> As that which Clymene's brain-sick son did guide
> When wandering Phoebe's ivory cheeks were scorched,
> And all the earth, like Aetna, breathing fire.
> Be warned by him, then; learn with awful eye
> To sway a throne as dangerous as his;   (V, 3, 228-35)

Despite his ambition and pride, Tamburlaine is no Macbeth to seek power "though the treasure / Of nature's germens tumble all together, / Even till destruction sicken. . . ."[24] Rather, he identifies himself with universal order, as does Seneca's Hercules. The very chariot which is a symbol of his cruel scourging is also the symbol of control and hence of order. Compared to the chariot of the sun, it is also the bringer of light.

In the depiction of the Herculean hero there is no relaxation of the tensions between his egotism and altruism, his cruelties and benefactions, his human limitations and his divine potentialities. Marlowe never lets his audience forget these antitheses. In the first scene of Act V this great benefactor orders the Governor of Babylon to be hung in chains on the wall of the town. He rises from his deathbed to go out and conquer one more army. It is Marlowe's triumph that, after revealing with such clarity his hero's pride and cruelty, he can give infinite pathos to the line, "For Tamburlaine, the scourge of God, must die" (V, 3, 248).

In obtaining a favourable reception for his hero among the more thoughtful members of his audience Marlowe could no doubt count on not only some familiarity with the heroic tradition in which he was working, but also on the often-voiced regard for the active life. Gabriel Harvey, it will be recalled, asks who would not rather be one of the nine worthies than one of the seven wise masters. He also expresses another attitude on which Marlowe could count, the Stoic regard for integrity—truth to oneself. Harvey prefers Caesar to Pompey because Pompey deserts himself, while Caesar remains true to himself. He notes that it was Aretine's glory to be himself.[25]

The last moments of the play appeal to the spectator's pity by insisting on the tragic limitation of Tamburlaine as a human being. "For Tamburlaine, the scourge of God, must die" is comparable to Achilles' lines: "For not even the strength of Herakles fled away from destruction, / although he was dearest of all to lord Zeus . . ." But the play's dominant appeal is to the wonder aroused by vast heroic potential. The very paradoxes of Tamburlaine's nature excite wonder, and this was supposed in Marlowe's time to be the effect of paradox. Puttenham, in his familiar *Arte of English Poesie*, calls paradox "the wondrer". Tamburlaine's "high astounding terms", for which the Prologue prepares us, clearly aim at the same effect. Many years later, Sir William Alexander, the author of several Senecan tragedies, wrote that the three stylistic devices which pleased him most were: "A grave sentence, by which the Judgment may be bettered; a witty Conceit, which doth harmoniously delight the Spirits; and a generous Rapture expressing Magnanimity, whereby the Mind may be inflamed for great Things." The last of these three he found in Lucan, in whose "Heroical Conceptions" he saw an "innate Generosity"; he remarked the power of "the unmatchable Height of his Ravishing Conceits to provoke Magnanimity".[26] Marlowe was undoubtedly influenced by the style of the *Pharsalia*, the first book of which he had translated, and in any case Alexander's words might justly be applied to *Tamburlaine*. The epic grandeur of the style,[27] with its resounding catalogues of exotic names, its hyperboles, and its heroic boasts and tirades, "expresses magnanimity", that largeness of spirit so consistently ascribed to the great hero. Alexander testifies that such a style may inflame the mind "for great things", and general as this description is, it serves well for the feeling aroused by the play. Another name for it was admiration.

4

Chapman

Farewell, brave relics of a complete man,
Look up and see thy spirit made a star;
Join flames with Hercules . . .

CHAPMAN'S Bussy D'Ambois is less of a demigod than
Marlowe's Tamburlaine—more clearly a man with human
failings. Nevertheless, Bussy is another Herculean hero. Chapman insists even more than Marlowe on the parallel,[1] translating a passage from *Hercules Oetaeus* for part of one of Bussy's
dying speeches and presenting in the lines quoted above a final
vision of the hero transfigured like his mythic prototype.

Some of the difference between Tamburlaine and Bussy
D'Ambois is due to the sources on which the two playwrights
drew. The history of an Oriental conqueror, who had already
become almost a myth in Marlowe's day, lent itself to the
portrayal of a man surpassing ordinary humanity. French
history of the late sixteenth century, to which Chapman turned,
was not apt to have in itself any such mythic suggestiveness for
an English audience in the first decade of the seventeenth
century.[2] Bussy was a much discussed nobleman who died in
1579, when Chapman was twenty. Monsieur, who plays such
an important part in the story, was the Duke of Anjou, well
known in England as a suitor for the hand of Queen Elizabeth.
In fact, the material which Chapman chose for this play looks
to be the most improbable basis for a Hercules play. What
Chapman saw in the material was a vision shaped by his
familiarity with the classics and with the work of Renaissance
scholars.

Though certain details are changed, the story of the play is
true to history in its main outlines.[3] It is the story of a brilliant
adventurer at the court of Henry III, notorious for his daring,
his insolence, his duels, his amours. Brought to court by
Monsieur, the king's brother, he flirts with the wife of the great
Duke of Guise, fights a duel in which he kills both his opponent
and one of the seconds, and then launches himself into an affair

with Tamyra, the Duchess of Montsurry. It is the discovery of this love-affair which brings about his end, for Monsieur, jealous of Bussy's success where he himself has failed, joins with Guise and the injured husband to set a trap in which Bussy is killed.

For the presentation of such swashbuckling romance the Elizabethan stage was well prepared by Kyd and others, who mixed Seneca with native tradition to produce a popular blend of love and blood and the supernatural. Far from avoiding the theatrical clichés of his day, Chapman exploits them to the hilt. Tamyra is made to be an active intriguer, employing a friar as pander (to the undoubted delight of English theatre-goers). To them alone is known a secret vault, through which Bussy is led, rising with the friar through a trap-door to make an impressive entrance. For the supernatural Chapman introduces conjuring scenes in the great tradition of Greene and Marlowe: spirits rise from the underworld, and in their turn conjure up visions for their masters. For good measure there is also a ghost in the last scenes of the play. Horror is generously provided in the scene where Montsurry stabs Tamyra's arms and finally puts her on the rack in order to compel her to write the letter which will draw Bussy into the trap. The letter is written in blood.

It is amazing that the dominant tone of a play drawn from such sources and utilizing such dramatic conventions should be one of quiet (and at times heavy) seriousness. For this tone the quality of Chapman's verse is partly responsible. Instead of Marlowe's insistent rhythms, his resounding catalogues, and the constructions which sweep the listener on to the conclusion, we have a style which is tough and dense, a learned vocabulary, sentences which are complex and long, reasoning which is hard to follow. At various times both compression and grammatical looseness seem to impede comprehension. Yet once one becomes somewhat accustomed to this difficult style, it attracts much more than it repels. It fascinates with its continual suggestion of further meaning to be unfolded, and in so doing it fulfils its major function. It persuades the reader or the spectator to look beyond the story and its theatrical trappings for the vision which the play embodies.

The Bussy with whom the audience is immediately confronted

at the opening of the first scene is dressed as a poor man (an unhistorical touch) and talks more like a philosopher than an adventurer. He talks, in fact, very like Plutarch, from whose ethical writings much of Bussy's first speech is translated.[4] The basis of the entire speech is a contrast between the man who is virtuous and poor and the man whom the world calls great. In the first part of the speech "great" men, the darlings of fortune, are memorably compared to "those colossic statues, / Which, with heroic forms without o'erspread, / Within are nought but mortar, flint, and lead". Their lack of the inner worth possessed by the virtuous man in his poverty seems to suggest to the speaker a yet more general reflection on the insubstantiality of man—"a torch borne in the wind; a dream / But of a shadow . . ." But he is still thinking mainly about the "great" man, for in the second half of his speech he offers himself the somewhat consoling thought that even those who seem outwardly most successful must eventually turn for help to Virtue, just as "great" seamen, after the most glorious of voyages, must call on "a poor, staid fisherman" to pilot them into port. The man who is later to be compared to Hercules is casting himself here in the unheroic role of the poor fisherman, while all the heroic comparisons, qualified though they may be by irony, are reserved for the ambitious man—by implication the politician of the type soon to be exemplified in Monsieur and the Guise. This initial view of Bussy as a despiser of the world becomes especially surprising in retrospect, when we see him in the midst of the "great" men he has described, a favourite at court, behaving in some respects very much like them. Unless the opening speech is taken as the hypocritical scorn of a jealous man, it eventually seems to present a paradox. It is only one of many.

The latter part of the speech exactly depicts the ensuing action. "*Procumbit*" says the Latin stage-direction, and as Bussy lies at one side of the stage, the picture of poor virtue, from the other side the great Monsieur sails on, accompanied by two pages, seeking Bussy as an aid in his ambitious schemes. As he says, "There's but a thread betwixt me and a crown", and though he does not admit that he wants to hasten his brother's death, he wants "resolved spirits" around him. D'Ambois is useful precisely because he is fearless, has nothing to lose, and is angry at the world for the way he has been treated. Monsieur is cynical enough to be sure that an attractive offer will bring him into the world he despises, and by the end of the scene this assurance has been justified. Bussy has accepted Monsieur's money and agreed to come to court: the poor fisherman has been hired to guide the great seaman to his destination.

In accepting Monsieur's offer, however, Bussy loses none of his antipathy to the politic man. He is willing to seize the opportunity because of his belief that "no man riseth by his real merit" but only when time or fortune is favourable to him (I, 1, 134-43). He sees well enough what Monsieur's game is, but determines to outplay his employer by remaining virtuous even at court:

> I am for honest actions, not for great:
> If I may bring up a new fashion,
> And rise in Court for virtue, speed his plow!
>
> (I, 1, 128-30)

The mere acceptance of service in Monsieur's train cannot be taken as proof of corruption, though it would seem to be so if it were not for the commentary of Bussy's speech. Action and speech taken together make quite another point—the extra-ordinary difficulties attending upon virtuous action in the world. If Bussy continues in the "green retreat" where Monsieur finds him he cannot act at all; in order to act he must enter an arena where virtue is only talked about. The problem, in its abstract formulation, is not unlike that faced by Bussy's con-temporary on the stage, Prince Hamlet. It grows out of that venerable topic of debate, the relative merits of the active and the contemplative life.

The activities of Bussy D'Ambois at court have already been referred to. The flirting, the duel, the affair with Tamyra, are characteristic of a wild adventurer such as the historical Bussy apparently was, but Chapman loads all of them with meanings far greater (and far other) than what these activities appear to signify. For instance, Bussy's extravagant attentions to the Duchess of Guise before the eyes of her husband and the rest of the court seem to be mere insolent rudeness. Monsieur in an aside interprets this defiance of the Guise as evidence of heroic self-sufficiency:

His great heart will not down, 'tis like the sea,
That partly by his own internal heat,
Partly the stars' daily and nightly motion,
Their heat and light, and partly of the place
The divers frames, but chiefly by the moon,
Bristled with surges, never will be won,
(No, not when th' hearts of all those powers are burst)
To make retreat into his settled home,
Till he be crown'd with his own quiet foam.   (I, 2, 157-65)

The parenthesis and the other qualifying phrases so characteristic of Chapman's style hold the meaning in suspension till the
very end, and shape it before our eyes. Even the great natural
force of the sea acts partly in response to external force and to
geographical circumstance, but once aroused, it alone determines its return to a state of calm. The weight of the meaning
is borne chiefly by two images in the latter half of the sentence,
"bristled with surges" and "crown'd with his own quiet foam".
The second of these, given the utmost force by the previously
interrupted flow of the sentence, pushes the entire episode to
which it refers into a new realm of meaning. Like the comment
of some Renaissance interpreter of one of Hercules' exploits, it
turns the attention quite away from what is outward and
physical to what is inward and spiritual. What seemed like an
irresponsible outburst of restless energy becomes a symbol for
majestic self-possession, manifest alike in fury and calm, a law
unto itself.

Immediately after this brush with Guise, and partly as a
result of it, Bussy avenges an insult by fighting a duel with
Barrisor. Not only is this encounter glorified by its presentation
in the heightened rhetoric of a Senecan *Nuntius* (II, 1, 35-137),
but it is made the occasion of further comments on the nature
of Bussy. Monsieur, in pleading for the King's pardon, calls
him "a man / In his uprightness, worthy to survive / Millions
of such as murther men alive" (II, 1, 177-9). Bussy, when he
has received his pardon, asserts the superiority of his virtue to
man-made laws:

          since I am free,
     (Offending no just law), let no law make
     By any wrong it does, my life her slave:
     When I am wrong'd, and that law fails to right me,

Let me be king myself (as man was made),
And do a justice that exceeds the law . . .   (II, 1, 194-9)

The suggestion in this speech that Bussy represents unspoiled
man is fully developed in the next act in a remarkable eulogy
of Bussy given by King Henry to the Guise, who continues to
regard the new favourite as a ruffian and a murderer:

Cousin Guise, I wonder
Your honour'd disposition brooks so ill
A man so good, that only would uphold
Man in his native noblesse, from whose fall
All our dissensions rise; that in himself
(Without the outward patches of our frailty,
Riches and honour) knows he comprehends
Worth with the greatest: kings had never borne
Such boundless empire over other men,
Had all maintain'd the spirit and state of D'Ambois . . .[5]
(III, 2, 88-97)

The speech is too long to be quoted in full. Bussy appears
once more as the man of intrinsic virtue, opposed to those whom
Fortune has rewarded. He belongs to the Golden Age, when
men were free and equal, before crime brought about the
development of restrictive legislation. His incomparable assets
are greatness of spirit and what Chapman calls "th'ingenious
soul", a soul both noble and strong by nature.

While such speeches as these make it clear that the Bussy of
Chapman's play is not to be taken as a despicable bully, they
raise a difficult problem in interpretation by the lengths to
which the praise of the hero is carried. Nothing he could possibly
do could fully merit such praise; what he does is far indeed from
meriting it. As we go through the play we seem to be moving on
two parallel lines, one of which is the adventures of the historical
Bussy, the other a progressive revelation of a mythic figure, a
Hercules disguised as Bussy. The distance between these lines
constitutes the chief problem for the critic. I shall mention
some of the solutions which have been offered before I give the
one which seems most acceptable to me, but first it is necessary
to present the central paradox, Bussy's relations with Tamyra,
on which any interpretation must be based.

Tamyra sums up in her own person many of the major
thematic contrasts of the play, for Chapman has managed to

associate her with all that is most defiantly individualistic in
Bussy and also with all the good and the bad in the society
which Bussy defies. She is both fatal enchantress and ideal
mistress—Acrasia and Gloriana, wrapped up in one person.
The affair is initiated in the second act when Monsieur tells
Bussy that he is going to lay siege to Tamyra and Bussy
announces in a brief soliloquy that his own love has long been
vowed to her in his heart, and that he does not fear Monsieur
as a rival. Immediately following is a scene in which the contradictions in Tamyra's character are fully displayed. First we see
her discussing Bussy with her husband and others, admitting
that his conduct in court has been rude, but also defending him:

> For though his great spirit something overflow,
> All faults are still borne, that from greatness grow . . .[6]

She has a reputation for virtue at court, which she defends by
saying that she would have been much more severe than the
Duchess of Guise if Bussy had made so bold with her, but at this
very moment, as it is soon made clear, she is planning to have
Bussy brought to her room by the Friar. There is no doubt that
she is fully aware of the moral implications of her plan, for on
two occasions during this scene she refers to the loss of virtue to
which her passion is leading her.[7] Shortly before Bussy arrives
she rejects the advances of Monsieur with a show of wifely
devotion, sternly refusing a chain of pearl which he offers her.
Somewhat later, parting from Bussy after their first assignation,
she gives him a chain of pearl as a token of her love.

Her behaviour shows Tamyra to be a deceitful and consciously
sinful woman; when Monsieur and, through him, Montsurry
find out about her, it is understandable that this is their view
of her. It is not, however, the only view that the play presents.
Bussy refuses to accept it, blames her for having a Puritan
conscience, and asserts the virtue of their love as a corollary
of his strength: "Sin is a coward . . ." (III, 1, 20). Like a knight
of romance he vows absolute secrecy as well as fealty, and
implies that Tamyra is virtuous as long as he can defend her
reputation. Surprisingly, this romantic idealization of the
affair receives some validation at the end of the play. Montsurry's torture of his wife is so horrible and his hiring of
murderers to dispatch Bussy so cowardly that sympathy is

thrown to the lovers, and their mutual devotion at the time of Bussy's death is far removed from lust or court intrigue. Against the clear symbolism of Tamyra's blood on the letter which draws Bussy to his destruction is balanced a contrary symbol when Bussy compares the soul and body of man to "two sweet courtly friends . . . / A mistress and a servant" (V, 4, 83-4). In this image, compounded of Platonism and courtly love, the mistress is identified with the hero's immortal part. A moment later, the spectacle of her suffering is the wound which finally breaks his heart (V, 4, 131-4). Tamyra remains acutely conscious of her sin to the end, but the nobility of her attachment to Bussy is equally stressed. In fact, her sense of sin becomes almost a guarantee of the purity of her feelings for her lover, for in one of her last speeches she bitterly observes that if her marriage vows had meant nothing to her she might easily have had the sort of affair which was common at court. Instead, it is her tragedy that, feeling equally her obligations to both men, she has equally betrayed both.

It is not easy to say whether Tamyra is a force for good or evil in Bussy's life. Like Iole, she is the object of passions which the world, but not the hero, regards as guilty; like Deianira, she is the most unwilling agent of the hero's destruction. Her use of the Friar as go-between and her association with night and the powers of darkness add further complexities to the interpretation of her part in the play.

The Friar appears to be a thoroughly hypocritical, scheming person when we first meet him—just a Protestant's idea of a Friar. Escorting Bussy to Tamyra's room in the night, he gives crafty instructions to the would-be lover to seem to have requested the interview for the purpose of explaining to her the reasons of his duel with Barrisor, a former admirer of hers. At the second assignation of the lovers the Friar proves to be an adept at conjuring, raising Behemoth to show them what Monsieur and Montsurry are doing. Yet he is by no means the wicked stereotype he seems. He is always spoken of with reverence; even when his complicity is discovered, Montsurry calls him nothing worse than a "strange creature" (V, 1, 191), and vents his outrage on the general wickedness of the world. The Friar's death is curious. Chapman might easily have shown him punished for his sins by Montsurry's sword. Instead, he dies of shock when he sees Tamyra put to the rack, and his death, as Parrott remarks (p. 559), breaks Tamyra's resolution when torture has not done so. When he reappears as a ghost, he bends his efforts first to the saving of Bussy's life, and then, when these fail, to reconciling Tamyra and Montsurry. His words in the last act are not those of a penitent sinner but of a divine agency. It is he who bids Bussy's spirit "join flames with Hercules", and in the first quarto this valedictory speech ends the play.[8] In the last analysis the irony of Tamyra's using this "holy man" as an "agent for her blood" cuts both ways. The suggestion that religion is being prostituted is certainly there, but for all that, the Friar's constant attendance upon the lovers tends to ennoble their affair. His admiration for both of them and Tamyra's respect and love for him are never undercut. In terms of the parallel actions of the play, it might be said that the Friar as a hypocritical churchman belongs to the adventures of Bussy, while the Friar as supernatural agency belongs to the revelation of Bussy as a mythic figure.

Before the first appearance of Bussy and the Friar in the secret vault Tamyra invokes the night in lines of compelling beauty:

> Now all ye peaceful regents of the night,
> Silently gliding exhalations,
> Languishing winds, and murmuring falls of waters,
> Sadness of heart and ominous secureness,
> Enchantments, dead sleeps, all the friends of rest,
> That ever wrought upon the life of man,
> Extend your utmost strengths, and this charm'd hour
> Fix like the Centre! Make the violent wheels
> Of Time and Fortune stand, and great Existence
> (The Maker's treasury) now not seem to be,
> To all but my approaching friends and me!   (II, 2, 108-18)

The conventional equation of light with good and dark with evil makes it quite logical that Tamyra, swayed by what she calls her "dark love" (II, 2, 96), should ask the night to protect her friends and her. Yet how different is this from the invocations of darkness in *Macbeth*! The night to which Macbeth and his Lady pray is "thick" and "seeling", palled "in the dunnest smoke of hell", and has a "bloody and invisible hand". Tamyra's night is a powerful enchanter, capable of arresting the violent motion of Time and Fortune and of establishing a calm like the central point of the revolving earth. The difference between the two is not mainly due to the fact that Macbeth is bent on murder and Tamyra on love; the two conceptions of night are radically different. Chapman's is a vital part of his strange presentation of the hero and heroine and of their involvement in the world of magic. The darkness with which they are associated is so important an element in the play that its significance must be explored before proceeding with the discussion of the characters. Chapman's attitude towards darkness underlies his presentation of the puzzling scenes of conjuration and, more generally, his practice of poetry.

It used to be said that Chapman and Marlowe belonged to a "School of Night", and though the notion of a "school" is no longer widely held[9] there is no doubt that for Chapman, at least, night had a special, mystical attraction. *The Shadow of Night*, composed of two poems, the "Hymnus in Noctem" and the "Hymnus in Cynthiam", is a *tour de force* in which night is praised and day disparaged. In the first of these hymns Night, the "Most sacred mother both of Gods and men" (l. 68) is contrasted with "A stepdame Night of minde" (l. 63).[10] The mental night or blindness of man has made a chaos of the corrupt world far worse than the original chaos which existed before creation. Since Day belongs to the created order which has so degenerated, Night becomes the patroness of virtue and truth. She is "deare Night, o goddesse of most worth" (l. 213) as opposed to "haughtie Day" (l. 217), "the whoredome of this painted light" (l. 249), "pale day (with whoredome soked quite)" (l. 329), "Dayes deceiptfull malice" (l. 339), and "shameless Day [who] doth marble us in ill" (l. 369). Hercules is asked to bend his bow against the sun:

Fall Hercules from heaven in tempestes hurld,
And cleanse this beastly stable of the world:
Or bend thy brasen bow against the Sunne,
As in Tartessus, when thou hadst begunne
Thy taske of oxen: heat in more extreames
Then thou wouldst suffer, with his envious beames:
Now make him leave the world to Night and dreames.
Never were vertues labours so envy'd
As in this light: shoote, shoote, and stoope his pride . . .
(ll. 255-63)

"Night and dreames." Night is repeatedly associated with the mysterious knowledge which comes in dreams and visions. It is peaceful and strong, a guide to virtuous conduct, a source of poetic inspiration, and a storehouse of learning.

Other writings of Chapman's, both prose and poetry, testify that this praise of night and darkness is not simply a *jeu d'esprit* or an example of that popular Renaissance exercise, the paradoxical encomium. In *The Tears of Peace*, for example, he speaks of how "the gaudie vulgar light / Burns up my good thoughts, form'd in temperate Night" (ll. 1003-4), and in the dedication of the Odyssey:

> *Truth* dwels in Gulphs, whose Deepes hide shades so rich,
> That *Night* sits muffl'd there, in clouds of pitch . . .
>
> *(Poems*, p. 409)

Only the poet who is strong enough can plumb these depths and arrive at the mysteries they contain.

For Chapman the pursuit of knowledge is a heroic and also ecstatic experience and one which he often describes in terms of the penetration of shadowy depths. He opens his dedication of *The Shadow of Night* by saying:

> It is an exceeding rapture of delight in the deepe search of knowledge, . . . that maketh men manfully indure th'extremes incident to that *Herculean* labour . . .[11]   *(Poems*, p. 19)

For the poet in quest of knowledge the darkness not only provides this rapture and attends upon revelation but also determines the manner in which the knowledge is to be transmitted. Style, too, should be somewhat dark. This is explained in the dedication of *Ovid's Banquet of Sense* in words which have often been quoted:

> The prophane multitude I hate, & onelie consecrate my strange Poems to these serching spirits, whom learning hath made noble, and nobilitie sacred; . . .
> But that Poesie should be as perviall as Oratorie, and plainnes her speciall ornament, were the plaine way to barbarisme. . . . That, *Enargia*, or cleerenes of representation, requird in absolute Poems is not the perspicuous delivery of a lowe invention; but high, and harty invention exprest in most significant, and unaffected phrase; it serves not a skilfull Painters turne, to draw the

figure of a face onely to make knowne who it represents; but hee
must lymn, give luster, shaddow, and heightening; which though
ignorants will esteeme spic'd, and too curious, yet such as have
the judiciall perspective, will see it hath, motion, spirit and
life. . . .

Obscuritie in affection of words, & indigested concets, is
pedanticall and childish; but where it shroudeth it selfe in the hart
of his subject, utterd with fitnes of figure, and expressive Epethites;
with that darknes wil I still labour to be shaddowed: rich Minerals
are digd out of the bowels of the earth, not found in the superficies
and dust of it . . .   (*Poems*, p. 49)

Though Chapman's vocabulary here is likely to provoke a
smile, it has the merit of illustrating the point he is making; it
avoids being indecently "perviall". In the *Justification of
Andromeda Liberata*, replying to criticism of his obscurity, Chapman goes so far as to say that poetry ought to be ambiguous[12]:

As *Learning*, hath delighted from her Cradle, to hide her selfe from
the base and prophane *Vulgare*, her ancient Enemy; under divers
vailes of *Hieroglyphickes*, Fables, and the like; So hath she pleased
her selfe with no disguise more; then in misteries and allegoricall
fictions of *Poesie*. . . . Yet ever held in high Reverence and
Aucthority; as supposed to conceale, within the utter barke (as
their Eternities approve) some sappe of hidden Truth. . . . Or else
recording some memorable Examples for the use of policie and
state: ever (I say) enclosing within the Rinde, some fruit of
knowledge howsoever darkened; and (by reason of the obscurity)
of ambiguous and different construction.   (*Poems*, p. 327)

I have quoted at length because the details of Chapman's
doctrine of obscurity relate it closely to the tradition, referred
to in Chapter 2, that the fictions of the poet *conceal* a truth which
would be desecrated by revelation to the ignorant majority, but
which the élite may see and delight in. This hieratic point of
view was understandably congenial to the Platonists, who were
fascinated by the occult and liked to think of the poet as a priest
whose divine inspiration (the *furor poeticus*) enabled him to
reveal the great mysteries to initiates.[13] Schoell has clearly
demonstrated Chapman's familiarity with the writings of
Ficino, and it is reasonable to suppose that his theory of style
owes a good deal to Ficino and his circle. His hatred of the
"prophane multitude", for instance, and his determination to

consecrate his poems to those who are worthy of them are not only reminiscences of Horace's "Odi profanum vulgus", but resemble even more closely, in thought and word, passages from Pico della Mirandola's Oration "On the Dignity of Man". To make the occult mysteries public, according to Pico, would be "to give a holy thing to dogs and to cast pearls before swine". Hence, the "Sphinxes carved on the temples of the Egyptians reminded them that mystic doctrines should be kept inviolable from the common herd (*a profana multitudine*) by means of the knots of riddles".[14] Plato and Aristotle figure in the list of those who have hidden their highest learning in riddles, and "so did Orpheus protect the mysteries of his dogmas with the coverings of fables, and conceal them with a poetic veil (*poetico velamento*), so that whoever should read his hymns would suppose there was nothing beneath them beyond idle tales and perfectly un-adulterated trifles".[15] Pico returns several times to the deliberate obscurity of poetic fables and to the difficulties which even he, an adept, has had in deciphering them. Edgar Wind, who believes that "a deliberate obliqueness in the use of metaphor" also characterizes a great deal of Renaissance painting, writes:

> The enjoyment Pico derived from occult authors was vicarious and poetical; they exercised his imagination in the employment of outlandish metaphors. It never occurred to him, as it did to less speculative minds, that the turgid lore of the dialectical magi might be put to a more nefarious use than for amplifying the Platonic *mystères littéraires*. Black magic, in the sense that it appealed to Agrippa of Nettesheim, he rejected as a vile superstition.[16]

Conti, whose writings Chapman knew well,[17] also speaks of the "occult way of philosophizing", which he says the Greeks took from the Egyptians to avoid publishing "admirable things" to the crowd ("*in vulgus*"); their solution was "*per fabulas philosophari*".[18]

From any of a large number of Renaissance authors Chapman may have derived his belief that the best poetry is deliberately contrived to yield its learning only to initiates.[19] Among the Florentine Platonists he would have found this theory combined with vast admiration for "man in his native noblesse" (sometimes expressed through the myth of Hercules), and with a keen interest in the occult. It is a combination very suggestive of the style and content of *Bussy D'Ambois*. Chapman, though certainly well aware of the "nefarious" uses of black magic, seems also to be aware that incantations, spells and spirits belong to the mysteries which it is man's privilege to penetrate and his duty to preserve inviolate. The darkness of the conjuring scenes, like the darkness of the style, is a means of giving to his hero an added dimension.

In Tamyra's invocation it seems to be assumed that the "peaceful regents of the night" have some of the extraordinary powers referred to in the "Hymnus in Noctem": a mystery surrounds them, they are opposed to Time and Fortune, and their calm is to be made available only to adepts—to Tamyra's friends. These are overtones, barely heard in the scene of the first assignation. In the conjuring scene they are sounded loudly along with other notes which recall the "Hymnus in Noctem". Bussy requests the Friar to use his "deep skill / In the command of good aërial spirits" (IV, 2, 8-9), and the Friar promises to do so "by my power of learned holiness" (l. 45). When Behemoth answers the summons he is shocked by the triviality of the task he is asked to perform:

> Why call'dst thou me to this accursed light,
> To these light purposes? I am Emperor
> Of that inscrutable darkness where are hid
> All deepest truths, and secrets never seen,
> All which I know, and command legions
> Of knowing spirits that can do more than these.
>
> (ll. 66-71)

After he has reluctantly obeyed instructions by revealing the activities of Monsieur and Montsurry, the Friar asks, "What shall become of us?" Behemoth replies:

> All I can say,
> Being call'd thus late, is brief, and darkly this:
> If D'Ambois' mistress dye not her white hand
> In his forc'd blood, he shall remain untouch'd;
> So, father, shall yourself, but by yourself:
> To make this augury plainer, when the voice
> Of D'Ambois shall invoke me, I will rise,
> Shining in greater light, and show him all
> That will betide ye all; meantime be wise,
> And curb his valour with your policies. (ll. 149-57)

Tamyra associates herself with the last piece of advice, urging Bussy to be politic, and Bussy agrees to cover his hate with smiles and fight policy with policy.

We seem to be witnessing in this scene the corruption of the hero by a combination of feminine wile, perverted religion, and the power of hell. Bussy has agreed to imitate what his nature is most opposed to, the politic man, whose appearance always belies his inner reality, as do the outsides of the "colossic statues". At the same time, to anyone familiar with Chapman's interest in the occult, the scene carries a totally different set of suggestions which cannot be dispelled by Behemoth's advocacy of policy just before his disappearance. Up to this time the emphasis is on knowledge. Behemoth and his cohorts are "knowing spirits" from the realm of darkness where truth is hidden, and Bussy, initiated into these mysteries by the Friar, is given the power to summon the spirits himself, and hence to see the "greater light" which comes from the darkness. Behemoth is an awe-inspiring figure but never horrible or repulsive like the cackling witches of *Macbeth*. He has the authority of Marlowe's Mephistophilis, and like him utters some indisputable truths. The Friar bids him to appear "*in forma spiritali, lucente, splendida & amabili*" (l. 58). Never is he presented as explicitly evil.

On the symbolic level, then, both Tamyra, who earlier invoked the "peaceful regents of the night", and Bussy are associated with darkness, to whose mysterious truth the daylight world is violently antagonistic. The opposition set up in the first scene of the play is given further meaning. Bussy's "green retreat" where he "neglects the light" and censures the great men of the world gives way to the secret vault or "Gulf", as it is once called in a stage direction; and to the darkness of Behemoth, from which the inner corruption of the world of great men is plainly seen as "Dayes deceiptfull malice", to use the words of the "Hymnus in Noctem".

The Prince of Darkness appears once more, in response to Bussy's demand. On this occasion the invocation is more impressive than the words spoken by the spirit—it is poetry of great distinction. An unusual feature of the invocation is that Bussy first calls upon Apollo, as god of the sun, though it is clear from the preceding lines that he means to summon Behemoth.

Apollo, though given high praise, is made to serve as a foil to
Behemoth; the light of day is once again portrayed as inferior
to darkness. The passage merits quotation in its entirety:

> Terror of darkness! O thou King of flames!
> That with thy music-footed horse dost strike
> The clear light out of crystal on dark earth,
> And hurl'st instructive fire about the world,
> Wake, wake the drowsy and enchanted night,
> That sleeps with dead eyes in this heavy riddle!
> Or thou great Prince of shades where never sun
> Sticks his far-darted beams, whose eyes are made
> To shine in darkness, and see ever best
> Where men are blindest, open now the heart
> Of thy abashed oracle, that, for fear
> Of some ill it includes, would fain lie hid,
> And rise thou with it in thy greater light.   (V, 3, 41-53)

It is impossible to read this speech as an unequivocal submission to the power of evil. In Chapman's strange terms it
expresses the initiate's passionate longing for inner illumination
and his courage to face a painful truth. The tone is extraordinarily different from that of the passages in *Doctor Faustus*
where Marlowe's hero is summoning the powers of darkness.
Marlowe constantly maintains the framework of Christian
morality in this play (as he does not in *Tamburlaine*), so that the
longing for obscure knowledge is clearly seen to be misguided.

> A sound magician is a demi-god:
> Here, tire my brains to get a deity!   (I, 1, 63-4)[20]

The eager zeal of Faustus is quite unlike Bussy's rapt earnestness
and anxiety. We scarcely need the Good and Bad Angels'
comments to show us what is wrong with the aspirations of
Faustus. His own words damn him. He is "glutted" with
thoughts of the material benefits he will reap when spirits bring
him pearls and "princely delicates", and "fill the public schools
with silk" (ll. 79-98). Furthermore, Mephistophilis, as Harry
Levin has observed, has somewhat the effect on Faustus that
Porfiry has on Raskolnikov, making him accuse and convict
himself.[21] Bussy's traffic with Behemoth is never undercut in this
way. It is a solemn moment in which salvation is offered and
tragically refused: Behemoth warns Bussy not to yield to

Tamyra's next summons; Bussy ignores the warning, and walks into the prepared trap.

The reasons for his doing so have an important bearing on the interpretation of his character. Behemoth has no sooner disappeared than Bussy decides that even if he knew Tamyra's summons must lead to death, he would have to obey:

> Should not my powers obey when she commands,
> My motion must be rebel to my will,
> My will to life.   (V, 3, 72-3)

This statement of the bond between them matches Bussy's later comparison of the soul and body of a man to "two sweet courtly friends". When Montsurry comes, disguised as the Friar, bearing the fatal letter, Bussy readily concludes that Behemoth is a "lying spirit", for Behemoth has told him that the Friar is dead. The deception practised by the worldly Montsurry causes distrust of an other-worldly agency. Bussy suffers not for involving himself with the powers of darkness but for not believing in them. The irony is underscored in the revised quarto by the addition of lines in which Bussy says that the "Prince of Spirits may be call'd / The Prince of liars", and Montsurry in his pious disguise answers, "Holy Writ so calls him" (V, 3, 97-8).

In his death Bussy rises to his greatest nobility. Shot in the back after he has killed one of the paid murderers and spared the life of Montsurry, he resigns himself to the inevitable with dignity and shows great fortitude by standing to the end, propped on his sword. The visual image he thus makes is magnificently appropriate to the Herculean allusions which are so abundant in this part of the play. The most striking of them is the passage on fame (V, 4, 98-111), which follows, at times word for word, a chorus in the fourth act of *Hercules Oetaeus*. His final thoughts are for his heroic reputation, for his mistress, for his failure to achieve what he believed himself capable of.

The most important question to be asked is about the nature of this failure, and to answer it is to deal with the problem raised earlier of the discrepancy between Bussy's actions and the extravagant praise of his spirit. Parrott, after pointing out the resemblance between Bussy and Marlowe's heroes, says:

If we look below the surface for the ground of Bussy's self-confidence, we come at once upon an element in his character which sharply distinguishes him from the Titanic, but simple, heroes of Marlowe. Bussy is not a mere bustling man of action, much less a braggart or *miles gloriosus*. Rather he is the embodiment of an idea which Chapman derived from the Stoics, that of the self-sufficiency, the all-sufficiency, of the virtuous man. Bussy, it is true, is far from virtuous in our modern sense of the word, but he is the very incarnation of *virtus*, as the Romans understood it, "the sum of all the bodily and mental excellences of man".[22]

Against this view John Wieler argues that Bussy is at least as far from virtuous in a Stoic sense as in a modern sense of the word, since self-sufficiency meant to the Stoic the ability to control the passions, as Bussy clearly fails to do. Wieler agrees with Theodore Spencer that "The tragedy of Bussy is just this; he is swayed by desires over which he has no control."[23] In general it might be said that critics favourable to Bussy have been willing to overlook his shortcomings, while those who have been most aware of the shortcomings have seen them as the tragic flaw. The most persuasive statement of the theory that Bussy represents a failure of control is that of Ennis Rees, who makes use of Chapman's comparison of Achilles and Ulysses. In the dedication of his translation of the *Odyssey*, Chapman distinguishes between the fortitude of Achilles and the wisdom of Ulysses, and states his preference for the *Odyssey*:

> In one, *Predominant Perturbation*; in the other, *over-ruling Wisedome*: in one, the Bodies fervour and fashion of outward Fortitude, to all possible height of Heroicall Action; in the other, the Minds inward, constant, and unconquerd Empire; unbroken, unalterd, with any most insolent, and tyrannous infliction.   (*Poems*, p. 406)

Rees points out the striking division of Chapman's tragedies "into two categories, roughly analogous to the *Iliad* and the *Odyssey*". Bussy and Byron, the hero of the next two tragedies, "correspond to Achilles, a character about whom Chapman was never able to feel quite comfortable"; Clermont, the hero of *The Revenge of Bussy D'Ambois*, Cato, of *Caesar and Pompey*, and Chabot correspond to Ulysses, and have "the poet's ethical sympathy". Emphasizing Chapman's frequently stated preference for the contemplative, as opposed to the active, life, Rees comes to the conclusion that Bussy and Byron are "monstrous characters", "abortions of nature", and "bestial servants of self-love", whose bad ends are used for moral instruction; "Bussy was made to express the frailty and fate of the natural man without true learning and religion."[24]

This distinction, though grounded in Chapman's stated opinions, greatly oversimplifies Chapman's attitude towards Achilles and Ulysses, and towards the two kinds of heroes in his own tragedies. It leads to a serious distortion of the meaning of *Bussy D'Ambois*. Bussy undoubtedly lacks complete control, like Achilles, but also like Achilles he is far from being monstrous or bestial.[25] There is not the slightest indication of irony in the words of the Friar's ghost, already partially quoted, which end the play in the first quarto:

> Farewell, brave relics of a complete man,
> Look up and see thy spirit made a star;
> Join flames with Hercules, and when thou sett'st
> Thy radiant forehead in the firmament,
> Make the vast crystal crack with thy receipt;
> Spread to a world of fire, and the aged sky
> Cheer with new sparks of old humanity.   (V, 4, 147-53)

The praise is anticipated in a scene which shortly precedes Bussy's death. Here Monsieur and Guise, involved as they are in the plot on Bussy's life, discuss him with a detachment which is quite out of character and which tends, therefore, to give their words even more weight. Monsieur says that the death they are about to witness will demonstrate the random operation of Nature, whose most valuable gifts often prove the ruin of a man, just as the stock of ammunition in a warship, the one thing which permits the ship to serve its function, may also blow up and destroy it, while the ship might sail longer, empty and use-less. When Guise disagrees with this view of Nature's operations Monsieur returns to his point with another comparison:

> here will be one
> Young, learned, valiant, virtuous, and full mann'd;
> One on whom Nature spent so rich a hand
> That with an ominous eye she wept to see
> So much consum'd her virtuous treasury.
> Yet as the winds sing through a hollow tree
> And (since it lets them pass through) let it stand;
> But a tree solid (since it gives no way

To their wild rage) they rend up by the root:
So this whole man
(That will not wind with every crooked way,
Trod by the servile world) shall reel and fall
Before the frantic puffs of blind-born chance,
That pipes through empty men, and makes them dance.
                                        (V, 2, 32-45)

These two speeches agree with too much else in the play to be
disqualified as evidence. From the beginning Bussy is shown to
be solid, his inner worth corresponding to his valour. His
decision to come to court and "rise by virtue" is not "winding
with every crooked way", whether or not it is a wise decision.
In spite of some lapses from perfect virtue, his actions at court
are not despicable, and at the end he is again the picture of self-
control and solidity. When he sees that he is mortally wounded
he forgives his murderers and prepares calmly for death. In the
first quarto the Friar's ghost tells Tamyra, "He hath the great
mind that submits to all / He sees inevitable" (Text Notes,
p. 568). Bussy is again like Hercules in submitting to his fate,
accepting his limitations. In this very acceptance there is a
strength for which the play has already provided an image in
the description of the sea retreating "into his settled home, . . .
crown'd with his own quiet foam" (I, 2, 164-5).

What is particularly striking is Chapman's failure to blame
Bussy for such shortcomings as he is shown to have. The affair
with Tamyra undoubtedly leads him into concealment and
finally to a decision to counter policy with policy. Parrott, in
his insistence on Bussy's *virtus*, may seem to pass too readily over
the implications of the affair. Chapman gives the world's
opinion of Bussy's conduct its full weight but does not allow
this opinion to stand unchallenged. Not only does he plant the
suggestions of a far more favourable symbolic interpretation of
the episode, but he makes the husband, Montsurry, a far worse
man than Bussy—scheming, cowardly, and cruel. The ghost of
the Friar, who lauds Bussy so highly, is severe with Montsurry,
addressing him as "Son of the earth", and urging a "Christian
reconcilement" with Tamyra (V, 4, 154-62). When we last see
Montsurry, he is refusing this reconcilement. Not the lover, but
the injured husband, appears in an unfavourable light.

The absence of blame for Bussy makes one important difference between Chapman's treatment of him and of Byron, the hero with whom Rees associates him. Though Byron is also an aspiring, impetuous hero at odds with the court, and though at the end he is also compared to Hercules, his faults and virtues are clearly distinguished. Despite his great spirit he is shown as a traitor, whose mistake, as Peter Ure says, is a "deliberate eschewal of virtuous action".[26] The Chancellor says of him, "A mighty merit and a monstrous crime / Are here concurrent" (*Byron's Tragedy*, V, 2, 277-8), and when he is imprisoned and confronted with death, Byron rages uncontrollably. To the extent that his crimes and weaknesses are blamed, Byron is less like Hercules than is Bussy, but even Byron is presented finally as a paradox:

> Oh of what contraries consists a man!
> Of what impossible mixtures! Vice and virtue,
> Corruption and eternnesse, at one time,
> And in one subject, let together loose!
> We have not any strength but weakens us,
> No greatness but doth crush us into air.
> Our knowledges do light us but to err. . . .
>
>   (V, 3, 189-95)

As one reads Chapman's tragedies it becomes increasingly clear that his preference for one type of man does not imply disapproval for all other types. The lines just quoted from *Byron's Tragedy* reveal a complex attitude toward human nature. Even where the vices and virtues are as clearly separated as they are there, they are seen to be joined fast. In Bussy's case one can hardly speak of vice or corruption. In *The Revenge of Bussy D'Ambois*, written several years later, Clermont D'Ambois is said to have his brother Bussy's valour, but a temper "so much past his, that you cannot move him" (*Revenge*, I, 1, 183). Later, in the same vein, Clermont is said to have not only valour but learning, "Which Bussy, for his valour's season, lack'd; / And so was rapt with outrage oftentimes / Beyond decorum" (II, 1, 88-90). Clermont is Chapman's "Senecal man", very close to the Stoic ideal, yet the difference between him and his brother is no matter of black and white. He reveres Bussy's memory and revenges his murder, which he considers most unjust. Like Bussy, he is opposed to the Machiavellians, but it requires the appearance of Bussy's ghost to make him take the necessary action of fighting Montsurry. The ghost reproaches Clermont for his "tame spirits", and urges him to imitate God by striking a blow for justice (V, 1, 78-99). The emphasis on virtue expressed in action is characteristic of Chapman, and coming from Bussy's ghost, it suggests that however superior Clermont may be, he has something to learn from his brother. The difference between Bussy and Clermont resembles the difference Tasso makes between Rinaldo and Goffredo. Goffredo is superior in reason, but he has need of Rinaldo in carrying out his enterprise. Rinaldo, without being perfect, is a most admirable hero. In the same way Bussy is admirable, and, though lacking Clermont's learning, is by no means entirely uncontrolled. In the earlier play he is not even entirely unlearned; Monsieur calls him learned, and the scenes with Behemoth suggest symbolically a pursuit of learning if not the acquisition of it.

The comparison of Bussy with Achilles is most instructive. As Donald Smalley has pointed out, Chapman has great respect for Achilles in spite of his preference for Ulysses. Like other Renaissance interpreters, he tends to think of "outward fortitude" as the expression of inward strength of mind, and furthermore shows Achilles as acquiring learning and control. Achilles is markedly different from Ulysses but not his opposite.[27] George Lord has shown that Ulysses, too, has to learn to control himself.[28] Though Achilles is characterized by "predominant perturbation" rather than "overruling wisdom", he still rises to the "height of heroical action", which is very high praise from a student of Homer. That Bussy is made to resemble Achilles is no argument that he is held up to censure.

Bussy's failure cannot be equated with moral failing and hence the meaning of his tragedy is not simply what might be suggested by the outlines of his story—that he must pay the penalty for pride, adultery and traffic with the devil. As Chapman dramatizes this story, the failure is rather Bussy's inability to reach his goal. Even so noble a warrior as Bussy cannot avoid a trap baited, however unwillingly, by his lady. The terrible pain expressed in Bussy's last speech is compounded of the bitterness of defeat and anguish for the suffering of Tamyra, who stands before him, still bleeding from Montsurry's torture. He is slain again by "this killing spectacle"; his "sun is turn'd to

blood". His lines also reflect the vastness of what he hoped to
accomplish:

> O frail condition of strength, valour, virtue,
> In me (like warning fire upon the top
> Of some steep beacon, on a steeper hill)
> Made to express it: like a falling star
> Silently glanc'd, that like a thunderbolt
> Look'd to have stuck and shook the firmament.
>
> (V, 4, 141-6)

This is the failure of a man like Tamburlaine, who must die,
leaving much unconquered, and of one like Hercules, whose
divine mission of purifying the world has not been fulfilled.

Tamburlaine more nearly succeeds in imposing his will on
the world; for the forces of tyranny and corruption are less
insidiously pervasive than in the world of Chapman's play. The
facts of contemporary history have a convincing, circumstantial
reality. But, like everything else in this play, they have also an
important symbolic value. Guise and Monsieur, the representatives of everything which Bussy opposes, become the embodiments of fate. Behemoth tells Bussy that fate prevents him from
giving all the information Bussy seeks.

> *Bussy.* Who are Fate's ministers?
> *Behemoth.* The Guise and Monsieur.
> *Bussy.*   A fit pair of shears
> To cut the threads of kings and kingly spirits,
> And consorts fit to sound forth harmony
> Set to the falls of kingdoms!   (V, 3, 63-7)

In one sense, then, this world of court intrigue which Bussy
opposes, yet the only world in which he can act, is his fate.[29]
Clermont, too, falls victim to this world in the end. Even his
virtues cannot assure victory over such odds.

It is characteristic of Chapman, thinking as he did about
poetry, to embody the tragedy of a Herculean hero overcome by
fate in a fiction which seemingly tells quite another story. For
the more ignorant members of the audience there is a story of
bloodshed, intrigue, and supernatural doings in a contemporary court. But the original audience for this play included
a large proportion of more knowing spectators, for Chapman
wrote *Bussy D'Ambois* for one of the "private houses", where the

audience, as Alfred Harbage has said, "was an amalgam of fashionable and academic elements, socially and intellectually self-conscious".[30] These more sophisticated spectators might be expected to share the author's delight in meanings artfully concealed beneath a deceptive surface. The play which resulted from this way of writing cannot be called an unqualified artistic success; the disparities between surface meaning and symbolic meaning, particularly in the conjuring scenes, too often suggest a *tour de force*. However, Chapman's procedure has its merits. Not only are there individual passages of high poetic quality, but the very disparities just referred to make a certain positive contribution to the meaning. Purity of motive and corruption of act are brought out by the ambiguity of every major incident: the decision to go to court is both a capitulation and a defiance, the duel both outrageous and noble, the affair with Tamyra both culpable and ideal, the association with Behemoth both a dabbling with evil and a mystical pursuit of the hidden truth. Together these paradoxes present the moving dilemma of a great-spirited man who attempts to live by a heroic code in a world dominated by Machiavellian policy.

The difference between Marlowe's and Chapman's portrayals of the Herculean hero appears constantly in the imagery of the two plays. The most brilliant images in *Tamburlaine*, such as that of the hero in his chariot, scourging tyrants, give form and concreteness to the hero's situation. They inevitably interpret that situation, but above all they present it. The poetry of *Bussy D'Ambois* characteristically works towards a different end. Its most brilliant images are those which make some thought about the hero concrete—the sea of his energy, which is both wild and yet contained within bounds—the fire of his spirit, which has the various qualities of a torch borne in the wind, a beacon, a falling star, a thunderbolt, and which, after death, returns to a world of fire. Marlowe's images keep the hero himself before our eyes; Chapman's focus the mind's eye on a problem of the heroic nature.

Shakespeare

Teach me,
Alcides, thou mine ancestor, thy rage.

BOTH Marlowe and Chapman place their heroes in the context of history, where the problem of individual worth is debated in an endless dialectic between society and the hero. The hero fights against the representatives of society—emperors, governors, dukes—in a struggle to impose his will upon the world, and yet he is not truly an enemy of society, for he fights against what he sees as corrupt. He is acclaimed as a benefactor like Hercules, who laid waste cities and committed murder, yet saved society from tyrants and monsters. Marlowe brings the contest between the hero and society into sharp dramatic focus in the episode of Tamburlaine at the siege of Damascus, where he is ruthless in his refusal of mercy, but ruthless in accordance with a principle on which his whole life is based. The stories of Antony and Cleopatra and of Coriolanus present just such a contest between a mighty individual and a city, and it is not in the least surprising that this kind of story should occur in Roman history, for Rome, as described by her historians, both encouraged the cultivation of individual valour and exacted the most complete devotion of her heroes.

Shakespeare wrote a pseudo-Roman tragedy at the beginning of his career in *Titus Andronicus*, whose hero bears some surprising resemblances to the type I have been describing. Titus is a military hero of inflexible integrity, opposed by the corrupt rulers of the city. Though the subservience to which he has been reduced prevents him from being an active hero through most of the play, at the end he is active enough in the perpetration of the Thyestean banquet for which the play is famous, and in spite of this revenge is clearly in some sense a restorer of order. What makes him an interesting character is Shakespeare's Ovidian presentation of a kind of metamorphosis of character brought about by violent outrage. The result, as I have suggested elsewhere,[1] is to place the hero almost beyond praise or blame, an object of admiration. In this respect, more than in any other, he bears a resemblance to Tamburlaine and Bussy D'Ambois.

The first of Shakespeare's plays to be set in the historical Rome, and the first one he drew from Plutarch, contains no Herculean figure. Caesar, who might be so presented, is more important in the play as an idea than as a man, and his hesitations about going to the senate are hardly heroic. Brutus, on the other hand, is far too reasonable (however mistaken) and too self-sacrificing to be called a Herculean hero. However, Antony, as he appears in *Antony and Cleopatra*, is explicitly compared to Hercules, and throughout most of the play is at war with Rome and all that Rome represents. While the importance given to Cleopatra and to Antony's final commitment to her makes the play as a whole something other than the tragedy of a Herculean hero, it nevertheless contains a major treatment of the type, and must be looked at before turning to the tragedy in which Shakespeare dealt most fully with a Hercules. This is, of course, *Coriolanus*, whose hero, like Tamburlaine and Bussy, is hated, feared, and loved as a kind of superior being.

1. *Antony and Cleopatra*

Two images of Antony dominate *Antony and Cleopatra*, the Roman and the Egyptian, Caesar's Antony and Cleopatra's. Caesar's is the tough soldier who could stand any hardship (I, 4, 56-71)[2]—the "plated Mars" of Philo's opening speech. To the Romans it seems that this Antony has melted under the influence of Cleopatra into an effeminate libertine, whose eyes "now bend, now turn / The office and devotion of their view / Upon a tawny front", and whose "captain's heart" is no more than "the bellows and the fan / To cool a gypsy's lust" (I, 1, 2-10). Later we hear from Cleopatra herself how she put her "tires and mantles on him" while she wore his sword, a prank which seems to symbolize all too exactly the transformation lamented by Caesar. It is Hercules unmanned by Omphale.

The Antony we see in Egypt is not merely the soldier debauched by a woman's influence, however, nor does Cleopatra want him to be anything less than the greatest of soldiers. His being the "demi-Atlas of this earth, the arm / And burgonet of men" (I, 5, 23-4) is part of his vast attractiveness as a lover.

H

Her grandiose imagination fashions an ideal for Antony which is not only larger but more complex than Caesar's. Excesses which seem to Caesar repellent and improper she finds becoming (as others find her passions and fits becoming to her), and she goads him into statements of his love which abolish all limits: "There's beggary in the love that can be reckon'd" (I, 1, 15). Thus the characteristics which adulterate the Antony of Caesar's military ideal serve to round out the heroic figure in the mind of Cleopatra, for whom Antony is not merely a soldier but a "man of men" (I, 5, 72), and finally a colossus, whose "legs bestrid the ocean"—a man "past the size of dreaming" (V, 2, 82, 97). In the contrast presented by Shakespeare, Caesar, the emblem of reasonable self-control, shrinks to a Machiavellian schemer as Antony grows to heroic proportions.

Antony's faults, like those of other Herculean heroes, are emphasized rather than glossed over: Maecenas says, "His taints and honours / Wag'd equal with him" (V, 1, 30-1).[3] But they are not the superb egotism nor the heartless cruelty of a Tamburlaine. The Antony who flees from the battle of Actium has offended not merely against a Roman code of values but against what he and everyone else recognize as a basic concept of his own integrity. He has told Octavia, "If I lose mine honour, / I lose myself" (III, 4, 22-3), and this violation of "experience, manhood, honour," as Scarus sees it (III, 10, 23) so shames Antony that he feels he has indeed lost himself. Plutarch comments that this failure to be himself proves the truth of an old man's jest, that "the soul of a lover lived in another body, and not in his own",[4] and Shakespeare has Antony tell Cleopatra, "O'er my spirit / Thy full supremacy thou knew'st" (III, 11, 58-9). At this moment there appears to be nothing in Antony to answer the expectations of either Caesar or Cleopatra. Shortly afterward she appears to be considering seriously the possibility of coming to terms with Caesar.

Cleopatra's part in this débâcle gives some colour of truth to the Roman view that the transforming power of a woman has destroyed what Antony was by taking possession of his soul, but the remainder of the play shows that destruction is not the end of the process of transformation. Out of the fragments of the Roman image of Antony grows the great image presented in Cleopatra's speeches in the fifth act—an image which owes as

much to the ideals of romance as to the older heroic ideal. The
hero is re-created and yet, as I have already insisted, not
entirely made anew, for the process in which Cleopatra has so
important a part is a reassertion of qualities Antony already
possesses, a shift of emphasis, a rediscovery of self.

The antony who commits suicide at the end of the play is no
longer a world-conqueror in the obvious sense of the term, yet
neither is he the defeated man we have seen after Actium. In
his own way he has conquered the world and himself. "So it
should be," as Cleopatra says, "that none but Antony / Should
conquer Antony" (IV, 15, 16-17). If in some respects he is no
longer Herculean, in others he is more so than ever. This
situation seems to be reflected in the allusions to Hercules, for
although "the god Hercules, whom Antony lov'd", is said to be
leaving him on the eve of one of his last battles (IV, 3, 15)[5] some
of the most striking identifications with Hercules are made
shortly before Antony's death. They emphasize certain
characteristics which he continues to share with his former
protector. Notable among these is Antony's violent rage, the
more conspicuous for being allied with an extravagant generosity, shown on occasion to those who have merited rage.
Bounty and rage, mingling and interacting, account for a large
share of Antony's heroic nature.

Antony displays his remarkable bounty immediately after
Actium, when he urges his loyal followers to divide his treasure
and go. Shortly afterwards he assures a penitent Cleopatra
that one tear is worth "all that is won and lost" (III, 11, 69-70).
On the eve of his next battle he moves his soldiers to tears by
his gifts and good wishes; Enobarbus dies of a broken heart,
overcome by a generosity which he can scarcely comprehend.
Indeed, from the Roman point of view these examples of
Antony's bounty are as patently unreasonable as his debauches.
In both cases Antony is spending his substance prodigally—in
effect, giving himself away. Looked at in this way, Antony's
generosity is closely allied to the self-destructiveness which leads
up to Actium, and an analogue to both is found in the melting
imagery first applied to the world Antony scorns, and finally to
himself, when he finds that he "cannot hold this visible shape"
(IV, 14, 14).

The same imagery of melting and disintegration is one of the means Shakespeare uses to affirm the positive value of Antony's giving. When the flood-waters of the Nile recede, they leave the adjacent land covered with mud and with insects which complete the dissolution of the creatures drowned in the water (III, 13, 166-7; V, 2, 58-60); yet "upon the slime and ooze" the seedsman scatters his grain, from which comes Egypt's rich harvest (II, 7, 24-6). When Antony hears the false news of Cleopatra's death, he strips off his armour, aided by Eros, completing by this action the destruction of the warrior image to which he has just alluded in his speech about the "visible shape" which is no more fixed than the cloud-shapes of dragons, bears or citadels. However, the act for which he prepares is an assertion more than a denial, and requires a warrior's courage. It is a final giving, which indicates strength rather than weakness. His words, addressed to Eros and to his own body, present the bursting forth of a greatness which can no longer be contained:

> Off, pluck off!
> The sevenfold shield of Ajax cannot keep
> The battery from my heart. O, cleave, my sides!
> Heart, once be stronger than thy continent,
> Crack thy frail case! Apace, Eros, apace.—
> No more a soldier. Bruised pieces, go;
> You have been nobly borne.   (IV, 14, 37-43)

The situation makes it clear that Antony speaks to a lover's heart as well as to a soldier's. He would end his life not only to recover a soldier's honour but to be worthy of Cleopatra. Once again it might be said that the lover's soul is not entirely his own, but where the pursuit of the beloved led to shameful self-betrayal at Actium, here it is the affirmation of an ideal exalted in romances and in Renaissance love-poetry generally: the lover finds only in the beloved the completing of himself.

To the largeness of Antony's spirit all his excesses testify—his prodigious feasting and lovemaking as well as his generosity and the final extravagance of suicide. Sensual indulgence, magnanimity and self-immolation appear to be manifestations of a single bent. So too, through its sheer intensity, does Antony's most Herculean trait, his rage.

It is ironical that Cleopatra seems less moved by Antony's generous forgiveness of her after Actium than by his outrageous behaviour in ordering Caesar's messenger whipped for kissing her hand. It is after he has gone on to rebuke her in some of the most violent and memorable language of the play that she makes hcr most positive declaration of love for him. When he sends a personal challenge to Caesar (as he had already done before Actium) and then makes plans for a battle on land, she speaks like one whose confidence has been restored: "That's my brave lord! . . . since my lord / Is Antony again, I will be Cleopatra" (III, 13, 176, 186-7). We cannot suppose that this change is due entirely to fear. Her equivocal answers to the offers from Caesar suggest that she has been bewildered and alarmed by the defeated and forgiving Antony, as if she could not be sure of the meaning of such abject behaviour. The Antony who whips a messenger she can understand, as her own treatment of another messenger shows well. The spectacle of Antony *furens* is one which she admires rather than fears. From this time she never wavers in her commitment.[6]

Antony's anger in this scene is a clear indication to the audience as well as to Cleopatra that he is in the process of rediscovering himself. Aware that "Authority melts from me" (III, 13, 90), he insists clamorously upon obedience from his servants while he rails at Cleopatra and the messenger. In all his relationships he is reasserting the authority of a leader. The re-emergence of this essential heroic quality is what Cleopatra applauds.

At the same time, the sceptical comments of Enobarbus, who has remained loyal up to this point, remind us that no practical benefits can be expected now from Antony's rage. When the messenger is sent to be whipped, he says, "'Tis better playing with a lion's whelp / Than with an old one dying" (III, 13, 94-5), and at the end of the scene:

> I see still
> A diminution in our captain's brain
> Restores his heart. When valour preys on reason,
> It eats the sword it fights with. I will seek
> Some way to leave him.   (III, 13, 197-201)

The irrational valour of the hero, exposed to the criticism of Roman practicality, is shown to be absurd—a posture which the logic of the situation will easily demolish. Enobarbus is

right, of course, for the one battle Antony wins has no great
military significance, and is succeeded by the final, crushing
defeat. The inevitability of disaster is orchestrated by the
unearthly music heard by the soldiers (IV, 3) and interpreted
as the departure of Antony's patron, "the god Hercules".

Antony's reassertion of his heroic self in the latter part of the
play is entirely personal. What he asserts is individual integrity,
not the integrity of a Roman general. The scene in which
Cleopatra and Eros help him to arm (IV, 4) presents a cheerful
ritual whose significance is mainly for the lovers themselves.
Antony alternately teases Cleopatra about her ineptitude and
praises her by way of chiding Eros. He wishes that she could
watch him fight and appreciate the fine points of "the royal
occupation". When he leaves, Cleopatra comments as might a
heroine of romance upon her knight's going forth to battle:

> He goes forth gallantly. That he and Caesar might
> Determine this great war in single fight!   (IV, 4, 36-7)

The entire scene (wholly invented by Shakespeare) emphasizes
the intimacy of the lovers and the importance to them of
Antony's behaving heroically. When he returns victorious it is
again the personal significance that is important. The contrast
between the "world" and the two lovers is apparent in Cleopatra's greeting to the victor:

> Lord of lords!
> O infinite virtue, com'st thou smiling from
> The world's great snare uncaught?   (IV, 8, 16-18)

The chief joy of the victory is that Antony, having demonstrated
his superiority, is not ensnared by the world. Despite Antony's
awareness of the continuing peril, he and Cleopatra treat the
victory as if it were absolute, but it is absolute only as a
demonstration to them of heroic quality. Heroism rather than
heroic achievement becomes the important thing in this part
of the play. Even Enobarbus recognizes this when his realistic
appraisal of Antony's situation gives way to the unbearable
perception of Antony's inherent nobility.

As the reward of the momentary victory is Cleopatra's
esteem, so the bitterness of the ensuing defeat is the suspicion
that she has compounded with Caesar. Here Antony closely

resembles Seneca's Oetaean Hercules, for even worse than the
pain of the poisoned robe is the thought that Deianira has been
responsible for his death rather than a worthy antagonist. Each
one feels that his death has been robbed of all honour. And each
longs passionately for revenge and then death. Hercules says:

> Would that with lifted club I might crush out her wicked life just
> as I smote down the Amazonian pest upon the slopes of snowy
> Caucasus. O well-loved Megara, wast thou wife to me when mad-
> ness came upon me? Give me my club and bow, let my right hand
> be defiled, let me put stain upon my glory, and let a woman be
> chosen as the last toil of Hercules.   (*Hercules Oetaeus*, ll. 1449-55)

Antony says, "When I am reveng'd upon my charm, / I have
done all", and when Cleopatra appears, he threatens:

> Vanish, or I shall give thee thy deserving
> And blemish Caesar's triumph. Let him take thee
> And hoist thee up to the shouting plebeians.
> Follow his chariot, like the greatest spot
> Of all thy sex. Most monster-like be shown
> For poor'st diminitives, for doits, and let
> Patient Octavia plough thy visage up
> With her prepared nails.   (IV, 12, 32-9)

In the latter part of this speech, made after Cleopatra has been
frightened away, Shakespeare makes the comparison to
Hercules explicit:

> 'Tis well th'art gone.
> If it be well to live; but better 'twere
> Thou fell'st into my fury, for one death
> Might have prevented many. Eros, ho!
> The shirt of Nessus is upon me. Teach me,
> Alcides, thou mine ancestor, thy rage.
> Let me lodge Lichas on the horns o' th' moon
> And with those hands that grasp'd the heaviest club
> Subdue my worthiest self. The witch shall die.
> (IV, 12, 39-47)

Rage is the characteristic response of the Herculean hero to an
attack on his honour. Both Hercules and Antony want more
than anything to recover some part of their lost honour in order
to make themselves worthy of a hero's death. Both of them wish
that revenge upon a perfidious woman might atone for their

guilt towards an innocent woman, as well as punishing an infamous betrayal.

From the vantage-point of this scene of Antony's Herculean rage one can appreciate the significance of a very early episode, in which this important trait is first established. There Cleopatra goads him, as part of her remarkable technique of seduction, to the verge of an angry outburst, and when he warns her to desist, comments:

> Look, prithee, Charmian,
> How this Herculean Roman does become
> The carriage of his chafe.   (I, 3, 83-5)

The words are mocking, yet they suggest, even here, a certain awe for Antony's heroic fury. Antony's rage at Cleopatra is brought to an abrupt end by the news that she has killed herself for his love, just as Hercules' rage at Deianira ends when Hyllus reveals her innocent intentions, her horror at the outcome, and her suicide. But the difference between Antony and Hercules is brought out by Antony's response to the news. To Hercules the full import of this news is that an old prophecy has been fulfilled, and that he is meeting the heroic death promised him. He is able to reassert his old self and muster the fortitude necessary to face the flames of his funeral pyre because it is clear that Deianira was merely instrumental in his undoing, and of no real importance. He then dismisses her from his thoughts. The news brought by Mardian means to Antony that Cleopatra, instead of betraying him, has given him a model of heroic death, and that life without so wonderful a woman is not worth living. There is Herculean fortitude in his suicide; there is also the final assertion of love. The meaning of Antony's tragedy does not lie entirely in the Herculean pattern.

Cleopatra both accentuates and modifies what is Herculean in Antony. Like Caesar, she admires the man of valour and noble rage, but she also encourages his carousals. To Caesar as Shakespeare portrays him even Hercules might have seemed excessive; every excess can be assimilated into Cleopatra's ideal of warrior and lover. What Caesar wants to see in Antony is less than a Hercules, but what Cleopatra wants is more. When she asks Dolabella if "there was or might be such a man / As this I dreamt of", he replies, "Gentle madam, no" (V, 2, 93-4).

Antony's suicide is in one sense a recognition of the impossibility of achieving Cleopatra's ideal in the world. It is a noble Roman's death, but more than that, it is a dedication of himself to Cleopatra, the final custodian of his heroic image.

The structure of the play does justice to the dimensions of the heroic portrayal. More episodic than any other play of Shakespeare's, *Antony and Cleopatra* ranges like *Tamburlaine* over vast areas and achieves the effect of the sort of magnitude which we normally associate with epic. The number of very brief scenes makes the technique seem to us almost cinematic,[7] though it was perfectly adapted to the stage of Shakespeare's day. Mark Van Doren remarks that the units of style are characteristically brief like the units of action. "This universe is too large to be rendered in anything but fragments."[8] Not only the universe but the hero. The dimensions of the world to which Antony is opposed serve as an analogue of his Herculean magnitude.

2. *Coriolanus*

As Coriolanus marches on Rome at the head of a Volscian army, the Roman general, Cominius, describes him thus to his old enemies, the tribunes:

> He is their god. He leads them like a thing
> Made by some other deity than Nature,
> That shapes man better; and they follow him
> Against us brats with no less confidence
> Than boys pursuing summer butterflies
> Or butchers killing flies.
>
>   .   .   .   .
>
>   He will shake
> Your Rome about your ears.   (IV, 6, 90-4, 98-9)

To which Menenius adds: "As Hercules / Did shake down mellow fruit." In these words Coriolanus is not only presented as a god and compared to Hercules; he is "like a thing / Made by some other deity than Nature". So extraordinary is he that even his troops, inspired by him, feel themselves to be as much superior to the Romans as boys to butterflies or butchers to flies. Like Menaphon's description of Tamburlaine ("Such breadth of shoulders as might mainly bear / Old Atlas' burthen") and Cleopatra's of Antony ("His legs bestrid the ocean"), this description of Coriolanus is central to Shakespeare's depiction of his hero. His superhuman bearing and his opposition to Rome are the two most important facts about him.

The god-like qualities of Shakespeare's Coriolanus need to be emphasized in an era which has tended to belittle him. He has been treated recently as a delayed adolescent who has never come to maturity, a "splendid oaf",[9] a mother's boy,[10] a figure so lacking in dignity that he cannot be considered a tragic hero.[11] The catastrophe has been said to awaken amusement seasoned with contempt. In spite of some impressive protests against this denigration,[12] the heroic stature of one of Shakespeare's largest figures remains somewhat obscured.

That he often cuts an unsympathetic figure (especially in the eyes of the twentieth century) is not surprising. His very superiority repels sympathy, while his aristocratic contempt of the plebeians shocks the egalitarian. His pride and anger provide a convenient and conventional basis of disapproval for those who share the tribunes' view that:

> Caius Marcius was
> A worthy officer i' th' war, but insolent,
> O'ercome with pride, ambitious past all thinking,
> Self-loving—   (IV, 6, 29-32)

Pride and anger, as we have seen, are among the distinguishing characteristics of the Herculean hero; without them he would not be what he is.

In one major respect the story of Coriolanus departs from that of his heroic prototype: Coriolanus submits to the entreaties of Volumnia and spares Rome. At this moment he is more human and more humane than at any other in the play, and it is the decision of this moment which leads directly to his destruction. Ironically, the one action of which most of his critics approve is "most mortal" to him. He is murdered not so much because he is proud as because of an intermission in his pride.

The portrait of Coriolanus is built up by means of contrasts. Some of them are absolute, such as those with the people and the tribunes. Others are modified by resemblances: the contrasts with his fellow-patricians, his enemy Aufidius, and his mother

Volumnia. Such a dialectical method of presentation is reminiscent of Seneca and recalls even more precisely the technique of Marlowe in *Tamburlaine*.[13] Something closely akin to it is used in *Bussy D'Ambois* and *Antony and Cleopatra*. In all of these plays sharply divergent views of the hero call attention to an essential paradox in his nature. The technique is brilliantly suited to the dramatization of such heroes, but, as the critical response to these plays has shown, it has the disadvantage of stirring serious doubts about the genuineness of the heroism. Readers, as opposed to spectators, have been especially susceptible to these misgivings, since they had before them no actor to counter by the very nobility of his bearing the devastating effect of hostile views. Readers of *Coriolanus* seem to have adopted some or all of the opposition views of the hero's character.

The contrast between Coriolanus and the citizens of Rome is antipodal. Whatever he most basically is they are not, and this contrast is used as the introduction to his character. The "mutinous citizens" who occupy the stage as the play begins are not entirely a despicable lot. It is clear enough that they represent a dangerous threat to the established order, but some of them speak with wisdom and tolerance. For one citizen who opposes Coriolanus because "he's a very dog to the commonalty" (ll. 28-9) there is another who recalls the warrior's services to Rome, and resentment of his pride is balanced against recognition of his lack of covetousness. These citizens, in their opening words and later in their conversation with Menenius, are neither remarkably bright nor stupid, neither models of good nature nor of malice. They are average people, and this may be the most important point about them. Their failings are as common as their virtues: in both we see the limitations of their horizons. Incapable of heroic action themselves, they are equally incapable of understanding a heroic nature. The more tolerant citizen in the first scene excuses the pride of Coriolanus by saying he cannot help it (l. 42), and hence should not be judged too harshly. In a later scene the citizens complain to Coriolanus that he doesn't love them. One of them tells him that the price of the consulship is "to ask it kindly" (II, 3, 81), a demand which has received enthusiastic approval from several modern critics. The citizens want the great warrior to be jolly and friendly with them, so that they may indulge in the luxury of treating him as a lovable eccentric. From the moment of his first entrance it is obvious that he will never allow them this luxury.

The first impression we are given of him is of his intemperance and his scorn of the people. Menenius Agrippa, one that, in the words of the Second Citizen, "hath always loved the people", has just cajoled them with his fable of the belly into a less rebellious mood when the warrior enters and delivers himself of a blistering tirade. The citizens are "dissentious rogues", "scabs", "curs", "hares", "geese", finally "fragments". He reminds them of their cowardice and inconstancy. But the most devastating part of his speech is the accusation that the citizens prefer to give their allegiance to a man humbled by a punishment which they will call unjust:

> Your virtue is
> To make him worthy whose offense subdues him
> And curse that justice did it.   (I, 1, 178-80)

What they cannot tolerate except in the crises of war is a greatness which lifts a man far beyond their reach.

In making his accusations Caius Marcius, as he is then called, reveals his reverence for valour, constancy and a great spirit, as well as his utter contempt for those who will never attain such virtues. We may suspect immediately what the rest of the play makes clear, that these are his own virtues. However, since they are displayed by a speech whose tone is so angry and contemptuous—so politically outrageous, when compared to the clever performance of Menenius—they are less apt to win liking than respect. We are confronted by the extraordinary in the midst of the average, a whole man amidst "fragments".

In succeeding scenes with the citizenry the indications of the first scene are developed. The battle at Corioles, where he wins his cognomen Coriolanus, is of course the key scene for the demonstration of valour, "the chiefest virtue", as Cominius later reminds the senators in describing the exploits of Coriolanus (II, 2, 87-8). Before the sally of the Volscians the Roman soldiers flee in miserable confusion, providing a pat example of their cowardice and bringing on themselves another volley of curses from their leader. Everything in the scene heightens the

contrast between him and them. "I'll leave the foe / And make
my wars on you!" he threatens; "Follow me!" (I, 4, 39-42).
When his courageous pursuit of the Volscians into their city is
followed by the closing of their gate we are presented with the
ultimate contrast and an emblem of the hero's situation: he is
one against the many, whether the many are enemies or fellow
countrymen. As Shakespeare presents this astounding feat it
borders on the supernatural. Coriolanus is given Herculean
strength. The simple statement of a soldier sums it up: "He is
himself alone, / To answer all the city (ll. 51-2).[14] Titus Lartius,
supposing him dead, adds an encomium in which the qualities
he has just demonstrated are converted into an icon:

> A carbuncle entire, as big as thou art,
> Were not so rich a jewel. Thou wast a soldier
> Even to Cato's wish, not fierce and terrible
> Only in strokes, but with thy grim looks and
> The thunder-like percussion of thy sounds
> Thou mad'st thine enemies shake, as if the world
> Were feverous and did tremble.   (I, 4, 55-61)

When the battle is won, the soldiers set about plundering the
city; Caius Marcius, matching his valour with generosity, refuses
any reward but the name of Coriolanus which he has earned.
No doubt there is a touch of pride in such conspicuous self-
denial, but the magnificence of the gesture is what counts. It
is not contrasted with true humility but with pusillanimity and
covetousness.

Coriolanus is not indifferent to the opinion of others, but he
insists upon being valued for his accomplishments, and not for
"asking kindly":

> Better it is to die, better to starve,
> Than crave the hire which first we do deserve.
>   (II, 3, 120-1)

The question of his absolute worth—the central question of the
play—is posed in an uncompromising form in the scenes where
Coriolanus is made to seek the approval of the citizens. Though
his reluctance to boast of his exploits, to show his wounds, or to
speak to the people with any genuine warmth does not immediately lose him their votes, it has cost him the approval of many
critics. In itself, however, this reluctance stems from a virtue

and a major one.[15] He refuses to seem other than he is and refuses to change his principles to suit the situation. The citizens, meanwhile, unsure what to think, first give him their "voices", and then are easily persuaded by the tribunes to change their minds. Again the contrast is pat, and however unlovely the rigidity of Coriolanus may be, its merit is plain when seen next to such paltry shifting. That it is a terrible and in some ways inhuman merit is suggested in the ironical words of the tribune Brutus: "You speak o' th' people / As if you were a god to punish, not / A man of their infirmity" (III, 1, 80-2). Later Menenius says without irony: "His nature is too noble for the world. / He would not flatter Neptune for his trident / Or Jove for's power to thunder" (III, 1, 255-7).

The greatness of Coriolanus is seen not only in his extraordinary valour and generosity but in his absolute rejection of anything in which he does not believe. In this scene he is urged to beg for something which he deserves, to flatter people whom he despises, and to conceal or modify his true beliefs. His refusal to do any of these things is manifested in a crescendo of wrath, defending his heroic integrity. The culmination is a violent denunciation of the plebeians for their ignorance, cowardice, disloyalty and inconsistency. Both friends and enemies attempt to stop the flow of this tirade, but Coriolanus rushes on with the force of an avalanche. The quality of the speech can be seen only in an extensive quotation:

> No, take more!
> What may be sworn by, both divine and human,
> Seal what I end withal! This double worship—
> Where one part does disdain with cause, the other
> Insult without all reason; where gentry, title, wisdom
> Cannot conclude but by the yea and no
> Of general ignorance—it must omit
> Real necessities, and give way the while
> To unstable slightness. Purpose so barr'd, it follows
> Nothing is done to purpose. Therefore, beseech you—
> You that will be less fearful than discreet;
> That love the fundamental part of state
> More than you doubt the change on't; that prefer
> A noble life before a long, and wish
> To jump a body with a dangerous physic
> That's sure of death without it—at once pluck out

The multitudinous tongue; let them not lick
The sweet which is their poison. Your dishonour
Mangles true judgment, and bereaves the state
Of that integrity which should become't,
Not having the power to do the good it would
For th'ill which doth control't.   (III, 1, 140-61)

It seems almost impertinent to object to the lack of moderation in this speech. In the great tumble of words, whose forward
movement is constantly altered and augmented by parenthetical
developments, excess is as characteristic of the presentation as
of the emotions expressed, yet one hardly feels that such excess
is a matter of degree. What is conveyed here could not be
brought within the range of a normally acceptable political
statement by modifying here and there an overforceful phrase.
It is of another order entirely, and excess is its mode of being.
The words of Coriolanus' denunciation of the plebeians are the
exact analogue of the sword-strokes with which he fights his way
alone into Corioles. Rapid, violent and unbelievably numerous,
they express the wrath which accompanies heroic valour. However horrifying they may be, they are also magnificent. Both
approval and disapproval give way to awe, as they do in the
terrible scenes of Hercules' wrath.

In the scenes which bring to a culmination the quarrel of
Coriolanus and the Roman people the great voice of the hero is
constantly surrounded by lesser voices which oppose it—the
friends, who urge moderation, the tribunes, who foment discord, and the people, who respond to each new suggestion. The
words "tongue", "mouth" and "voice" are reiterated, "voice"
often having the meaning of "vote". We hear the scorn of
Coriolanus for the voices of the many in his words: "The
tongues o' th' common mouth", "Have I had children's
voices?" "Must these have voices, that can yield them now /
And straight disclaim their tongues? ... You being their mouths,
why rule you not their teeth?" "at once pluck out / The
multitudinous tongue" (III, 1, 22, 30, 34-6, 155-6). As for the
hero, we are told by Menenius, "His heart's his mouth; / What
his breast forges, that his tongue must vent" (III, 1, 257-8), and
when, shortly after, the "multitudinous tongue" accuses him
of being a traitor to the people, he makes the speech which leads
directly to his banishment: "The fires i' th' lowest hell fold-in

the people!" (III, 3, 68). It is the final answer of the heroic voice to the lesser voices.

The contrast is also realized dramatically in the movement of these scenes, for around the figure of Coriolanus, standing his ground and fighting, the crowd swirls and eddies. Coriolanus and the patricians enter to a flourish of trumpets; to them the tribunes enter. After the hero's lengthy denunciation of the people, they are sent for by the tribunes. The stage business is clearly indicated in the directions: "Enter a rabble of *Plebeians* with the *Aediles*." "*They all bustle about Coriolanus*." "*Coriolanus draws his sword*." "*In this mutiny the Tribunes, the Aediles, and the People are beat in*." "*A noise within*." "Enter *Brutus* and *Sicinius* with the *Rabble* again" (III, 1, 180, 185, 223, 229, 260, 263).

If Shakespeare does not make the many-voiced, ceaselessly shifting people hateful, he also makes it impossible to respect them. M. W. MacCallum shows that while the people are given more reason to fear Coriolanus than they are in Plutarch, their original uprising is made considerably less justifiable.[16] Whether or not Shakespeare reveals a patrician bias in his portrayal of them, there can be no doubt that he shares the distrust of popular government common to his time. Condescension qualifies whatever sympathy he shows.

Coriolanus cannot be condescended to. He belongs to another world, as he makes clear in his final denunciation of the people in response to their verdict of banishment:

> You common cry of curs, whose breath I hate
> As reek o' th' rotten fens, whose loves I prize
> As the dead carcasses of unburied men
> That do corrupt my air, I banish you!
>
> .   .   .   .
>
> Despising
> For you the city, thus I turn my back.
> There is world elsewhere.   (III, 3, 120-3, 133-5)

That world is the forbidding world of heroes, from which he promises his friends:

> you shall
> Hear from me still, and never of me aught
> But what is like me formerly.   (IV, 1, 51-3)

The tribunes are portrayed much less favourably than the

people, though, surprisingly, they have eager apologists among the critics. Less foolish than the plebeians, they are more malicious. Motivated by political ambition, they provoke sedition, encouraging the plebeians to change their votes, and baiting Coriolanus with insults.[17] When the exiled Coriolanus is marching on Rome "like a thing / Made by some other deity than nature", they appear almost as small and insignificant as the people themselves.

The contrast with these scheming politicians establishes the honesty of Coriolanus and his lack of ulterior motives. He has political convictions rather than ambitions. Though he believes that his services to Rome deserve the reward of the consulship, the wielding of political power does not in itself interest him, nor is it necessary to him as an expression of authority. He is dictatorial without being like a modern dictator. The tribunes, who accuse him of pride, are fully as jealous of their prerogatives as he is, and far more interested in increasing them. Coriolanus' nature, compared to theirs, seems both larger and more pure.

Certain aspects of this heroic nature come out most clearly in contrasts between Coriolanus and his fellow patricians. Menenius is to Coriolanus what Horatio is to Hamlet. Horatio's poise and his freedom from the tyranny of passion show him to be what would be called today a "better adjusted" person than Hamlet; yet Hamlet's lack of what he admires in his friend reveals the stresses of a much rarer nature. No one mistakes Horatio for a hero. Similarly, Menenius is far better than Coriolanus at "getting on" with people. In the first scene of the play his famous fable of the belly, told with a fine combination of good humour and firmness, calms the plebeians. When Coriolanus, after his glorious victory, objects to soliciting votes by showing his wounds in the Forum, Menenius urges, "Pray you go fit you to the custom" (II, 2, 146). After the banishment he says to the tribunes in a conciliating fashion, "All's well, and might have been much better if / He could have temporiz'd" (IV, 6, 16-17). Menenius' ability to temporize and fit himself to the custom has made him liked on all sides, but this striking evidence of political success does not guarantee him the un-qualified respect of the spectator. Dennis erred only in exaggerat-ing, when he called Menenius a buffoon.

In contrast to this jolly patrician, always ready to compromise,

I

the austerity and fixity of Coriolanus stand out. To Plutarch, writing as a moralist and historian, it is lamentable that Coriolanus lacks "the gravity and affability that is gotten with judgement of learning and reason, which only is to be looked for in a governor of state", but though the lack is equally apparent in Shakespeare's tragedy, the conclusion to be drawn differs as the point of view of tragedy differs from that of history. Plutarch judges Coriolanus as a potential governor. He finds that a deficient education has made him "too full of passion and choler" and of wilfulness, which Plutarch says "is the thing of the world, which a governor of a commonwealth for pleasing should shun, being that which Plato called solitariness".[18] The tragedy of *Coriolanus*, for all its political concern, is not contrived to expose either the deficiencies of the protagonist as a governor (though all the evidence is presented) or the unreliability of the plebeians and their representatives (which could be taken for granted). What Shakespeare insists on is an extraordinary force of will and a terrible "solitariness" characteristic of this hero. No contrast in the play brings these out more clearly than the contrast with Menenius.

The change in emphasis from history to the heroic is clearly evident in Shakespeare's treatment of Aufidius. In Plutarch's account he is not mentioned until the time of the banishment, when Coriolanus offers himself as a general to the Volsces. At this point, however, Plutarch states that Aufidius was noble and valiant, that the two had often encountered in battle and that they had "a marvellous private hate one against the other".[19] From these hints Shakespeare makes the figure of the worthy antagonist, who is a part of the story of so many heroes. The rivalry is mentioned in the very first scene of the play, and is made one of the deepest motives of the hero's conduct. He envies the nobility of Aufidius,

> And were I anything but what I am,
> I would wish me only he. . . .
> Were half to half the world by th'ears, and he
> Upon my party, I'd revolt, to make
> Only my wars with him. He is a lion
> That I am proud to hunt. (I, 1, 235-40)

To fight with Aufidius is the ultimate test of Coriolanus' valour

—of his warrior's areté. And because the rival warrior most
nearly shares his own ideals, the relationship takes on an intense
intimacy. Shakespeare introduces Aufidius unhistorically into
the battle at Corioles. We discover that although Aufidius
reciprocates the feelings of Coriolanus, he is prepared after his
defeat at Corioles to use dishonourable means, if necessary, to
destroy his enemy, but of this Coriolanus knows nothing, nor
is there any hint of it when Aufidius later welcomes Coriolanus
as an ally:

> Let me twine
> Mine arms about that body whereagainst
> My grained ash an hundred times hath broke
> And scarr'd the moon with splinters. . . .
>
> .   .   .   .   .
>
> Know thou first,
> I lov'd the maid I married; never man
> Sigh'd truer breath. But that I see thee here,
> Thou noble thing, more dances my rapt heart
> Than when I first my wedded mistress saw
> Bestride my threshold.   (IV, 5, 111-14, 118-23)

Plutarch's Aufidius makes only a brief and formal speech
acknowledging the honour Coriolanus does him. Shakespeare's
invention of a long speech, loaded with the metaphors of love,
is the more striking at this point, since the preceding speech by
Coriolanus follows Plutarch very closely indeed. The strong
bond between the rival warriors is obviously important.

It is sometimes thought highly ironic that Coriolanus, who
prides himself on his constancy, should be guilty of the supreme
inconstancy of treason to his country. In fact, however reprehens-
ible he may be, he is not inconstant. Shakespeare makes it clear
that his first allegiance is always to his personal honour. The
fickleness of the mob and the scheming of the tribunes have
deprived him of his deserts, much as Agamemnon's seizure of
Briseis deprives Achilles. Both this threat to his honour and an
ambivalent love-hatred draw Coriolanus to the enemy whom
he considers almost an alter ego.

Resemblances or fancied resemblances between the two
warriors establish the supremacy of the heroic ideal in Coriolanus' scale of values, but we cannot doubt which of them more
nearly encompasses the ideal. As we watch the progress of their

alliance, we see Aufidius becoming increasingly jealous and finally working for the destruction of his rival even while he treats him almost as a mistress. In defence of his conduct he asserts that Coriolanus has seduced his friends with flattery, but there is no evidence to support this unlikely accusation. Malice and double-dealing are quite absent from the nature of Coriolanus.

The ill-will mixed with Aufidius' love serves another purpose than contrast, however: it adds considerable weight to his praise of Coriolanus to other characters, such as that contained in a long speech to his lieutenant:

> All places yield to him ere he sits down,
> And the nobility of Rome are his;
> The senators and patricians love him too.
> The tribunes are no soldiers, and their people
> Will be as rash in the repeal as hasty
> To expel him thence. I think he'll be to Rome
> As is the osprey to the fish, who takes it
> By sovereignty of nature. First he was
> A noble servant to them, but he could not
> Carry his honours even. Whether 'twas pride,
> Which out of daily fortune ever taints
> The happy man; whether defect of judgment,
> To fail in the disposing of those chances
> Which he was lord of; or whether nature,
> Not to be other than one thing, not moving
> From th' casque to th' cushion, but commanding peace
> Even with the same austerity and garb
> As he controll'd the war; but one of these
> (As he hath spices of them all, not all,
> For I dare so far free him) made him fear'd,
> So hated, and so banish'd. But he has a merit
> To choke it in the utt'rance. So our virtues
> Lie in th' interpretation of the time;
> And power, unto itself most commendable,
> Hath not a tomb so evident as a chair
> T'extol what it hath done.
> One fire drives out one fire; one nail, one nail;
> Rights by rights falter, strengths by strengths do fail.
> Come, let's away. When, Caius, Rome is thine,
> Thou art poor'st of all; then shortly art thou mine.

(IV, 7, 28-57)

Surely, what is most remarkable in this account of failure is the emphasis on virtue. One thinks of Monsieur, telling Guise that Nature's gift of virtue is responsible for the death to which Bussy hastens at that very moment, led on by plots of Monsieur's contriving. In both cases the interests of the speaker are so exactly contrary to the tenor of their remarks that the character-analysis is given the force of absolute truth. Aufidius' speech has to be taken in its entirety, so dependent are its component parts on one another. Its frame is a realistic appraisal of the situation at Rome and of his own malicious purposes. Within is an intricate structure of praise and blame. First comes the recognition of "sovereignty of nature", which underlies the entire speech: the superiority of Coriolanus to Rome is as much in the order of nature as is the predominance of the osprey, who was thought to have the power of fascinating fish. Next comes Coriolanus' lack of equilibrium, a point which the play has thoroughly established. Aufidius then mentions three possible causes of failure, carefully qualifying the list by saying that in all probability only one was operative. Pride, the first, is presented as the natural temptation of the happy man, as it is in the medieval conception of fortune's wheel. The defect of judgment, mentioned next, recalls the contrast with Menenius, and the patent inability of Coriolanus to take advantage of his situation—to dispose "of those chances / Which he was lord of". Thus, the first cause of failure is a generic fault of the fortunate, while the second is a fault which distinguishes Coriolanus from a lesser man. The third is the inflexibility which makes him austere and fierce at all times. This is not only the most persuasive as an explanation of his troubles but is also the most characteristic of him. The comments which follow immediately —on the "merit to choke it in the utt'rance" and the virtues which "lie in th' interpretation of the time"—suggest redeeming features. They are not simply good qualities which can be balanced against the bad, but virtues inherent in some of the faults which have just been enumerated, or qualities which might be interpreted as either virtues or faults. The inflexibility is the best example. It is closely related to the other faults, to the lack of equilibrium, the pride, and the defect of judgment. Yet it is impossible to regard Coriolanus' refusal to compromise as entirely a fault. It is also his greatest strength. The concluding lines of the speech put forth a paradox even more bewildering, that power, rights and strengths often destroy themselves. Aufidius need only wait for his rival's success to have him in his power. The final emphasis falls entirely on virtue, with no mention of weakness or deficiency.

The eloquent couplet which sums up this paradox,

> One fire drives out one fire; one nail, one nail;
> Rights by rights falter, strengths by strengths do fail

is very like the lines, already quoted, from Chapman's nearly contemporaneous *Tragedy of Charles, Duke of Byron*:

> We have not any strength but weakens us,
> No greatness but doth crush us into air.
> Our knowledges do light us but to err. . . .

From this melancholy point of view the hero is only more certainly doomed than the average man.

Next to Coriolanus Volumnia is the most interesting character in the play—the Roman mother, whose influence over her son is so great and ultimately so fatal. In the first scene a citizen says of Coriolanus' services to Rome, "Though soft-conscienc'd men can be content to say it was for his country, he did it to please his mother and to be partly proud, which he is, even to the altitude of his virtue" (ll. 37-41). In the last act Coriolanus says,

> O my mother, mother! O!
> You have won a happy victory to Rome;
> But for your son—believe it, O believe it!—
> Most dangerously you have with him prevail'd,
> If not most mortal to him.   (V, 3, 185-9)

But powerful and obvious as this influence is, it should not be allowed to obscure the major differences between mother and son. Volumnia belongs to the world which Coriolanus, as hero, both opposes and seeks to redeem. She represents the city of Rome much more completely than Zenocrate represents the city of Damascus. She is by far the strongest of the forces which Rome brings to bear on him, and much of her strength derives from the fact that she seems at first so thoroughly committed to everything in which he believes. Only gradually do we discover what she truly represents.

In her first scene she is every inch the mother of a warrior, shocking timid Virgilia with grim speeches about a soldier's honour. We next see her welcome Coriolanus after his victory at Corioles, and make the significant remark that only one thing is wanting to fulfil her dreams—one thing "which I doubt not but / Our Rome will cast upon thee" (II, 1, 217-18)—obviously the consulship. Her son's reply foreshadows the conflict between them:

> Know, good mother,
> I had rather be their servant in my way
> Than sway with them in theirs.   (II, 1, 218-20)

Volumnia wants power for her son as much as Lady Macbeth wants it for her husband. Coriolanus wants above all to do things "in his way".

Close to the centre of the play occurs the first of the two conflicts between mother and son. There is no basis for the scene in Plutarch. It is an addition of great importance,[20] contributing to the characterization of the principals and preparing for the famous interview in which Coriolanus is deterred from his vengeance on Rome. The issues engaged here are what separate Coriolanus from every other character.

He has just delivered his lengthy excoriation of the people, and is being urged by his friends to apologize. As Volumnia enters he asks her if she would wish him to be milder—to be false to his nature, and she, who proclaimed to Virgilia that life was not too great a price to pay for honour, gives him an answer based solely on political expediency: "I would have had you put your power well on, / Before you had worn it out" (III, 2, 17-18). She observes with great shrewdness, "You might have been enough the man you are / With striving less to be so", but she adds a sentence which shows that what she is advocating is politic concealment of Coriolanus' true nature:

> Lesser had been
> The thwarting of your dispositions, if
> You had not show'd them how ye were dispos'd
> Ere they lack'd power to cross you.   (ll. 19-23)

In the previous scene, where Coriolanus defied the people and the tribunes, the sincerity of his voice as compared to theirs was expressed in Menenius' words, "His heart's his mouth; /

What his breast forges, that his tongue must vent." The same imagery is caught up here in the words in which Volumnia characterizes her attitude towards apologizing:

> I have a heart as little apt as yours,
> But yet a brain that leads my use of anger
> To better vantage.   (ll. 29-31)

It is not in the least surprising that Menenius applauds this speech, as he does a later and longer one in which Volumnia urges Coriolanus to speak to the people not what his heart prompts,

> But with such words that are but roted in
> Your tongue, though but bastards and syllables
> Of no allowance to your bosom's truth.   (ll. 55-7)

Heart opposes the politician's brain and the orator's tongue in these speeches as honour opposes policy, even though Volumnia tries, by a specious parallel with the tactics of war, to persuade her son that honour can be mixed with a little policy and no harm done. Coriolanus, whom she accuses of being "too absolute", sees plainly that the two are not compatible:

> Must I
> With my base tongue give to my noble heart
> A lie that it must bear?   (ll. 99-101)

Volumnia has aligned herself firmly with the advocates of policy: that is, of compromise and hypocrisy. Without admitting it, she is one of the enemies of the "noble heart".

Under the stress of her passionate urging (she does not hesitate to mention that she will undoubtedly die with the rest of them if he refuses to take her advice), Coriolanus finally agrees to conceal his true nature, as Bussy, at the request of Tamyra, agrees that "policy shall be flanked with policy". Some critics, taking a line similar to that of Volumnia, have chided Coriolanus for going from one extreme to another in his response to his mother. He says:

> Well, I must do't.
> Away, my disposition, and possess me
> Some harlot's spirit!   (ll. 110-12)

It is very difficult, however, to deny the keenness of his perception. He has agreed with great reluctance to do as his mother wishes, but he is well aware that she is asking him to betray an ideal and to sell himself.

The drama of this confrontation is infinitely heightened by our awareness that Volumnia desires more than anything else the honour of her son, though she, rather than his enemies, moves him towards the loss of it. In the following scene the tribunes are largely responsible for Coriolanus' reassertion of his heroic integrity. In words which fit into the now familiar imagery Brutus announces their strategy for provoking another outburst:

> Put him to choler straight . . .
>   Being once chaf'd, he cannot
> Be rein'd again to temperance; then he speaks
> What's in his heart, and that is there which looks
> With us to break his neck.   (III, 3, 25, 27-30)

The successful execution of their plan makes Coriolanus go back on his promise to dissimulate, and leads to his banishment. The city on which he turns his back to seek "a world elsewhere" is made up of his friends and his foes, but at this point in the play it is clear that they all belong almost equally to the world which he rejects.

The last two acts of the play are illuminated by the implications of the words, "There is a world elsewhere". The world which Coriolanus now inhabits is neither the world of the Romans nor that of the Volscians. It is a world of absolutes— the world, as I have already suggested, of heroes. When Cominius comes to intercede for Rome, he refuses to answer to his name, insisting that he must forge a new name in the fire of burning Rome; he sits "in gold, his eye / Red as 'twould burn Rome" (V, 1, 11-15, 63-4). The fierceness of his adherence to his principles has translated him almost beyond humanity. Menenius is rejected in his turn, with the comment: "This man, Aufidius, / Was my belov'd in Rome; yet thou behold'st." "You keep a constant temper," Aufidius replies (V, 2, 98-100). The loss of humanity is brought out again in the half-humorous description given by Menenius:

> The tartness of his face sours ripe grapes. When he walks, he moves like an engine, and the ground shrinks before his treading. He is able to pierce a corslet with his eye, talks like a knell, and

his hum is a battery. He sits in his state, as a thing made for
Alexander. What he bids be done is finish'd with his bidding. He
wants nothing of a god but eternity and a heaven to throne in.
(V, 4, 18-26)

The hard metallic imagery which G. Wilson Knight has noted
throughout the play is very telling in this passage.[21] Coriolanus
has steeled himself to become a Tamburlaine and administer
divine chastisement, refusing to be softened by considerations of
friendship.

Unlike Tamburlaine, however, Shakespeare's Herculean hero
finds that in despising a petty and corrupt world he is also
denying nature. Tamburlaine is obliged to accept the limitations
of nature only when he is faced with death; the situation forces
Coriolanus to submit sooner. As Hermann Heuer says,
" 'Nature' becomes the key-word of the great scene"[22] of the
hero's second conflict with his formidable mother. As he sees
them approach, the battle is already engaged in his mind
between nature and heroic constancy:

> Shall I be tempted to infringe my vow
> In the same time 'tis made? I will not.   (V, 3, 20-1)

And a moment later:

>   But out, affection!
> All bond and privilege of nature, break!
> Let it be virtuous to be obstinate.   (ll. 24-6)

>   I'll never
> Be such a gosling to obey instinct, but stand
> As if a man were author of himself
> And knew no other kin.   (ll. 34-6)

Nowhere in the play is the conflict between the heroic and the
human more clear-cut. Only the demigod which Coriolanus
aspires to be could resist the appeal made by Volumnia and
Virgilia. Tamburlaine could refuse Zenocrate before the gates
of Damascus, but Marlowe made him more nearly the embodiment of a myth. Coriolanus belongs to a more familiar world
and his tragedy can be put very generally as the impossibility
in this world, as in the world of Bussy D'Ambois, of reliving a
myth. Heroic aspiration is not proof here against the urgent
reality of human feelings. Already sensing his weakness, Corio-

lanus begs Virgilia not to urge forgiveness of the Romans, and
to Volumnia he says:

> Do not bid me
> Dismiss my soldiers or capitulate
> Again with Rome's mechanics. Tell me not
> Wherein I seem unnatural. Desire not
> T'allay my rages and revenges with
> Your colder reasons.   (ll. 81-6)

There is unconscious irony in the phrase, "colder reasons",
for Volumnia's appeal is nothing if not emotional. It begins and
ends with the pitiable plight of Coriolanus' family—a direct
assault upon his feelings and instincts. Enclosed in this context
is the appeal to his honour. No longer does Volumnia urge
mixing honour with policy. It is her strategy now to make the
course she recommends appear to be dictated by pure honour.
She suggests that if he makes peace between the two sides, even
the Volscians will respect him (presumably overlooking his
abandonment of their cause), while if he goes on to conquer
Rome he will wipe out the nobility of his name. Honour as she
now presents it is a god-like sparing of offenders:

> Think'st thou it honourable for a noble man
> Still to remember wrongs?   (ll. 154-5)

The final, and successful, appeal, however, is personal:

> This fellow had a Volscian to his mother;
> His wife is in Corioles, and this child
> Like him by chance.   (ll. 178-80)

Aufidius, shortly after, shows that he has understood perfectly
the essential nature of the appeal:

> I am glad thou hast set thy mercy and thy honour
> At difference in thee. Out of that I'll work
> Myself a former fortune.   (ll. 200-2)

I have emphasized Volumnia's rhetorical strategy more than
the validity of her arguments, because it is important that
Coriolanus is broken by a splendid oration. Eloquence, as is
well known, was highly prized by the Elizabethans, and we have
seen it in Tamburlaine as a further evidence of heroic superiority. But the rhetorical training of the Elizabethans made them

acutely aware of the trickiness of oratory, and eloquence on their stage could be a danger-signal as well as a badge of virtue. The case of Volumnia's appeal to Coriolanus is as far from being clear cut as it could be. The plea for mercy and the forgetting of injuries commands assent; yet one is well aware that the nature of the injuries, and hence the validity of the vow Coriolanus has taken, are never mentioned.[23] If the matter were to be discussed in the manner of the debate in the Trojan council in *Troilus and Cressida*, it would be a question of whether true honour lay in revenging or forgiving an undoubted injury, and whether the hero's loyalty at this point should be to the city which exiled him or to the city whose forces he now leads. As it is, Volumnia's rhetoric identifies the cause of mercy with the lives of the pleaders, and Coriolanus must choose between his vow and his family. He must indeed defy nature if he resists his mother's plea. Of this she is very well aware, and she plays on her son's attachment to her just as she had done previously, when urging on him a course of moderate hypocrisy. After her victory, judgment between the conflicting issues remains as puzzling as it was before.

When Volumnia's lack of principle and her association with the political world of Rome are fully perceived, it becomes more difficult to be sure of the significance of Coriolanus' capitulation.[24] We know from him that it is likely to be "most mortal", and we know that Aufidius will do whatever he can to make it so. We know, that is, that the hero is now a broken man, but has he been ennobled by choosing the course glorified by Volumnia's eloquence? This is not the impression made by the last scenes. MacCallum says, "Still this collapse of Coriolanus' purpose means nothing more than the victory of his strongest impulse. There is no acknowledgement of offence, there is no renovation of character . . ."[25] His choice is a recognition of the claims of nature, but this recognition makes possible no new affirmation such as Antony's after the bitterness of his defeat. Nature, as amoral as fecund, seems to melt the valour and stoic integrity of Antony, but in the new growth stimulated by this nature, valour and integrity appear again, transformed. To Coriolanus nature comes in the guise of a moral duty, which is also a temptation to betray his principles. The idea of fecundity is present only as Volumnia uses it for a persuasive weapon, threatening him with the horror of treading on his mother's womb. The melting that follows this persuasion leads to mere destruction. Nature, instead of opening a new way to the hero, blocks an old one and teaches him his mortal finitude.

The decision Coriolanus is asked to make is an impossible one. In the situation as Shakespeare presents it, it is almost inconceivable that he should deny the claims made by Volumnia; yet in acknowledging them he accomplishes nothing positively good. He avoids an act of shocking inhumanity and thereby surrenders control of his world to the forces of policy and compromise—the enemies of the "noble heart". Volumnia and Virgilia are hailed by the Romans, whose one thought is gratefulness to be alive. In Corioles Aufidius contrives the assassination of the hero, who is of no further use. What Coriolanus says of the scene of his submission might be applied to the entire ending of the play:

> Behold, the heavens do ope,
> The gods look down, and this unnatural scene
> They laugh at.   (V, 3, 183-5)

For if the natural order seems to be preserved when Coriolanus decides to spare his country, it is wrecked when the one man of principle is defeated and then murdered. The colossal folly of destroying what far outweighs everything that is preserved is sufficient to provoke the laughter of the gods.

Yet the play does not end on the note of ironic laughter. The final note is affirmation. There is no new vision to affirm and no transcendent world to which the hero willingly goes. Coriolanus will not "join flames with Hercules". What the last scene of the play affirms with compelling force is the value of what the world is losing in the death of the hero. The incident of the assassination dramatizes the essential heroism which Coriolanus has displayed throughout the action. Instead of the comfort of an apotheosis we are given the tragic fact of irremediable loss. After the success of the conspiracy even Aufidius is "struck with sorrow", and closes the play with the prophecy: "Yet he shall have a noble memory."

The handling of the assassination scene restores a much needed clarity after the puzzling ambiguities of Coriolanus' submission to his mother. Envy, meanness, and an underhand way of seeking revenge all make Aufidius the equivalent of the tribunes in earlier scenes. He baits Coriolanus in a similar way and provokes an exactly comparable self-assertion on the part of the hero. As the accusation "traitor" inflamed him before, it does so again, but here there is an interesting difference. After calling him traitor, Aufidius addresses him as Marcius, stripping him of his title of Coriolanus, and finally calls him "thou boy of tears" (V, 6, 84-99), referring of course to his giving in to his mother's plea. Coriolanus protests each term, but it is "boy" which raises him to the height of his rage:

> Boy! O slave!
>
> . . . . .
>
> Cut me to pieces, Volsces. Men and lads,
> Stain all your edges on me. Boy? False hound!
> If you have writ your annals true, 'tis there,
> That, like an eagle in a dovecote, I
> Flutter'd your Volscians in Corioles.
> Alone I did it. Boy?   (V, 6, 103, 111-16)

What hurts most is the impugning of his manhood—his heroic *virtus*. He asserts it by the magnificently foolhardy reminiscence of his singlehanded victory over the very people he is addressing —"Alone I did it." His words recall the earlier description of him, "He is himself alone, / To answer all the city" (I, 4, 51-2). Shakespeare's alteration of history, making Coriolanus "alone" is one of the touches which reveals most unequivocally his heroic conception of the character. In Coriolanus the opposition of the individual might of the hero to the superior forces of nature and fate is pushed to the uttermost.

It is characteristic of Shakespeare's Coriolanus that he resents "boy" more than "traitor", for it is clear throughout that the honour and integrity to which Coriolanus is committed are intensely personal. In this respect he resembles Antony in his final moments. When James Thomson wrote his *Coriolanus* in the middle of the eighteenth century, he reversed the order of the accusations. Thomson's Tullus does not call Coriolanus "boy", but he reminds him of his capitulation and condescendingly offers to protect him from the Volscians. Coriolanus, in return, recalls his victory at Corioles, though he says nothing of being alone. Tullus then insults the Romans and finally

accuses Coriolanus of being a traitor both to them and to the
Volscians. To the slurs on Rome Coriolanus replies:

> Whate'er her blots, whate'er her giddy factions,
> There is more virtue in one single year
> Of *Roman* story, than your *Volscian* annals
> Can boast thro' all your creeping dark duration![26]

This patriotic emphasis, which Thomson presumably felt
necessary as a means of getting sympathy for his hero, makes all
the plainer the consequences of Shakespeare's climactic
emphasis on Coriolanus as an individual who can never be
completely assimilated into a city, his own or another.

John Philip Kemble's acting version combined Thomson and
Shakespeare. He kept the patriotic defence of Rome from
Thomson, but followed it with the speeches from Shakespeare
prompted by the accusation "traitor". The culmination of the
interchange is once more the hero's indignant repetition of
"boy!", which Kemble made memorable by his way of saying
it. Slightly later, Macready was especially pleased that he could
rival Kemble's success in the inflection of this crucial mono-
syllable.[27] These actors, who made "boy!" the high point of
their portrayal of heroic dignity, were much closer to the core
of Shakespeare's character than are the critics who see him as
in fact boyish and small. The whole effect of the last scene
depends on a recognition very similar to Cleopatra's after the
death of Antony:

> The soldier's pole is fall'n! Young boys and girls
> Are level now with men. The odds is gone,
> And there is nothing left remarkable
> Beneath the visiting moon.   (IV, 15, 65-8)

Coriolanus is angular, granitic, and hence unlovable. Antony's
faults are much more easily forgiven than this obduracy.[28] Yet
of the two it is Coriolanus who more certainly commands
respect and veneration.

Shakespeare to Dryden

IT is a well-known fact that the drama of the period between Shakespeare and Dryden contributed in many ways to the formation of the heroic plays which enjoyed such popularity after the Restoration of Charles II. Since Hercules was one of the greatest embodiments of the heroic ideal, it is surprising to find that the Jacobean and Caroline stage provided no noteworthy heroes of the Herculean mould. One explanation is the vastly increased popularity of the theme of love and hence the greater importance of women.[1] Some of the ablest playwrights, such as Webster, Middleton and Ford, took comparatively little interest in warrior heroes, and are remembered today chiefly for the extraordinary dramatic life of their portraits of women— the Duchess of Malfi, Vittoria Corombona, Beatrice-Joanna, Livia, Annabella, Calantha. Though some of these women— certainly the Duchess, Vittoria and Calantha—have a heroic greatness of spirit, and though the Duchess and Vittoria stand up courageously to the forces of a corrupt society, it would be futile to seek further points of resemblance between them and the Herculean hero. The most memorable male characters of these playwrights have, if anything, still less in common with Hercules. Bosola, Flamineo, De Flores, Giovanni belong to traditions far removed. Ford's Perkin Warbeck, the pretender to the English throne, comes closer to the type, but the fascination of this play lies in the complete subjectivity of Warbeck's concept of his greatness. That he is not in fact the man he claims to be is clear, but whether he is self-deluded or a deliberate impostor remains an enigma. The problem of the play has more to do with the nature of reality than the nature of heroism. Ford's interest in such psychological subtleties relates him closely to Webster and Middleton. Ambiguities of motive, delicate shadings of evil, problems to perplex moral judgment are typical of the plays of all three men. Whereas the author of a Herculean play looks beyond the failings of his hero to virtues so awesome that the world can ill afford to lose them, these authors look squarely at the power of evil, whether it operates inside or outside of their characters. But in the midst of sin they see goodness or greatness—pure love in the heart of an incestuous girl, courage in a "white devil". Sometimes they focus attention on a hardening into sin, such as Beatrice-Joanna's in *The Changeling*; sometimes on a venial wrongdoing which leads so great a woman as the Duchess of Malfi to a horrible death.

Among the characters mentioned so far only four might be considered heroic: Webster's Duchess and Vittoria, Ford's Calantha and, perhaps in a special way, his Perkin Warbeck. All four inspire some degree of "admiration". Among the protagonists of Beaumont and Fletcher and Massinger several are not only "admirable" but are also more familiar heroic types. For example, Caesar, in *The False One*, is of course a great conqueror; Archas, the marvellously noble hero of *The Loyal Subject*, is a successful general; Miranda, the Knight of Malta, is to be admired (his name is no accident) not only for the purity of his love but for his chivalric prowess; both the embattled queen, Bonduca, and her general, Caratach, are warriors of surpassing nobility and courage. Malefort, in Massinger's *The Unnatural Combat*, is the saviour of his city and at the same time a man who bows to no authority. The brilliant rhetoric of these three playwrights aids them in elevating such heroes to a dazzling height above common humanity. Here are characters more obviously akin to the protagonists of the later heroic plays.

However, these great-spirited characters, whether or not they are warriors, are either decidedly more evil or decidedly more innocent than the Herculean hero. Miranda is not only brave but pure; Archas cannot be swayed from loyalty; and Caesar, fortified by a most honourable Cleopatra, is a pattern of nobility. Malefort, on the other hand, is so thoroughly possessed by a guilty passion (so recognized by him) that he is driven from outrage to outrage until, in a highly melodramatic scene, he is struck dead by a bolt of lightning. In Webster one sees the contrast between the great Duchess, whose naturalness and even naïveté make her seem innocent in comparison to those around her, and Vittoria, whose guilt is clear from the start.

I have made a great deal of the fact that "admiration", rather than a strict moral accounting, is the expected response

K

to a Herculean hero. The briefest consideration of these Jacobean and Caroline heroes is enough to remind one that it is also the expected response to heroes of a different sort. The more the hero is elevated—the more largeness of spirit is emphasized —the greater the appeal to wonder. For this reason, the incestuous Malefort is more awesome than the incestuous Giovanni. Ford does comparatively little to increase the stature of his hero; on the contrary, he makes him understandable in human terms. Massinger shows Malefort consumed by the flames of an "infernal brand" (IV, 1, p. 190),[2] "possessed with whirlwinds", "each guilty thought . . . a dreadful hurricano" (V, 2, p. 225), and at the last cursing God (*ibid.*, p. 227)—a prodigy of evil. In a similar fashion Miranda is a character of astonishing goodness—a more admirable lover than Romeo. These extraordinary heroes, both the monsters and the saints, leave an important legacy to the heroic play of the Restoration, but they contribute only indirectly to the development of the sort of hero with whom we have been concerned. A glance at a few more pronouncements on admiration suggests some broad divisions in the heroic tradition which help to define the position of the Herculean hero.

In *L'Arte Poetica* Minturno says that "whoever suffers a marvelous thing, if it is horrifying or causes compassion, will not be outside the scope of tragedy, whether he be good or whether he be evil".[3] The operative word is "marvelous", and the emphasis is not surprising in the critic who has so much to say about the admiration roused by wonderful actions in tragedy and epic. By specifying that the tragic hero may be either good or evil, Minturno justifies the choice of even a thoroughly evil character rather than the mainly but not absolutely good character recommended by Aristotle. Even a Richard III can arouse admiration. A very similar attitude is found in the more practical realm of Renaissance history and political theory. Machiavelli, in his *Discourses on Livy*, discusses the failure of Giovanpaolo Baglione to murder Pope Julius II when he had him in his power. Machiavelli attributes this to some lack in Baglione, for he notes that some people do not know how to attempt a crime when it "has in itself some grandeur or magnanimity".[4] The clear implication is that Baglione was too small a person to carry out this enterprise. The "grandeur and magnanimity" he looks for in a man who is to shape history are the qualities Minturno requires for tragedy.

When a playwright gives these qualities to a villainous protagonist even more liberally than Shakespeare gives them to Richard III, the result is a hero not only wicked but monumental. Thorough disapproval exists side by side with recognition of extraordinary greatness. It is possible that Marlowe so regarded his Jew of Malta, but T. S. Eliot's uneasiness about the play, shared by many other readers, reflects some lack of sureness and control in the execution. Malefort is a much more impressive example, though Massinger also fails to make his portrayal entirely convincing. Sejanus and Cataline belong to this line of development, and Jonson even raises Cethegus, a secondary villain, to heroic status by language which Dryden refers to in his essay "Of Heroic Plays" as a precedent for the extravagance of Almanzor. Though much of the language in the tragedy of *Catiline* is derived from Sallust and other Latin authors, the phrases cited by Dryden appear to be Jonson's own. The appeal to admiration through extravagance of language was not as foreign to him as is sometimes thought.

On the Restoration stage the best-known successor to such admirable bad-men is Maximin, the anti-Christian emperor of Dryden's *Tyrannic Love*. Phrases reminiscent of Tamburlaine are put in the mouth of this character whom Dryden designed, as he said, to set off that of the martyr, St Catherine:

> What soul is this which empire cannot stir!
> (IV, 1, p. 442)

> Our Gods are Gods, 'cause they have power and will;
> Who can do all things, can do nothing ill.
> Ill is rebellion 'gainst some higher power:
> The world may sin, but not its emperor.   (V, 1, p. 456)

> What had the Gods to do with me or mine?
> (V, 1, p. 463)[5]

Here atheistical ranting is set in a moral framework which explicitly condemns it, however grand it may be.

The theory which justified the villain as a tragic hero also justified his diametrical opposite, the man of extraordinary goodness, equally repugnant to strict Aristotelian theory. Minturno even argued that Christ was a suitable protagonist for tragedy.[6] Though few tragic heroes have ever been truly Christ-like, an increasing number in the seventeenth century were astoundingly good. In fact, as vastly admirable heroes began to crowd the stage, many more good ones were to be found than bad, possibly because extraordinary goodness was more astounding than extraordinary badness. Some of the model characters in Beaumont and Fletcher and Massinger have already been mentioned. In Ford's *The Broken Heart* a striking example is Calantha, whose Stoical suppression of her personal feelings in the interest of the public good provides the amazing scene which Lamb praises so highly.

Corneille's emphasis on admiration, though not so much of a departure from Renaissance tradition as it used sometimes to be called, remains a prominent feature of his plays.[7] Since Dryden and his contemporaries were considerably indebted to the theory and practice of Corneille,[8] what he has to say about admiration of virtue and vice is pertinent to the development of these attitudes in England. Discussing the problem of moral instruction in his First Discourse ("De L'Utilité et des Parties du Poème Dramatique"), he argues against the notion that wicked or vicious characters should not be treated in tragedy, and reminds his readers of Horace's advice to show Medea proud, Ixion treacherous, and Achilles angry, defying law. As a modern instance Corneille mentions the Cléopatre of his *Rodogune*, who is very wicked, as he admits; but, he says, "tous ses crimes sont accompangés d'une grandeure d'âme qui a quelque chose de si haut, qu'en même temps qu'on déteste ses actions, on admire la source dont elles partent".[9] The point could not be more clearly made. Corneille's words could be applied without change to Malefort or Maximin. The wicked hero is the exception in Corneille, however. As Paul Bénichou remarks, in most cases there is no conflict between the hero and moral law.[10] If Rodrigue in *Le Cid* is almost entirely admirable in every sense of the word, Nicomède is absolutely so. In the Examen prefixed to *Nicomède* Corneille says, "Dans l'admiration qu'on a pour sa vertu, je trouve une manière de purger les passions dont n'a point parlé Aristote, et qui est peut-être plus sûre que celle qu'il prescrit à la tragédie par le moyen de la pitié et de la crainte. . . . La grandeur de courage de Nicomède nous laisse une aversion de la pusillanimité. . . ."[11]

By reference to these heroic personages, both English and French, the uniqueness of the Herculean hero is seen more readily. He is admirable in a very special way. He is regarded from a point of view which seems to correspond in part to Corneille's description of Nicomède, in part to his description of Cléopatre. As in Nicomède, "grandeur de courage" is certainly the virtue which is admired, and it is exactly opposed to pusillanimity. If the hero orders the slaughter of innocent citizens or turns against his own city, his crimes, like those of Cléopatre, are so much a part of a great spirit that, shocking as they are, they seem to have their origin in something admirable. Yet this attempt to explain the attitude toward a Herculean hero misrepresents it by dividing it into neat sections. The character is a monolith, and the attitude towards him, though complex, is single. Recognition of whatever crimes may be charged to him is included within admiration for his extraordinary virtue.

What Werner Jaeger says about areté throws light on this way of regarding a hero. The aristocratic Greek ideal, with its unqualified respect for the honour of the individual, allows for the highest possible regard for a hero who in certain circumstances goes quite contrary to what is good for the community.[12] In later times an exclusive concern with personal honour was thought of as the sin of ambition or pride, and the heroic ideal came under the sway of more democratic ethics. Christian ethics reinforced a tendency which was already under way. The earlier concept relied more on a rationally indefinable grandeur; the later one tended to explain heroic virtue in terms of what was demonstrably good for the community. Jonson brings the rigorous clarity of his style to the definition of this public and Christian ideal of heroism. In *The New Inn* Lovel is asked to say "what true valour is"; the standard of conduct he erects, logical down to the last detail, is clearly not that of the Hercules we have seen. The very absence of paradox in Lovel's concept of valour brings out the distinctive contradictions in the Herculean concept:

> It is the greatest vertue, and the safety
> Of all mankinde, the object of it is danger.
> A certaine meane 'twixt feare, and confidence:
> No inconsiderate rashnesse, or vaine appetite

Of false encountring formidable things:
But a true science of distinguishing
What's good or evill. It springs out of reason,
And tends to perfect honesty, the scope
Is alwayes honour, and the publique good:
It is no valour for a private cause.   (IV, 4, 38-47)

Under the influence of the later attitude the truly villainous
hero develops as a kind of distortion—a hero whose opposition
to society is made gross and clear-cut, and whose largeness of
soul is almost a travesty of heroic grandeur. He is clearly
separated from the virtuous hero, whose exemplary conduct
endears him to society and typically culminates in an act of
self-sacrifice. The Herculean hero, then, might be called a
survival of an older concept of the heroic in which devotion to
an ideal self, rather than submission to the demands of society,
is the proper goal of the high-minded man. It is assumed that
such a man is the greatest treasure a society can possess; yet in
honouring him that society grants him his claim to almost unqualified freedom. In Renaissance treatments of Hercules the
ideals of glorious individualism and service to society are held
in perilous equilibrium. Consciously or unconsciously influenced
by this tradition, the English playwrights we have been studying
maintain the equilibrium, but the least shift of emphasis produces the very different heroes briefly mentioned in this section.

In France the movement called *préciosité* contributed to the
formation of the heroic ideal.[13] A programme for refining
manners and letters was closely allied to enthusiasm for the
noble ideals of honour, valour and love expressed in romances
such as D'Urfé's *L'Astrée*. The effects of this combination of
interests are to be seen in the drama of Corneille not only in the
importance given to the theme of love but in the self-conscious
concern with ideals of conduct, from the sphere of manners to
that of ethics. While the *précieux* encouraged individualism, the
loftiness of their idealism was obviously congenial to the
development of a concept of heroism in which the individual
did not challenge the accepted canons of morality. Thus
préciosité was probably in part responsible for the outstanding
virtue of the usual Cornelian hero.

A somewhat comparable development took place in England
in the reign of Charles I, whose French queen exposed the court

to the influence of *préciosité*. Alfred Harbage discusses the concern with love, the noble ideals, and the refinement of Caroline
drama, and shows how important these were in shaping the
dramatic tradition which was passed on to the Restoration
writers.[14] Like their French counterparts, these characteristics
may help to explain the absence of that older, more primitive
heroic ideal which appeared occasionally on the Elizabethan
and the early Jacobean stage. The intellectual climate favoured
the development of a gentlemanly hero who did not rage unduly
and whose desire for glory and greatness could be formulated
in a way quite acceptable to society.

On the Restoration stage Dryden is unique in revivifying the
older heroic ideal. Though we might expect to find many
Herculeans in an age when the heroic play was the characteristic form of serious drama, in fact the vast majority of the
heroes belong to other strains of the heroic tradition. As in the
preceding period, and possibly for the same reasons, many of
the heroes are exemplary. Orrery, for example, characteristically portrays such a model of filial and patriotic devotion as
Mustapha. Otway creates the fiery Don Carlos, who in a
Herculean moment, contemplates rebellion against his unjust
father, but comes finally to generous forgiveness. Lee delights
in the portrayal of heroes distracted from their pursuit of glory
by one or more enchantresses, and some of his most grandly
heroic characters, whether good or evil, are women: Sophonisba,
Roxana, Statira. If some of the heroes of Restoration heroic
plays occasionally approach the Herculean type, few of them
conform to it at all closely. In three important plays of Dryden's,
however, the Herculean hero is presented fully and brilliantly.
To these plays the next chapter is devoted.

6

Dryden

Yours is a Soul irregularly great,
Which, wanting temper, yet abounds with heat . . .

THE Herculean hero in Dryden's plays is both the sum of all
his predecessors and a new creation, suited to the ideals and
the stage conventions of a new age. In Dryden's major con-
tributions to serious drama, *The Conquest of Granada*, *Aureng-Zebe*
and *All for Love*, certain elements present in all the earlier
"Herculean" plays stand out with the dazzling clarity of points
made by a good debater, fully aware of the significance of his
material. As Chaucer in *Troilus and Criseide* and the *Knight's
Tale*, while in certain respects modifying the medieval romance,
produces a distillation of its essential character, Dryden seizes
upon the essentials in the tradition we have been considering,
and in the very process of transforming, gives them a kind of
ideal statement by making explicit what was before implied.

The hero's extraordinary stature is never more emphatically
clear than in these plays. "Vast is his courage, boundless is his
mind," says an admiring observer of Almanzor (1 *Conquest*, I,
253), and Ventidius expatiates on the "vast soul" of Antony
(*All for Love*, I, 125).[1] In "A Parallel of Poetry and Painting"
Dryden writes, "When we view these elevated ideas of nature,
the result of that view is admiration, which is always the cause
of pleasure."[2]

The protagonists of these plays are prime examples of the
Herculean hero's self-reliance and determination to guard his
own integrity at whatever cost. Each of them is imbued with
the areté of an Achilles or a Coriolanus. In the dedication of *All
for Love* Dryden is eloquent on this subject, and the words he
addresses to his noble patron apply perfectly to his heroes:

> The highest virtue is best to be trusted with itself; for assistance
> only can be given by a genius superior to that which it assists;
> and 'tis the noblest kind of debt, when we are only oblig'd to God
> and nature. This, then, my Lord, is your just commendation, that

you have wrought out yourself a way to glory, by those very means
that were design'd for your destruction. . . .   (Noyes, p. 224)

In one of the most famous passages of *The Conquest of Granada*,
Almanzor proclaims: "I alone am king of me. / I am as free as
nature first made man" (1 *Conquest*, I, 206-7). As Tamburlaine
plays fast and loose with Cosroe and Coriolanus deserts Rome
for the Volsces, Almanzor changes sides so often that it was easy
for Dryden's enemies to ridicule the fickleness of the hero.
Dryden replied by asking, "what tie has he on him to the
contrary?" (Ker, I, 157). Though the reply does not settle the
question of artistic propriety, it stresses the main point:
Almanzor has a freedom of action granted only to gods and
heroes. His only obligations are those which he chooses to
recognize.

The superiority to ordinary mortals, such a conspicuous trait
in Tamburlaine and Coriolanus, is again illustrated in Almanzor, whose contempt for the "unthinking crowd" is matched
only by his power over them. In the first scenes of *The Conquest
of Granada* a sentence or two and a few sword-strokes suffice to
establish his absolute authority. Aureng-Zebe, also, is distinguished from the average by something approaching the
supernatural—"Sure *Aureng-Zebe* has somewhat of Divine" (III,
SS, 249).

As to the fierceness of the Herculean hero, it was doubtless
impossible to surpass Marlowe either in degree or in the clarity
of presentation, but Dryden has not skimped on this characteristic in his portrayal of Almanzor, who inspires terror by his very
looks (as do Tamburlaine and Coriolanus), and flies into a rage
whenever his purpose is thwarted. The fierceness of Morat in
Aureng-Zebe is equally conspicuous.[3] In these two instances
Dryden may fairly be accused of exaggerating a Herculean trait
almost to the point of caricature.

His essays—particularly the essay "Of Heroic Plays"—reveal
Dryden's awareness of the confluence of traditions which produced this genre and also his preference for the kind of heroic
character which I have called Herculean. His often-quoted
genealogy of Almanzor is the core of his ideas on this subject:

I must therefore avow, in the first place, from whence I took the
character. The first image I had of him was from the *Achilles* of

Homer; the next from Tasso's *Rinaldo* (who was a copy of the former), and the third from the *Artaban* of Monsieur Calprenède, who has imitated both. (Ker, I, 155)

By emphasizing his debt to Homer and Tasso Dryden wishes to dissociate himself from a tendency in the French romance which seems to him a falsification of the heroic tradition, the exaggerated importance of the "point of honour". Of Homer and Tasso he says:

They made their heroes men of honour; but so as not to divest them quite of human passions and frailties: they contented themselves to show you, what men of great spirits would certainly do when they were provoked, not what they were obliged to do by the strict rules of moral virtue. For my own part, I declare myself for Homer and Tasso, and am more in love with Achilles and Rinaldo, than with Cyrus and Oroondates. (*Ibid.*, pp. 156-7)

Although Dryden goes on to say that Almahide, Ozmyn and Benzayda are "patterns of exact virtue" which may challenge comparison with the best of the French, Almanzor is deliberately excluded from this category. The distinction Dryden is making brings out his love for a greatness which is irregular. This is the greatness of Antony, for whom virtue's path is too narrow (*All for Love*, I, 124-5). It is equally Almanzor's:

A soul too fiery and too great to guide:
He moves eccentric, like a wand'ring star
Whose motion's just, tho' 'tis not regular.
(1 *Conquest*, V, 3, 37-9)

But this attribute is never more succintly put than in Indamora's lines to Morat:

Yours is a Soul irregularly great,
Which, wanting temper, yet abounds with heat . . .
(*Aureng-Zebe*, V, SS, 281)

Dryden's heroes are legitimate descendants of the earlier Herculean heroes.[4] However, it requires no argument to persuade any reader of the plays that these descendants speak and behave very differently from their forebears. One of the reasons why they do so is the acknowledged influence of the romance, and especially of the French romance.[5] The emphasis on the theme of love is the most obvious contribution of the

romance tradition. As we have seen, a romantic concept of love
does not occur at all in the Hercules plays of Sophocles,
Euripides and Seneca. In *Tamburlaine* it is distinctly secondary,
but considerably more important in *Bussy D'Ambois*. In *Coriolanus* it is again almost non-existent, but so important in *Antony
and Cleopatra* that the play cannot be considered exclusively as
the tragedy of a Herculean hero. At the outset, then, it might
seem that the romance influence, which largely accounts for
the major roles of the women in Dryden's plays, makes the hero
too much a lover to be a Hercules. In Dryden's hands, however,
the love of the hero is often a means of completing his heroic
duty, rather than an alternative or an obstacle.[6] The presence
of such an element modifies, but does not destroy the Herculean
pattern. The case of *All for Love*, like that of *Antony and Cleopatra*,
is a special one, but I shall argue that Dryden's play is even
more affected than Shakespeare's by the concept of the
Herculean hero.

The emphasis on romantic love may be traced all the way
back to Virgil and Heliodorus, but for Dryden it was the more
recent examples of the tradition which counted most.[7] He had
the opening pages of *Orlando Furioso* open before him when he
reflected that

> . . . an heroic play ought to be an imitation, in little, of an heroic
> poem; and, consequently, that Love and Valour ought to be the
> subject of it.   (Ker, I, 150)

but the courtliness of some of the speeches and actions of his
lovers comes more directly from French romance than from
Ariosto or Tasso. Artaban is one of the models for Almanzor,
and despite Dryden's primary allegiance to Achilles and
Rinaldo, the influence of Artaban is powerful.

The romance not only increases greatly the importance of
love in the hero's life. Sometimes it also leads to the resolution
of a major paradox in the situation of the Herculean hero, the
opposition between his freedom and the demands of society.
In *Tamburlaine, Bussy D'Ambois* and *Coriolanus* this paradox is
left unresolved. We can sympathize with Zenocrate's pleas for
Damascus and at the same time respect Tamburlaine's refusal
to heed them—see that Bussy has no right to Tamyra, yet wish
for his victory over the French court which seeks to restrain

him—respond to Volumnia's arguments while perceiving that they are aimed at the destruction of the hero's integrity. In *The Conquest of Granada* the same opposition is again dramatized, but at the end Almanzor, who has boasted that "I alone am king of me", has come to acknowledge not only certain moral obligations but even fealty to King Ferdinand. In the character of Aureng-Zebe a careful balance of personal honour and filial duty is preserved.[8] In both cases the influence of the heroine is largely responsible for the reconciliation of these opposites.

1. *The Conquest of Granada*

Through the ten acts of *The Conquest of Granada* (1670) in the midst of an impressively large cast of characters Almanzor is kept as surely in the centre of the stage picture as is Tamburlaine. Thanks to Dryden's contrivance, the number of characters surrounding the hero only serves to emphasize his uniqueness. The type situation in the play is one in which a chaos of conflicting energies is turned, at least temporarily, into order by the lone might of Almanzor. His first entrance is brilliantly prepared. We hear of the bull fight in which "the champions of the salvage kind" (already Augustan diction is beginning to serve its purpose) are pitted against Moorish horsemen who "gracefully" command "their proud ginnets". But the dexterity of the best of the Moors is surpassed by that of a "brave unknown", whose performance dazzles the spectators as he puts an end to the contest between man and beast (1 *Conquest*, I, 20-98). This description is cut short by the eruption of fighting between two families, the Zegrys and the Abencerrages. In the midst of the mêlée Almanzor, the "brave unknown", appears, brings victory to the Abencerrages, and shortly afterwards persuades both sides to lay down their arms.

The impression of uniqueness made by his valour is of course heightened by the mystery surrounding him and by his often-quoted self-description:

> I am as free as nature first made man,
> Ere the base laws of servitude began,
> When wild in woods the noble savage ran. (I, 207-9)

There is an inescapable suggestion that Almanzor himself belongs to an incorruptible world, remote in time and space.

To put the matter differently, the portrayal of Almanzor is coloured by what Lovejoy calls "hard" primitivism—the glorification of a rough and simple life, opposed in every way to corrupt civilization.[9] For the Cynics and Stoics the Scythians were the ideal representatives of such a life. A similarly "primitive" colouration is seen in the portrayal of Tamburlaine, the Scythian shepherd, and Bussy, who is said to "uphold / Man in his native noblesse".

In *The Conquest of Granada* this primitivism and several of the circumstances of Almanzor's first appearance are derived from La Calprenède. In *Cléopâtre* Artaban is first presented as an unknown knight who arrives in the midst of a fray and triumphs in each of his encounters. When the "valiant Unknown" is asked to give some account of himself, Artaban tells of his youth in the woods of Gaul (the setting of the romance is the Roman empire in its early years), where he was nourished "like Achilles", and trained as Chiron, the centaur, trained Achilles.[10] Though unaware of it at the time of this narration, Artaban is actually the illegitimate son of no less a worthy than Pompey. The conventions of romance thus enable La Calprenède to revivify an idea inherent in the legend of Achilles' divine parentage and education by the centaur: that some great natural force makes the hero superior to ordinary mortals.[11] A mysterious (and as it turns out, noble) parentage replaces the divine, and an ancient Gaul replaces the centaur. A similar mystery surrounds Almanzor's origins. He is at first "the brave unknown"; later we hear that he was "rais'd by valor from a birth unknown" (*Ibid.*, I, 257). Only at the end does Almanzor discover that he is the son of the Duke of Arcos, and hence a Christian. Like Artaban, he has grown up far from the centres of civilization. His youth in pagan Africa is the equivalent of Artaban's in Gaul. He therefore shares the rough purity and the mysterious power of the hero of La Calprenède's romance.

Introduced as an almost mythic embodiment of certain heroic qualities, Almanzor is seen in the rest of the play in an astonishing variety of relationships, each of which contributes to the definition of his character. If Chapman's play is more reflective than Marlowe's—more a dramatization of the *idea* of a hero— then Dryden's is still more so. The action becomes a kind of continuous discourse on heroism. Dryden proceeds by means of intricately related contrasts, reminiscent of those in *Tamburlaine* and *Coriolanus* but more elaborately wrought. To point them all out would be tedious. I shall concentrate on some of the most important—the contrasts with Boabdelin, Almahide, Ozmyn, the warring chieftains in Granada, and Lyndaraxa.

Boabdelin is represented as an almost psychopathically inept king, a second Mycetes, whose weakness encourages not only foreign attack but civil strife. Wishing to impose peace on the feuding Zegrys and Abencerrages, Boabdelin can say nothing more forceful, even surrounded as he is by his own guard, than "A king intreats you". (I, 274). Almanzor, relying only upon the display of valour which he has just given in the scuffle, says:

> What subjects will precarious kings regard?
> A beggar speaks too softly to be heard:
> Lay down your arms! 'Tis I command you now.
>
> (I, 275-7)

Only through him is the authority of this "precarious" king (the word is brilliantly exact) maintained. The innate royalty of Almanzor is contrasted at the outset with the mere show of royalty in a corrupt king. At the end Almanzor finds that, through his mother, he has royal blood in his veins, and an aristocratic audience was free to interpret Almanzor's behaviour as the inevitable revelation of good blood. Royalty, like murder, will out. But Boabdelin also has royal blood, and the difference between the two men lies in the greatness of spirit which makes Almanzor's royalty genuine. Boabdelin's claim on Almahide, like his claim to the throne, has the sanction of legality; it has not, by the standards of romance, the sanction of true love. Almahide is already promised to him at the opening of the play and marries him at the end of Part I, but from the moment in Act III when Almanzor sees her, he has her heart. The paths of Almanzor and Boabdelin cross and recross throughout the ten acts of the play. At each intersection the true lover confronts the merely legal possessor, and the true king the mere office-holder.

The reading of the head-title: *Almanzor and Almahide, or The Conquest of Granada* makes clear the centrality of this love relationship. It is customary to think of the love and honour of heroic plays as the opposites which they sometimes are.

Abdalla, for example, is tempted by his love for Lyndaraxa, to revolt against his brother, Boabdelin.

> Betwixt my love and virtue I am toss'd;
> This must be forfeited, or that be lost.   (II, 185-6)

Precisely this sort of conflict is burlesqued in *The Rehearsal* (III, 5) when Prince Volscius debates which of his boots to pull on, the one representing love, or the one representing honour. Though Almanzor at first conceives of his passion for Almahide in these same terms, her ultimate effect on him is anything but the destruction of his honour. In the first scene we hear of him:

> Vast is his courage, boundless is his mind,
> Rough as a storm, and humorous as wind:
> Honor's the only idol of his eyes;
> The charms of beauty like a pest he flies. . . .
>   (I, 253-6)

where it will be noted that Almanzor's honour is associated with the free exercise of his power. When he meets Almahide he compares the effect of her eyes, in one of the least happy of Dryden's similes, to the sting of a tarantula, and adds:

> Honor burns in me, not so fiercely bright,
> But pale, as fires when master'd by the light.
>   (III, 332-3)

In the event, however, his honour is burning at least as bright when, after rescuing Almahide from the revolted Zegrys and restoring Boabdelin to his throne, he leaves her free to choose him or remain faithful to her engagement to the king. As his ability to sway the victory first to the Zegrys, then back again to the Abencerrages, demonstrates his heroic prowess, so this refusal to exploit his power reveals a moral sensibility quite different from that of a Tamburlaine. Almahide comments:

> Almanzor can from every subject raise
> New matter for our wonder and his praise.
> You bound and freed me; but the difference is,
> That show'd your valor; but your virtue this.
>   (IV, 2, 373-6)

Almanzor's acquisition of this moral dimension of his *virtus* is a gradual process which extends through most of the two parts of the play and is mainly due to the influence of Almahide. At the beginning, though his inclinations are of the best, his discrimination is overwhelmed by his impetuosity. At his first entrance, in the midst of the mêlée between the rival factions, he announces that he has no time to find out which cause is best, but chooses to help the underdog. At this point his nobility is decidedly rough-hewn. Almahide says of him:

> Mark but how terrible his eyes appear!
> And yet there's something roughly noble there,
> Which, in unfashion'd nature, looks divine,
> And, like a gem, does in the quarry shine.
>
> (III, 304-7)

Later she addresses a tentative criticism to him:

> Might I not make it as my last request,
> (Since humble carriage suits a suppliant best,)
> That you would somewhat of your fierceness hide—
> That inborn fire—I do not call it pride?
>
> (IV, 2, 467-70)

A still more favourable view of his "inborn fire" comes from Almahide's father, Abenamar:

> What, in another, vanity would seem,
> Appears but noble confidence in him;
> No haughty boasting, but a manly pride;
> A soul too fiery and too great to guide:
> He moves eccentric, like a wand'ring star
> Whose motion's just, tho' 'tis not regular.
>
> (V, 3, 34-9)

The images of gem and fire convey the impressions of value, vitality, and power; the roughness and fierceness with which they are qualified combine with the idea of eccentricity contained in the image of the "wand'ring star". The last speech is notable for its plain insistence on propriety. While the rough gem may need polishing and the inborn fire controlling, the orbit of the "wand'ring star" is exact, however unlike that of a planet. Throughout the play a delicate balance is maintained between the hero's "irregularity" and his rightness. It would be a misrepresentation to say that Almanzor in Act I is mainly good but in need of a little discipline, for Dryden never allows the problem to be formulated that simply. Even Almanzor's errors testify to his areté, but he learns to redefine his idea of the good. He is not so much disciplined as he is educated towards a larger vision. A figure which Almahide uses when she is urging him to find another love applies well to this process of education and to her part in it. Comparing his ravaged heart to a city laid waste by fire, she advises him:

> Build love a nobler temple in my place;
> You'll find the fire has but inlarg'd your space.
>
> (V, 3, 273-4)

The most important effects of Almahide on Almanzor are seen in Part II, but the contrast between the two is established at their first meeting, after the celebrations of Almahide's imminent marriage have been interrupted by the Zegry revolt. The stage-direction reads, "After the dance, a tumultuous noise of drums and trumpets" (III, 232). To Almahide both the noise and the discord it symbolizes are torture: "The noise my soul does thr'o my senses wound" (III, 251). Her love of quiet and peace are juxtaposed with Almanzor's warlike fierceness— her love of order with his irregularity. Though she asks him to hide "somewhat of his fierceness", he does not strictly obey her, for after he has freed her, he asks Boabdelin to renounce her, and flies into a rage when the king refuses. By the end of Part I he has been banished (shouting, like Coriolanus, "Where'er I go, there can no exile be; / But from Almanzor's sight I banish thee" [V, 3, 107-8]), but in Part II Boabdelin is obliged to ask Almahide to reconcile Almanzor in order to save the city from the Spaniards. Her father brings him back to Granada from where he "found him, like Achilles on the shore" (2 *Conquest*, II, 3, 3), unmoved by the plight of the city until the queen's name was mentioned. When Almahide is left alone with Almanzor she accomplishes the remarkable feat of overcoming his jealousy and persuading him, as the proof of his virtue, to fight, unbribed, to "preserve a mistress and a king" (II, 3, 100). Almanzor accepts this abstract obligation, and thus, through the force of love, acknowledges after all a "power above his own".[12]

At the same time, it must be noted that Almanzor has an effect on Almahide. If she is responsible for enlarging his vision

L

of the good, he also alters hers. After she has had the chance to
contrast Boabdelin with him she soliloquizes:

> How blest was I before this fatal day,
> When all I knew of love, was to obey!
> 'Twas life becalm'd, without a gentle breath;
> Tho' not so cold, yet motionless as death;
> A heavy, quiet state; but love, all strife,
> All rapid, is the hurrican of life.
> Had love not shown me, I had never seen
> An excellence beyond Boabdelin.
> I had not, aiming higher, lost my rest;
> But with a vulgar good been dully blest:
> But, in Almanzor, having seen what's rare,
> Now I have learnt too sharply to compare . . .
>   (1 *Conquest*, V, 3, 198-209)

The quiet order, for which she seems to stand at first, is here
associated with dullness, and compared unfavourably with the
motion and even discord brought into her life by Almanzor.

Comparison between Almanzor and Almahide's brother,
Ozmyn, is inevitable. It will be remembered that Dryden refers
to both brother and sister as "patterns of exact virtues", which
may challenge comparison with the French. Ozmyn is indeed
irreproachable. His valour is very great, but no greater than his
love for Benzayda or his devotion to his father, his family, and
his country. All of these qualities are repeatedly tested in a
series of harrowing situations growing out of the hatred between
his family (who are Abencerrages) and Benzayda's (who are
Zegrys). In each crisis the behaviour of Ozmyn is exemplary.
Yet there can be no doubt that Almanzor outshines this paragon.
The difference between them is indicated in the opening
description of the bull-fight in which they have both performed.
Abenamar says:

> My son did well, and so did Hamet too;
> Yet did no more then we were wont to do;
> But what the stranger did was more then man.
>   (1 *Conquest*, I, 46-8)

Almanzor's "irregularity" is part of what raises him above even
the best of men.

Dryden attempts to explain this aspect of his hero in the

dedication of the play to the Duke of York. As in the essay "Of Heroic Plays", he cites the precedents of Homer and Tasso for the imperfect hero, and defends such a character by saying: "But a character of an eccentric virtue is the more exact image of human life, because he is not wholly exempted from its frailties" (Noyes, p. 5). This does scant justice to Dryden's achievement, and is even somewhat misleading, for the Aristotelian formula of all-too-human frailty present in an otherwise good man applies rather better to an Oedipus, an Othello, or a Lear than it does to Almanzor. Dryden goes on to say that Almanzor's roughness, impatience, and self-confidence "approaching to an arrogance" are errors "incident only to great spirits", and that they may be passed over without strict examination when they are accompanied by such "greater graces" as Almanzor's "frank and noble openness of nature, an easiness to forgive his conquer'd enemies, and to protect them in distress; and, above all, an inviolable faith in his affection". Here we are much closer to an explanation of Almanzor's superiority to Ozmyn. He is not more appealing because more humanly fallible but because of an exceptional force of spirit, which manifests itself both as generosity and as something "approaching to an arrogance"—that force which is persistently imaged in the play as fire.

The contrivance of the plot invites comparisons between Almanzor and the three factious lords at Boabdelin's court, his brother, Abdalla; Abdelmelech, the chief of the Abencerrages; and Zulema, the chief of the Zegrys. All three are military leaders; all three are self-assertive power-seekers; all three are lovers. But in the course of the play we see them becoming more and more the victims of their lust and their drive to power. In pursuit of Lyndaraxa, Abdelmelech and Abdalla sacrifice their friendship, and Abdalla also abandons his loyalty to the king, while the fickleness of Lyndaraxa, carried in some scenes to the point of absurdity, brings out the futility of their frantic efforts. The harder they try to gain power in order to command love, the more they seem like puppets, operated by Lyndaraxa, who loves neither one. Meanwhile, the love of Zulema for Almahide appears more and more clearly as lust until, near the end, losing all control, he attempts to rape her. Here are energetic men, swayed by strong passions, who yet are made to seem mean rather than great. The difference between them and Almanzor is much the same as the difference Dryden describes in the dedicatory epistle to *Aureng-Zebe* between the courtier without wit and the master of wit, the Earl of Mulgrave, whom he is addressing. He is discussing the opposition at court to artistic worth:

> For in all Courts, there are too many, who make it their business to ruine Wit: And Montaign, in other places, tells us, what effects he found of their good Natures. He describes them such, whose Ambition, Lust, or private Interest, seem to be the onely end of their Creation. . . . Dulness has brought them to what they are; and Malice secures them in their Fortunes . . . these are they, who wanting Wit, affect Gravity, and go by the name of Solid men: and a solid man is, in plain English, a solid, solemn Fool.[13]

The bracketing of dullness with malice, lust, and self-interest is revealing. *Per contra*, the witty man is generous and devoted to the public interest. He is also a lover of liberty, and in the person of the earl he is a despiser of popular acclaim, a constant friend, and one whom only generosity keeps from being an equally constant enemy (for "he who is too lightly reconcil'd, after high Provocations, may recommend himself to the World for a Christian, but I should hardly trust him for a Friend").[14] Almanzor's flame is thus analogous to the true spark of wit, which is opposed to dullness, the enemy of all that is great. If the flame burns sometimes with an unruly brilliance, such excesses are comparable to those of the genius who breaks the rules to "snatch a grace beyond the reach of art", as Pope was to write:

> Great wits sometimes may gloriously offend,
> And rise to faults true Critics dare not mend.[15]

Almanzor rises to his faults; Abdalla, Abdelmelech and Zulema stoop to theirs; and where mere restraint might make them better men, he needs only to be shown how his heroism might be put to an even better use.

One more contrast remains to be discussed, that between Almanzor and Lyndaraxa. It is the subtlest of all and is managed for the maximum dramatic effect. Superficially, Lyndaraxa appears to be a female Almanzor. Early in the play she owns that her soul's ambition is "to live without control" (1 *Conquest*,

II, 148-9). The martial music which dismays Almahide has a
"sprightly sound" to her, and warms her blood (III, 252-4).
During a portion of the action she controls one of the forts of
Granada and attempts to influence the outcome of the war. Her
one aim is to be queen. As Almanzor changes sides, she favours
first one suitor, then another, and without hesitation joins with
the Spaniards when it seems to be in her interest to do so. But
these likenesses only help to define the qualities which distinguish her from the hero. Lyndaraxa carries Hobbesian
materialism to the point of caring for nothing but her own
advancement. A generous thought never crosses her mind.
Almanzor at his most arrogant never seeks power purely for
himself or for its own sake. Lyndaraxa is constant only in her
ambition, waiting to see which of her suitors can help her attain
her goal. She is therefore obliged to temporize and dissemble
with them. Here Almanzor is her polar opposite. When
Abenamar at one time suspects him of duplicity, he says:

> My kindness and my hate unmask'd I wear:
> For friends to trust, and enemies to fear.
> My heart's so plain
> That men on every passing thought may look,
> Like fishes gliding in a crystal brook. . . .
>
> (IV, 1, 41-5)

Throughout Part I we are free to perceive such contrasts in the
successive scenes in which Almanzor and Lyndaraxa appear.
They do not appear together until the third act of Part II, by
which time the counterpoint of their careers has generated a
keen desire to see them confront each other. Lyndaraxa now
sees that no one is so apt to make her a queen as Almanzor, and
as she lays her plans she brings out the cardinal difference
between them:

> In gaining him, I gain that fortune too,
> Which he has wedded, and which I but woo.
>
> (2 Conquest, III, 3, 61-2)

In the final analysis, her ambition is a continual restless pursuit,
which obliges her to await the outcome of the actions of others.
Almanzor creates and dominates situations. In this scene, as
she makes the advances and he repels them, her weakness and
his strength are more apparent than ever. The final emphasis is

upon constancy. She twits him with the futility of his love for Almahide, which she says is merely a mask for despair. He replies that the love she offers is merely a mask for inconstancy. When she makes fun of the very idea of constancy in love, he tells her that even hopeless loyalty is nobler than change, and that the unchanging soul is free of fate. That Lyndaraxa is completely at the mercy of fate is brought out at the very end when, just as the Spaniards are about to entrust the government of Granada to her, she is stabbed by her rejected suitor, Abdelmelech. Though her character is manipulated too mechanically to be convincing, there is a moment of genuine pathos when she finally realizes that her painful pursuit of fortune has been in vain.

The tournament which takes place in the fifth act of Part II, just before Lyndaraxa has gone over to the Spaniards, is a perfect dramatization of some of the basic contrasts and is also an effective means of drawing together the separate strands of the plot. After the failure of Zulema's attempt on Almahide, he and Lyndaraxa and their brother Hamet falsely accuse Almahide of unchastity. Although Almanzor himself suspects her, he fights to defend not only her honour but his own, and is joined by Almahide's brother Ozmyn. In the lists these champions of honour are opposed by the contrivers of dishonour, Zulema and Hamet, whose defeat leads to the vindication of Almahide and the banishment of Lyndaraxa.

Dryden's arrangement of his materials in *The Conquest of Granada* is one of the most remarkable and distinctive features of the play. Though the duration of the action is severely restricted, its ten acts comprehend many episodes and have, therefore, something of the epic sweep of *Tamburlaine*. But where the chief structural units of Marlowe's play correspond to so many different groups of enemies whom the hero encounters and defeats, the structure of *The Conquest of Granada* is based on the interaction of several plots (and in this regard is again indebted to the French romance). The love of Almanzor and Almahide, the love of Ozmyn and Benzayda, the rivalry between the suitors of Lyndaraxa, and the strife between the Moorish factions are all related to the Spaniards' ultimately successful campaign against Granada. Episodes of one plot are alternated with episodes of the others in such a way that the contrasts discussed above are brought out and through them various aspects of the heroic character. The unlikeness of Almanzor to Ozmyn reveals traits not emphasized by his unlikeness to Boabdelin; his apparent similarity to Lyndaraxa is a totally different thing from his true affinity to Almahide, which not only reveals but in some measure alters him. As Dryden's presentation is more schematic than that of the playwrights previously considered, the portrayal of his hero is correspondingly more exact.[16] The ways in which he departs from the social norm are precisely defined; the question of whether he is to be praised or blamed for these departures is explicitly discussed. Almahide, important in herself as the heroine of romance must be, is also a means of dramatizing the conflict between the Herculean hero's opposition to a corrupt world—the world of tyrants and petty men—and his obligation to an ideal society. For Almahide is both sympathetic and critical. She makes him see (at least at moments, for there are backslidings) the idea of a king behind the corrupt mask, and she persuades him to fight unbribed for this idea. In this way the paradox of the hero as both outcast and saviour is rationally resolved.

The principal movement of the action is the development of Almanzor under the influence of Almahide. Part I carries the story from Almanzor's first appearance through several sudden reversals of fortune to his banishment from Granada—from the first image of him as the brave unknown in the bull-fight, who did "more than man", to that of "a dying conqueror", to whom he compares himself as he takes leave of Almahide. Part II presents the complementary series of events which transform a sulking Achilles into a victorious hero. His decision to help Boabdelin in the defence of Granada is an important stage in his moral development. His defence of Almahide in the tournament is a reassertion of heroic honour.

The episodes of Part II are framed within scenes dominated by Ferdinand and Isabella, who never appear in Part I. In the opening scene the queen spares the life of Ozmyn, who has been captured in battle, because he is a true lover. Love, she says, defining the play's ideal, is a "heroic passion" which "kindles all the soul with honor's fire, / To make the lover worthy his desire" (2 *Conquest*, I, 1, 145-8). In the last scene she persuades Almahide to accept Almanzor as a husband. He has made himself "worthy his desire" by defending both Almahide and her husband, even though the defence of his own honour is in both instances a major consideration. As the queen of a court of love, Isabella reinforces and calls attention to the role of Almahide in the hero's education.

The ending of the play, with Boabdelin dead, Ferdinand and Isabella in command of Granada, and Almahide promised to Almanzor, is of course a typical romance ending, and a typical ending for tragicomedy. Far more than the mere presence of Almahide in the play, it alters the Herculean pattern. The only happiness for Hercules is to be made a star; Almanzor gets his reward in this world. Nevertheless, allowing for this important difference, it is not hard to see that certain elements of Dryden's ending correspond to elements in the endings of the Herculean tragedies. The Christian king and queen are rather shadowy and remote figures who finally, after long opposition, accept Almanzor into their society. He discovers that by birth he was already a Christian. Thus Almanzor is in effect translated into another world, but one in which he belongs. More important, the ending is quite consonant with Dryden's development of his theme. Almanzor's acknowledgement of fealty to Ferdinand is a logical conclusion to his education by Almahide. At the same time, his words recall the Almanzor of Act I, who admits no power above his own:

> I bring a heart which homage never knew;
> Yet it finds something of itself in you:
> Something so kingly that my haughty mind
> Is drawn to yours, because 'tis of a kind.
> (2 *Conquest*, V, 4, 153-6)

The style of *The Conquest of Granada* is as extravagant as the character of its hero. His brags provide excellent examples :"I alone am king of me", "I have not leisure yet to die", "The Moors have heav'n, and me, t'assist their cause". In the pro-logue to *Tyrannic Love* Dryden had been rash enough to say, paraphrasing Horace, that the poet "should be bold and dare" rather than creep servilely after sense. That there are moments in *The Conquest of Granada* when sense is unduly sacrificed to boldness cannot be denied, but it should be noted that the aim is consonant with the conception of the hero. It should also be recognized that although Dryden's brand of extravagance has not been popular in recent times, much of the merit of this play is a verbal merit. I shall not attempt a thorough-going analysis of the style nor an answer to each point made by its critics. My discussion of style will deal chiefly with the ways in which it serves the purposes of a Herculean play.

Dryden's misgivings about the excesses of *Tyrannic Love* and *The Conquest of Granada*, expressed in the dedication of *The Spanish Friar*, have often been quoted, but they are too important to take for granted. They are the more interesting for being directly associated with his equally well-known strictures on Chapman's style:

> I have sometimes wondered, in the reading, what was become of those glaring colours which amazed me in *Bussy D'Amboys* upon the theatre; but when I had taken up what I supposed a fallen star, I found I had been cozened with a jelly; nothing but a cold, dull mass, which glittered no longer than it was shooting; a dwarfish thought, dressed up in gigantic words,[17] repetition in abundance, looseness of expression, and gross hyperboles; the sense of one line expanded prodigiously into ten; and, to sum up all, uncorrect English, and a hideous mingle of false poetry, and true nonsense; or, at best, a scantling of wit, which lay gasping for life, and groaning beneath a heap of rubbish. A famous modern poet used to sacrifice every year a Statius to Virgil's *Manes*; and I have indignation enough to burn a *D'Amboys* annually, to the memory of Johnson. But now, My Lord, I am sensible, perhaps too late, that I have gone too far: for, I remember some verses of my own *Maximin* and *Almanzor*, which cry vengeance upon me for their extravagance, and which I wish heartily in the same fire with Statius and Chapman.   (Ker, I, 246)

The context is a discussion of the difference between seeing and reading a play—the effects of costumes and scenery and, above all, of the actors. In the theatre, he is saying, Chapman's extravagance and his own are tolerable; in the study the discerning critic will look for a purity, clearness, boldness, and just elevation, which cannot be appreciated in "the vehemence of action" (Ker, I, 248). Dryden's later plays are, in fact, less extravagant than his earlier ones, but from the perspective of the twentieth century, they all resemble each other more than any of them resembles Chapman. Except for the mere fact of their extravagance, Bussy and Almanzor talk a totally different language. With Almanzor's

> . . . know that I alone am king of me.
> I am as free as nature first made man,
> Ere the base laws of servitude began,
> When wild in woods the noble savage ran.
>
> (1 *Conquest*, I, 206-9)

may be compared Bussy's

> . . . since I am free,
> (Offending no just law), let no law make
> By any wrong it does, my life her slave:
> When I am wrong'd, and that law fails to right me,
> Let me be king myself (as man was made),
> And do a justice that exceeds the law;   (II, 1, 194-9)

In Chapman the antitheses between freedom and slavery, right and wrong, just and unjust law are teased into a kind of play on words—a blend of virtuosity and serious thought approaching the metaphysical. The flow of the sentence is somewhat slowed by modifying phrases, though not so much so as in many other passages of the same play. Dryden's lines are smoother, clearer and even more extravagant. They are free of any ambiguity of tone.

A better illustration of the looseness and amplification of which Dryden complains might be Bussy's first speech, which begins:

> Fortune, not Reason, rules the state of things,
> Reward goes backwards, Honour on his head;
> Who is not poor, is monstrous; only Need
> Gives form and worth to every human seed.
> As cedars beaten with continual storms,
> So great men flourish; and do imitate
> Unskilful statuaries, who suppose,
> In forming a Colossus, if they make him
> Straddle enough, strut, and look big, and gape,
> Their work is goodly: . . .   (I, 1, 1-10)

Almanzor, in a similarly gloomy moment, says:

> O heav'n, how dark a riddle's thy decree,
> Which bounds our wills, yet seems to leave 'em free!

Since thy foreknowledge cannot be in vain,
Our choice must be what thou didst first ordain.
Thus, like a captive in an isle confin'd,
Man walks at large, a pris'ner of the mind:
Wills all his crimes, while heav'n th'indictment draws,
And, pleading guilty, justifies the laws.

(2 *Conquest*, IV, 3, 143-9)

Compared to Chapman, who carries the comparison to a colossus through six more lines after those quoted, Dryden is economical and neat. And again, his comparison is clear, while Chapman somewhat obscures his by the rapid shift from cedars to statues, and by the misleading introduction of the creators of the statues, who are, strictly speaking, irrelevant. Dryden is pointed where Chapman is vastly suggestive. Rhymed couplets further sharpen the effect of Dryden's lines, and give them a formality quite lacking in Chapman's.

Some of Dryden's comments on Chapman may be taken as rhetorical flourishes—even from a neo-classic point of view they obviously exaggerate the badness of Chapman's style; and one may surely question the sincerity of Dryden's wish that *The Conquest of Granada* were in the fire with *Bussy D'Ambois*—some of it, perhaps, but not all. Yet Dryden's attraction to Chapman and his dissatisfaction with him are both significant critical data. In theme, in concept of heroic character, the two plays are remarkably close. In style, despite the fact that Dryden seems to accuse himself of Chapman's faults, they are remarkably different. In comparing them, one is particularly struck by Dryden's simplicity and formality. Both of these characteristics of style are integral parts of Dryden's presentation of the Herculean hero.

The suitability of heroic verse to the stage has been much discussed (Dryden and Howard debated it at length), and we are always reminded that Dryden himself, after an enthusiastic and able defence, tired of writing plays in rhyme. Without entering into theory or into Dryden's reasons for changing his practice, one can see that the formality of the couplet was well suited to Restoration theatrical conditions. The elaborate scenery, used largely as a backdrop, the heavy, lace-trimmed costumes, with plumes for the hero and a great train for the heroine,[18] the stiff postures (in part forced by the costumes), all contributed to a ceremonial effect which heroic verse supports.

Other characteristics of the language add to its formality. The court, where so many scenes are laid, has its decorum of polite usage—verbal equivalents to bows and curtseys—and (at least in a poetic imitation of the court) of a language freed from vulgarity. The debates in which Dryden's characters, like their prototypes in French romance, take such delight, induce pointedness and careful balance. Even Almanzor, rough and fierce as he is supposed to be, is master of most of these courtly procedures. He shows considerable finesse in his debates with Almahide and Lyndaraxa. He is much more of a courtier than is Bussy D'Ambois.

This formality of language is one part of the heightening which was considered essential to serious drama,[19] but although it imposes an artificial pattern on the language of conversation,[20] it does not lead to the tortured syntax or the obscure shifts of imagery by which Chapman raises the level of his poetry to the height of a discriminating audience. In fact, much of Dryden would undoubtedly have seemed to Chapman altogether too "perviall". Even to the twentieth century some of the speeches analysing character are apt to seem too explicit.[21] Self-analyses are conspicuous: "My boiling passions settle and go down" (1 *Conquest*, II, 180), "Like him, who on the ice / Slides swiftly on, and sees the water near, / Yet cannot stop himself in his career, / So am I carried" (*Ibid.*, III, 90-3), "I scarcely understand my own intent: / But, silkworm-like, so long within have wrought, / That I am lost in my own web of thought" (2 *Conquest*, I, 2, 224-6). The combination of explicitness and formality seems fatal. Tossed off informally, without benefit of similes, such comments might pass on the modern stage. If the meaning were entrusted more wholly to the figure of speech, as in Bussy's soliloquy, "My sun is turned to blood" (*Bussy D'Ambois*, V, 4, 135 ff.), they would pass for more interesting poetry.

As they stand, however, these clear and formal statements perform the important function of fixing with great precision various points in the pattern of Dryden's contrasting characters. It is a complex pattern, dependent on the interrelationships of many delicately distinguished traits. Where the perception of the thematic development is so important, such deliberate and precise statement is wholly appropriate, however little it accords with the artistic preferences of another age. It is of a piece with the adroit dialectic which Dryden makes the basis of so many scenes. There too, the exact definition of an idea or a state of mind is essential to the effect.

What seems most strange about the self-analyses of Dryden's characters is the impression they give that the characters have stepped out of themselves to comment in the fashion of a presenter. When they quarrel or make love, they sometimes seem to be discussing the emotions they feel rather than expressing them. Almanzor asks Almahide to give him back his heart, which

> lion-like, has been in desarts bred,
> And, us'd to range, will ne'er be tamely led.
>   (1 *Conquest*, III, 356-7)

and later in the same scene comments:

> There's something noble lab'ring in my breast:
> This raging fire which thro' the mass does move
> Shall purge my dross, and shall refine my love.
>   (*Ibid.*, 422-4)

The immediacy which one expects in such scenes is not there. The emotions on which the dramatic tension is based are not destroyed but they are distanced. Since the technique of presenting them is description, the effect approaches that of narrative, and reminds us of Dryden's deliberate imitation of epic. At the same time one must constantly recall how the speaking of the lines by the actors would counterbalance this influence of narrative devices. From the accounts that have come down to us, it would seem that Restoration actors and actresses excelled in conveying the emotional vitality of the big scenes. In the theatre, then, the emotions of these speeches would presumably lose nothing of their force, but would have the definition given them by extended description, as an aria in opera may define emotion.

The most conspicuous of Dryden's figures of speech is the simile, mercilessly parodied in *The Rehearsal* and *Tom Thumb*. It is in the greatest danger of being absurd when it is extended in imitation of Homeric or Virgilian epic, stopping the

action, and increasing the impression that we are listening
to a discussion, rather than witnessing an enactment. The
danger of absurdity is not avoided when Boabdelin says to
Almahide:

> As some fair tulip, by a storm oppress'd,
> Shrinks up, and folds its silken arms to rest;
> And, bending to the blast, all pale and dead,
> Hears from within the wind sing round its head;
> So, shrouded up, your beauty disappears . . .
>
> (1 *Conquest*, V, 3, 129-33)

The strain on the conventions of conversational discourse is
intolerable, and one has the impression that Boabdelin, instead
of Dryden, is being literary. The impression is heightened when
Almahide takes up the figure in her reply. A less offensive
example is another speech of Almahide's to Boabdelin:

> So two kind turtles, when a storm is nigh,
> Look up, and see it gath'ring in the sky . . .
>
> (2 *Conquest*, I, 2, 128-9)

The comparison is inept as applied to Boabdelin, who is not in
the least dovelike, and it is as literary as the first example. What
makes it different is the fact that Almahide offers it as an
observation on the dangerous plight of Boabdelin and herself,
and that it conveys something of her feelings in this plight. It
can be accepted more readily than the tulip passage as the
poetic equivalent of thought.

The more frankly reflective such passages are—the further
removed from the pretence that they form part of a conversation—the easier they are to justify in artistic terms.
Almanzor, seeing Almahide approach, says, more to himself
than to her:

> So Venus moves, when to the Thunderer,
> In smiles or tears, she would some suit prefer;
> When with her cestos girt,
> And drawn by doves, she cuts the liquid skies,
> And kindles gentle fires where'er she flies . . .
>
> (2 *Conquest*, II, 3, 29-33)

The poetic convention here is basically that which underlies
Romeo's lyric transports when he sees Juliet at the window: "It

is the east, and Juliet is the sun." Like Romeo's metaphors, the epic simile presents the beloved in terms which reflect the lover's emotions and also affirm the qualities for which she stands in the play. The gentleness and power of the queen of love are appropriately ascribed to Almahide.

In this instance the simile operates successfully to maintain the elevation of tone required by the characters and the situation, and extends the perspective beyond the immediate present. It performs these functions with a gravity and deliberateness borrowed from epic. One further example of such elevation and extension may be cited from a passage of self-description. Lyndaraxa, taken prisoner by her rejected suitor, vows to revenge herself and die:

> But, like some falling tow'r
> Whose seeming firmness does the sight beguile,
> So hold I up my nodding head awhile,
> Till they come under; and reserve my fall,
> That with my ruins I may reach 'em all.
>
> (2 *Conquest*, IV, 2, 136-40)

One may wince at the "nodding head", but the heroic dimension given to Lyndaraxa's passion is wholly in keeping with her character, and corresponds to the importance in the play of the destructive force she represents.

The epic simile is merely a special case of the explicit analysis we have been considering. At best, some insight is provided which assigns a value to an emotion, a thought, a character, or an entire situation. When this occurs, the pause in the action, the loss of immediacy, are sacrifices worth making in the interest of the total design.

Critics have sometimes complained that Dryden's characters are mere types and their emotions unreal. What has been said about style may partially explain this effect. Bonamy Dobrée's comment that Restoration tragedy "mapped out, not the actualities of human emotion, but its ideals . . ."[22] applies particularly to *The Conquest of Granada*. It is a "mapping out" of ideals, and Dryden's style often points away from the "actualities of human emotion" to the map on which their relative positions may be studied. The ideal with which the play is mainly concerned is what is loosely called the heroic ideal, but in this instance may be called more specifically the concept of the Herculean hero. Though Almanzor has, to be sure, some of the characteristics of the seventeenth-century gentleman, he is compelling, not as an imitation of familiar human behaviour, but as the recreation of an ideal. Thus certain aspects of Dryden's style combine with the conventions of romance and with Dryden's structure of comparisons and contrasts to remove the focus of attention from the immediate to the realm of ideas. The hero is thus returned to the world of myth, but the myth of a rational age.

2. *Aureng-Zebe*

Dryden has been accused of repeating in play after play the same character-types. Martin Clifford, in his *Notes upon Mr Dryden's Poems in Four Letters* (1687), observed sarcastically that he was strangely mistaken if he had not seen Almanzor in town previously in some disguise. "Prithee tell me true, was not this huff-cap once the Indian Emperor, and, at another time, did not he call himself Maximine?" (Quoted in SS, I, 132). Montague Summers, without considering it a fault, points to the resemblance of Almanzor both to preceding heroes and to Aureng-Zebe, and mentions several other "stock types" who appear in the heroic plays.[23] The half-truth contained in these observations is both helpful and misleading. It is true that there are certain recurring types, and hence the familiarity with one example advances one towards an understanding of another. Yet the most interesting part of these relationships is the differences between the corresponding characters. When *The Conquest of Granada* is compared to *Aureng-Zebe*, these differences reveal Dryden's inventiveness in dealing with essentially similar heroic material. In most respects *Aureng-Zebe* is a better play, though Dryden never recaptures the exuberance and spaciousness of his depiction of the Herculean hero in *The Conquest of Granada*.

Aureng-Zebe appeared in 1675, five years after *The Conquest of Granada*, and four years after the publication of *Samson Agonistes*, of which there are several verbal echoes.[24] Both in the dedication and in the prologue Dryden refers to his growing impatience with rhyme, and this is the last of his plays written

in heroic verse. It provides a stylistic transition to the blank
verse of *All for Love*, for the couplets are handled rather more
freely than in *The Conquest of Granada* and the extravagance is
much modified. For the plot, Dryden turned to almost contemporary events in India, which he altered drastically to
suit his purposes. His procedure here is remarkably similar to
Chapman's in *Bussy D'Ambois*.

The old Emperor of India is like Boabdelin in that he can no
longer rule effectively. His capital, Agra, is threatened as the
play opens by the armies of four factions, each led by one of his
sons. He also resembles Boabdelin in being constantly distracted
from his duties by amorousness. Married for the second time to
Nourmahal, a prodigy of jealousy and ambition, he is infatuated
by a captive queen, Indamora, whom he has betrothed to his
son, Aureng-Zebe. Though he is at the mercy of his passions
until almost the end of the play, there is always the suggestion
that he has been more of a man, and that he might again become
more. He is therefore a more impressive and a more sympathetic
figure than Boabdelin. His tirades against Nourmahal have a
satirical wit which gives him something of the appeal of the
libertine hero of a Restoration comedy:

> Such virtue is the plague of humane life:
> A virtuous Woman, but a cursed Wife
> In vain of pompous chastity y'are proud:
> Virtue's adultery of the Tongue, when loud.
>
> (II, SS, 228)

Nourmahal is a grander and more terrible Lyndaraxa. Seeking power for her son, Morat, jealous of Indamora, and
incestuously enamoured of her step-son, Aureng-Zebe, she is
the incarnation of disordered passion. What the Emperor, with
some restraint, calls her "unquietness" is contrasted with Indamora's serenity, as Lyndaraxa is contrasted to Almahide. The
burning poison which actually destroys Nourmahal's reason
in the final scene of the play is also a metaphor for her
passion.

Two of the Emperor's four sons never appear on the stage.
The remaining two, Aureng-Zebe and Morat, are the most
important male characters. They are distinguished at the outset
by the following descriptions:

M

Morat's too insolent, too much a Brave,
His Courage to his Envy is a Slave.
What he attempts, if his endeavours fail
T'effect, he is resolv'd no other shall.

But *Aureng-Zebe*, by no strong passion sway'd,
Except his Love, more temp'rate is, and weigh'd:
This *Atlas* must our sinking State uphold;
In Council cool, but in Performance bold:
He sums their [i.e. the other sons'] Virtues in himself alone,
And adds the greatest, of a Loyal Son . . .

                                        (I, SS, 206)

One has almost the impression that Almanzor has been split in
two, his irregularity going to Morat, his self-discipline to
Aureng-Zebe.

The love of Aureng-Zebe, his one extravagance, is fixed upon
Indamora. Morat is married to Melesinda, but conceives a
passion for Indamora. These two women are models of virtue,
but differentiated by temperament and fortune. Indamora, like
Almahide, is a powerful force in the play. Melesinda's is the
harder lot, and she accepts it with a meekness and a melancholy
resignation which make her less effectual but more pathetic.

These are the principal characters. Some of the contrasts are
carried over from *The Conquest of Granada* but are presented with
far greater economy of means in the actions of this smaller group
of characters. The structure is also tighter. The epic sweep of ten
acts is reduced to the usual five, each a single scene, whereas
some acts in *The Conquest of Granada* are divided into two or three
scenes. The influence of epic form is less pronounced, though
in the dedication, Dryden asserts the relationship again in
referring to *Aureng-Zebe* as "a Tragedy; the Characters of which
are the nearest to those of an Heroick Poem" (SS, 197).

The strange contraries of which the Herculean character is
composed have never been more clearly dramatized than in the
contrasting natures of the brothers, Aureng-Zebe and Morat.
Morat has the boundless ambition, the strong passion, and the
contempt for moral convention; Aureng-Zebe has the generosity
and loyalty which make him a saviour of society—the "Atlas"
who is to uphold the state. Both have infinite courage and greatness of mind. As Melesinda says:

Too truly *Tamerlain's* Successors they,
Each thinks a World too little for his sway.

(III, SS, 241)

Morat uses a rumour of the Emperor's death as a pretext for a
revolt and then, when Aureng-Zebe has successfully defended
the capital on behalf of their father, exploits the Emperor's
jealousy of his loyal son to get both of them in his power. His
ruthless pursuit of power is strikingly like Tamburlaine's:

Me-thinks all pleasure is in greatness found.
Kings, like Heav'ns Eye, should spread their beams around,
Pleas'd to be seen while Glory's race they run:
Rest is not for the Chariot of the Sun.
Subjects are stiff-neck'd Animals, they soon
Feel slacken'd Reins, and pitch their Rider down.

(III, SS, 243-4)

Aureng-Zebe fights only to maintain his father's power, and
though he refuses to give Indamora up, remains loyal even
when the Emperor has disinherited him and called on Morat.
He is generous to his plotting step-mother up to the time when
he is obliged to fend off her advances. As one of the minor
characters observes:

Sure *Aureng-Zebe* has somewhat of Divine,
Whose virtue through so dark a clowd can shine.

(III, SS, 249)

Two halves of the Herculean hero. Yet neither Morat nor
Aureng-Zebe by himself seems to qualify thoroughly for the
term when we are first introduced to them. Morat's disregard
for others is more cynical and more materialistic than Tamburlaine's. Machiavelli and Hobbes seem to be mixed in equal
proportions in the observations:

'Tis not with me as with a private Man.
Such may be sway'd by Honour, or by Love;
But Monarchs, onely by their int'rest move.

(III, SS, 252)

and

Crimes let them [i.e. the gods] pay, and punish as they please:
What Pow'r makes mine, by Pow'r I mean to seize.
Since 'tis to that they their own greatness owe
Above, why should they question mine below?

(IV, SS, 270)

These speeches have the ring of Maximin, the Roman tyrant in Dryden's earlier *Tyrannic Love*, a character designed, as he said, to set off the virtue of the Christian martyr, St Catherine.[25] Morat seems to be presented like Maximin as a foil to goodness —the goodness of his brother or of his wife—and hence as a character basically unlike the Herculean hero, who is often immoral in certain respects, but who is never presented as outright evil. At such moments one is aware that the compensating characteristics of the true Herculean hero seem to be left out of Morat and given entirely to Aureng-Zebe.

By his very perfection Aureng-Zebe seems to be as far from qualifying as his brother. His extraordinary generosity to his enemies and his refusal to be disloyal to his father, no matter what is done to him, remind one of Dryden's witticism in the dedication of the play, that "he who is too lightly reconcil'd after high Provocations, may recommend himself to the World for a Christian, but I should hardly trust him for a Friend". He appears to be like Corneille's Nicomède, admirable in every sense of the word. He is not above righteous wrath, however. Confronted in court by his brother's outrageous behaviour, he denounces him in words which recall the Hobbesian state of nature:

> When thou wert form'd, Heav'n did a Man begin;
> But the brute Soul, by chance, was shuffl'd in.
> In Woods and Wilds thy Monarchy maintain:
> Where valiant Beasts, by force and rapine, reign.
>
> (III, SS, 248)

Aureng-Zebe's unremitting loyalty eventually leads to a scene of reconciliation which belongs to quite another strain of the heroic than the Herculean. In the course of the play the Emperor gives several indications of the battle within him between virtue and his unseemly passion. When, at the end of Act IV, Morat is openly seeking his life and Aureng-Zebe offers to fight for him again, he says:

> Can you forgive me? 'tis not fit you shou'd.
> Why will you be so excellently good?   (IV, SS, 277)

Otway echoed these words the next year in a scene of reconciliation between Don Carlos and his father, where the latter says:

Why wert thou made so excellently good;
And why was it no sooner Understood?
(*Don Carlos*, V, 415-16)[26]

Much later in his career, Dryden himself constructed the more
famous scene of reconciliation between Dorax and Sebastian,
in which such overwhelming goodness is given its most memorable line:

Oh, stop this headlong torrent of your goodness . . .
(IV, 3, SS, VII, 442)

Thus if Morat has characteristics which relate him to the
wicked tyrants of the stage, Aureng-Zebe has much in common
with heroes of outstanding goodness in a Cornelian line which,
in England, leads to Cato and to sentimental drama.[27]

In describing the polarity of Morat and Aureng-Zebe, however, I have left out of reckoning certain very important traits
which appear in them either immediately or by the end of the
play. It is these traits which justify discussing both brothers as
versions—and not merely as complementary halves—of the
Herculean hero.

Of the two brothers Morat is much the more complete
embodiment of the type. It is he of whom it is said, "Yours is a
Soul irregularly great, / Which, wanting temper, yet abounds
with heat . . ."—words which I have taken to typify Dryden's
concept of this sort of hero. But Aureng-Zebe, though he is
considerably more "regular" than either his brother or Almanzor, has Rinaldo-esque moments of uncontrolled passion—of
fury and love. Most of these occur in his scenes with Indamora,
for the plot is so arranged that her actions repeatedly arouse his
suspicions. In the first of these scenes she brings him to the verge
of despair by advising him to give her up; for the Emperor has
warned her to conceal his passion for her on the peril of her life
and her lover's. When Aureng-Zebe is about to leave her, however, she makes the forbidden revelation and is seized by guards.
Aureng-Zebe goes from disillusionment with her to fury at his
father, and is only saved by her entreaty from attacking his
father's soldiers.

In this scene the paradox of his relationship to Indamora is
revealed: she is the one being who raises his passions beyond his
control, and the one who can enable him to regain control. His

father's injustice and caprice in the immediately preceding scene have aroused nothing beyond restrained protests of innocence; here he is ready for armed defiance until she persuades him to "stand the blameless pattern of a Son" (I, SS, 218). The violence of his feeling for her is prepared for in the initial description, which makes his love an exception to his general temperateness. The imagery of some of his speeches reflects this violence:

> If Love be Vision, mine has all the fire
> Which, in first Dreams, young Prophets does inspire:
> I dream, in you, our promis'd Paradice:
> An Ages tumult of continu'd bliss.   (I, SS, 216)

Yet she is also the "calm Harbour" where his "Tempest-beaten Soul may safely rest" (*Ibid.*, 215).

When he next sees her he has been told that he owes his life to her making terms with Morat. Again his jealousy gets the better of him, so that he denounces her fiercely in words which echo another great denouncer of women, Milton's Samson:

> Ah Traitress! Ah ingrate! Ah faithless mind!
> Ah Sex, invented first to damn Mankind!
> Nature took care to dress you up for sin:
> Adorn'd, without; unfinish'd left, within.   (IV, SS, 274)

He is brought out of his jealous fit by Indamora's withering observation that his "mean suspitions" are even worse than his brother's pride, but jealousy is replaced by an expression of love which is extravagant even by heroic standards:

> Love mounts, and rowls about my stormy mind,
> Like Fire, that's born by a tempestuous Wind.
> Oh, I could stifle you, with eager haste!
> Devour your kisses with my hungry taste!   (*Ibid.*, 275)

and more of a similar nature.

Arranging the plot in a manner reminiscent of Fletcher, Dryden contrives a third and final misunderstanding between the lovers. Aureng-Zebe, returning from a battle in which he has been reported dead, finds Morat dying at Indamora's feet. Once again he is bitter and once again reconciled, but his apology suggests that his love will never be completely tamed:

Forgive those foolish words—
They were the froth my raging folly mov'd,
When it boil'd up: I knew not then I lov'd;
Yet then lov'd most.   (V, SS, 299)

Indamora's control is asserted, but the force of Aureng-Zebe's
love, even as manifested in "raging folly", is not really con-
demned. It is like the pride of a Tamburlaine or a Coriolanus
in that its very excesses seem to be a virtue. Although Aureng-
Zebe apologizes to Indamora, it is she who finally yields to him,
accepting him as he is. In his capacity of lover, he comes closest
to the pattern of a Herculean hero.

Several quotations have already shown Morat's resemblances
to Tamburlaine. He defies "all mankind", promises to vanquish
all his father's foes alone, (III, SS, 245, 247), and announces:

I'm in Fate's place, and dictate her Decrees.
                                                  (IV, SS, 263)

In the early scenes he appears rather the tyrannical villain than
a character who might arouse sympathy. His inhuman treatment of Melesinda, a veritable saint of a wife, recalls the
cruelty of Maximin to St Catherine. To Indamora, however, he
reveals something other than villainy even in his attempt to
seduce her. He first meets her after coming to power, when she
intercedes with him for Aureng-Zebe's life. When he makes the
time-honoured condition that she become his mistress, she of
course refuses, and in refusing states her position with the
customary clarity of Dryden's characters:

If, Sir, I seem not discompos'd with rage,
Feed not your fancy with a false presage.
Farther to press your Courtship is but vain:
A cold refusal carries more disdain.
Unsetled Virtue stormy may appear;
Honour, like mine, serenely is severe.   (III, SS, 255)

The contrast between tempest and calm is even sharper here
than in the interviews of Aureng-Zebe and Indamora, and
properly so, since Morat is the son of Nourmahal, the stormiest
of all the characters. Although her words describe two possible
ways to refuse his advances, they also suggest the difference
between their two temperaments. Morat is always tempestuous,

but as the play progresses, his energy shows itself in different ways. As yet there is no indication that he is moved by anything but lust, but in subsequent scenes, as the influence of Indamora grows, he begins to merit the phrase "unsettled Virtue", which she applies differently here. His energy becomes that of the Herculean hero.

His next encounter with her marks the transition. By this time he believes that he has secured his position by routing the forces of his father and Aureng-Zebe from the citadel, and he comes to claim Indamora. She turns their interview into an attack on his morality, forcing him to state and defend his principles. He would prefer to mount the throne without guilt, he says, "But yet 'tis necessary to be great" (V, SS, 281). The next three speeches define two concepts of greatness and reveal, somewhat unexpectedly, a latent sympathy on the part of Indamora for her would-be seducer:

> *Ind.*   All Greatness is in Virtue understood:
>   'Tis onely necessary to be good.
>   Tell me, what is't at which great Spirits aim,
>   What most your self desire?
> *Mor.*   Renown, and Fame,
>   And Pow'r, as uncontrol'd as is my will.
> *Ind.*   How you confound desires of good and ill!
>   For true renown is still with Virtue joyn'd;
>   But lust of Pow'r lets loose th'unbridl'd mind.
>   Yours is a Soul irregularly great,
>   Which wanting temper, yet abounds with heat:
>   So strong, yet so unequal pulses beat.
>   A Sun which does, through vapours dimly shine:
>   What pity 'tis you are not all Divine!   (V, SS, 281)

This is Dryden's dialectic at its best. The two positions are distinct, and yet it is clear that they are not diametrically opposed. The most basic motives of Morat's actions are not so different from Aureng-Zebe's as they have appeared to be. Indamora sees and appreciates the greatness of his ambition, though she wants to put it at the service of a higher ideal. To Morat the vision she opens up is "the distant prospect of a Shore, / Doubtful in mists" (*Ibid.*, 281). He admits that in pursuing fame he has been "directed Wrong".

In the story of Morat Dryden maintains an exceedingly

delicate balance between the value of heroic energy and the value of control. In the scene just discussed Morat is converted by Indamora; at the end of the play he dies at her feet. Both episodes testify to the strength of Indamora's guiding hand. Between them is a scene which emphasizes her timidity—her lack of the sort of strength Morat has in abundance. In this scene she kneels before an enraged Nourmahal who threatens her life. Here it is the jealous empress who displays a kind of heroic grandeur and despises Indamora for her weakness:

> Disdain my mercy, and my rage defie;
> Curse me with thy last breath; and make me see
> A Spirit worthy to have Rival'd me.   (V, SS, 289)

Dryden explains in the dedication that Indamora's fear of death is a human frailty by which she is distinguished from some of the heroines of romance, but whether or not verisimilitude was part of Dryden's concern in this scene, there can be no doubt that a highly effective contrast was another—a contrast not only between the two women, but between the strength and weakness of Indamora.

Dryden is presenting in Morat and Indamora a complementary relationship similar to that of Almanzor and Almahide. Both women recognize an untamed force of which they do not wholly approve but to which they are drawn because of the absence of such a force in themselves. In Morat the force is much wilder than in Almanzor; in Indamora the weakness is more pronounced than in Almahide. Hence, the dramatic contrast of the scenes in *Aureng-Zebe* where this relationship is presented is greater than in the scenes of Almanzor and Almahide.

The scene of Morat's death is very powerful. It combines the ideas of transcendence and limitation as do the final scenes of *Tamburlaine, Bussy D'Ambois* and *Coriolanus,* but as the ending of *The Conquest of Granada* does not. There all is hope for a future in which the qualities of Almanzor and Almahide will be happily combined. The power of the scene of Morat's death derives from a complex awareness that even though a comparable synthesis of values has been partially achieved, complete fulfilment is forestalled by death and, in another way, by the prior commitment of Morat to Melesinda and Indamora to Aureng-Zebe. When Morat makes his final entrance, mortally

wounded, he sinks at Indamora's feet, illustrating with this
action the words he addresses to her:

> I can no more; yet, ev'n in death, I find
> My fainting body byass'd by my mind:
> I fall toward you; still my contending Soul
> Points to your breast, and trembles to its Pole.
>
> (V, SS, 289-90)

It is ironical that this ennobling love of Morat's should also be
illicit, and the irony is underscored by pathos when Melesinda
arrives on the scene to beg for one parting look from her husband. Her lines fall into a sentimentality which is below the
artistic level of the rest of the dialogue, and yet perhaps
appropriate to the melodramatic action of the scene. Dryden
makes use of every theatrical device to make his point.

Morat now protects Indamora from a final attempt on her
life by Nourmahal, but Indamora, who believes Aureng-Zebe
to be dead and sees Morat dying, has lost her own fear of death.
The effect on her of both brothers is seen in her lines:

> No, let me die; I'm doubly summon'd now;
> First by my *Aureng-Zebe*; and, since, by you.
> My Soul grows hardy, and can death endure:
> Your Convoy makes the dang'rous way secure.
>
> (*Ibid.*, 290-1)

Shortly afterward, she begs Morat to take her with him, since
there is no longer anything worth living for. And he, although
he has begged his wife's forgiveness, addresses his last words to
Indamora:

> I leave you not; for my expanded mind
> Grows up to Heav'n, while it to you is joyn'd:
> Not quitting, but enlarg'd! A blazing Fire,
> Fed from the Brand.   (*Ibid.*, 293)

It is a splendid statement of his final development. One recalls
Almahide's "You'll find the fire has but inlarg'd your space."
As with other Herculean heroes, it is this largeness which is
remembered and bitterly missed when it has gone.

Morat's death is enclosed in an ironic frame. Not only is
Melesinda present to remind us of his unfaithfulness, but before
the end, Aureng-Zebe arrives, unseen by the others, and over-

hears the speeches of his brother and Indamora. The result is
the last quarrel and reconciliation, which have already been
described. After the genuine elevation of the death scene they
seem anti-climactic and almost trivial. The issues they raise are
far less absorbing.

When the characters of the two brothers are compared in
their totality, Morat's is seen to be the more brilliant creation.
Here the inherent opposition in the Herculean hero between
the drive for personal aggrandizement and the desire to serve
some divinely high purpose is pushed to an extreme. While
these contradictory qualities exist in Tamburlaine, they are
never explicitly distinguished, and the character remains a
monolith. In Morat they are made into warring qualities which
drive the hero to destruction, for he is killed by his mother's
soldiers when he returns from a skirmish to save Indamora from
her: almost successful in battle, he is ruined by his love.

Aureng-Zebe, because his personal ambition is so much more
nearly under control from the start, appears more often in the
role of victim than of aggressor. To him is given the mournful
wisdom of many of the *sententiae*, including the famous "When I
consider Life, 'tis all a cheat" (IV, SS, 258). As the tone of these
observations is philosophical and resigned, so his character, in
spite of some flashes of fire, tends to seem passive and a little
dull, when compared to that of his brother. When, as a lover,
he shows some mettle, it is only to be captiously jealous, so that
the spectator is apt to feel as Indamora does when she compares
the brothers:

> His Pride, and Brutal fierceness I abhor;
> But scorn your mean suspitions of me more.
>
> (IV, SS, 274)

Colley Cibber's comments on the acting of Morat reveal
something of the impression the character made. Speaking of the
actor, Kynaston, he says:

He had a piercing Eye, and in Characters of heroick Life a quick
imperious Vivacity in his Tone of Voice that painted the Tyrant
truly terrible. There were two plays of *Dryden* in which he shone
with uncommon Lustre; in *Aureng-Zebe* he play'd *Morat*, and in
Don Sebastian, Muley Moloch; in both these Parts he had a fierce,

Lion-like Majesty in his Port and Utterance that gave the Spectator a kind of trembling Admiration![28]

Looking back on Kynaston from the perspective of 1740, Cibber compares him in the part of Morat with Booth, who was inferior because he was too restrained.

There are in this fierce Character so many Sentiments of avow'd Barbarity, Insolence, and Vain-glory, that they blaze even to a ludicrous Lustre, and doubtless the Poet intended those to make his Spectators laugh while they admir'd them; but Booth thought it depreciated the Dignity of Tragedy to raise a Smile in any part of it, and therefore cover'd these kind of Sentiments with a scrupulous Coldness and unmov'd Delivery . . .[29]

The example Cibber gives is Morat's ranting reply to Nourmahal, when she asks him why he spares the life of his brother: "I'll do't, to show my Arbitrary pow'r" (IV, SS, 263). Whether or not Cibber is right in thinking that Dryden anticipated an approving smile or laugh at such lines, his understanding of the part is excellent, and it seems right to insist that the "bold Flights of the Author" should be followed by the actor.[30] Surely the effect should be "trembling Admiration".

Morat, then, in some respects eclipses his brother, but it would be wrong to suggest that Aureng-Zebe does not remain the central figure Dryden obviously intended him to be. His story begins and ends the play, and is never lost to sight. In him Dryden presents something much closer to a "pattern of exact virtue" than he had done in Almanzor—closer than any of his major heroes with the possible exception of Cleomenes. As Morat reveals the difficulty of controlling heroic energy, Aureng-Zebe, even more than Almanzor, presents a golden possibility. Tragic limitation is included within a design which centres on heroic potentiality.

3. All for Love

The comparison of *All for Love* with Shakespeare's *Antony and Cleopatra* has been an exercise for innumerable students, the subject of at least one German dissertation,[31] and of a few sentences in every history of the drama. Here, aside from an occasional reference to Shakespeare, the context will be

Dryden's other plays. It is easy to exaggerate the differences between *All for Love* and the two heroic plays already discussed. Dryden himself led the way towards putting it in a category apart not only by abandoning couplets to "imitate the divine Shakespeare",[32] but by his comment in the late essay, "A Parallel of Poetry and Painting", that he never wrote anything (presumably meaning any of his plays) for himself but *Antony and Cleopatra* (Ker, II, 152). Since Dryden's time critics have considered it exceptional in having an artistic merit which they deny to *The Conquest of Granada* or *Aureng-Zebe*, and one of the most astute of the recent critics has seen it as an exception in Dryden's thematic development.[33] There can be no doubt that there are differences, but the resemblances which bind *All for Love* to its predecessors, if less obvious, are very strong. The verse is certainly much freer; yet it retains often the anti-thetical balance common to heroic couplets, as when Cleopatra says of Caesar:

> He first possess'd my person; you, my love:
> Caesar lov'd me; but I lov'd Antony.   (II, 353-4)

Though emotion is presented with more immediacy in this play than in *The Conquest of Granada*, the basic concerns from which the emotions arise remain very similar, and the entire framework of feeling and thought within which the characters discuss their problems is the same. If the characters of *All for Love* are less stylized in presentation, they are still of the same family as the characters in Dryden's other heroic plays.

One of the family connections is seen in the traits of the Herculean hero which reappear in Antony. Though the title of the play leaves no doubt about the primacy of the theme of love, the hero, like his prototype in Shakespeare's play, is a warrior whose nobility and generosity are combined with strong passion and a contemptuous disregard for the mores of his society. Dryden's Antony manifests these characteristics in ways which relate him even more closely to Almanzor and Morat than to Shakespeare's hero. And Cleopatra is much more closely related to other Dryden heroines than to Shakespeare's Cleopatra. These relationships must now be examined in more detail.

The first extended description of Antony is given by his general, Ventidius, who is known to the Egyptians as one who does not share in Antony's debauches, "but presides / O'er all his cooler hours" (I, 103-4):

> Virtue's his path; but sometimes 'tis too narrow
> For his vast soul; and then he starts out wide,
> And bounds into a vice, that bears him far
> From his first course, and plunges him in ills:
> But, when his danger makes him find his fault,
> Quick to observe, and full of sharp remorse,
> He censures eagerly his own misdeeds,
> Judging himself with malice to himself,
> And not forgiving what as man he did,
> Because his other parts are more than man.   (I, 124-33)

Here again is an "irregular greatness" which cannot be quite contained within the bounds of virtue. Antony is farther than Almanzor from being a "pattern of perfect virtue", much farther than Aureng-Zebe, and not so far as Morat. The admiration of Ventidius is apparent, but equally so is his Roman attempt to distinguish neatly between what is to be praised and blamed in Antony. As Aureng-Zebe tries to dissect the paradox of Morat into man and brute, Ventidius divides Antony into erring man and "more than man", but in spite of this logical division the implication of the speech is that virtue and vice are distinctions of secondary importance when discussing so vast a soul. Later in the play, echoing the "taints and honours" speech of Shakespeare's Maecenas, he says:

> And sure the gods, like me, are fond of him:
> His virtues lie so mingled with his crimes,
> As would confound their choice to punish one,
> And not reward the other.   (III, 48-51)

The impossibility of confining Antony's spirit is the essence of his heroic individuality. When his fortune has ebbed to its lowest point, he compares his fortitude to a "native spring" which again fills the dried river-bed to overflowing:

> I've still a heart that swells, in scorn of fate,
> And lifts me to its banks.   (III, 133-4)

The image recalls Shakespeare's Antony, but echoes Almanzor more closely:

I cannot breathe within this narrow space;
My heart's too big, and swells beyond the place.
(1 Conquest, V, 3, 23-4)

In Ventidius' initial description Antony's love is sharply differentiated from his virtue. It is obviously the vice into which the great man has "bounded"—an unruly, excessive infatuation. It may be compared with the "wild deluge" of the opening lines of the play, where Serapion is talking of "portents and prodigies". To stem this disastrous flow is the task which Ventidius has set himself, regardless of the admiration he has for Antony's largeness of spirit.

It is a commonplace of criticism that the first act of Dryden's play is dominated by Ventidius. Never again are we so completely in the warriors' world. From a dramatic point of view the showpiece of this act, and indeed one of the best scenes of the entire play, is the quarrel and reconciliation of Antony and his general. It has always been thought to derive from the famous quarrel and reconciliation of Brutus and Cassius, and Hart and Mohun, who took these parts in Shakespeare's play, distinguished themselves as Antony and Ventidius. Dryden preferred the scene, as he states in the preface, to anything he had written "in this kind". It bears a certain resemblance to the reconciliation of Aureng-Zebe with his father and more to the quarrel and reconciliation of Dorax and Don Sebastian, written many years later. In all of these scenes the generosity of the heroic mind triumphs over amour propre.

The significance of Antony's scene with Ventidius, however, is totally different from that of Aureng-Zebe's scene with the Emperor. Not only is the hero in this instance more sinning than sinned against, but the result of the dialogue is to arouse, not to pacify, the party at fault. The Emperor had to be induced to give up the senseless persecution of his son; Antony has to be roused from the torpor of remorse. Antony's change is presented in a highly dramatic contrast. At the beginning of the scene he throws himself on the ground, calling himself the "shadow of an emperor" and thinking of the time when he will be "shrunk to a few cold ashes". At the end, standing with Ventidius, he says:

O, thou has fir'd me; my soul's up in arms,
And mans each part about me.   (I, 438-9)

The vital spark which makes him great has been restored.

In *All for Love* appears again the contrast between the fiery spirit and the cold one, analogous, as I have suggested, to Dryden's familiar contrast between wit and dullness. Though Antony is cold and torpid at the beginning, he is by nature fiery, and is brought to himself by the force of friendship. Caesar, his opposite, is "the coldest youth", who gives "so tame" an answer to Antony's challenge, has not even warmth enough to die by a fever, and rather than risk death will "crawl upon the utmost verge of life" (II, 113-30).

> O Hercules! Why should a man like this,
> Who dares not trust his fate for one great action,
> Be all the care of heav'n?   (II, 131-3)

The task that Ventidius accomplishes in the first act may be looked at in two ways. It is in one sense a curbing and controlling of Antony. This aspect is suggested early by Ventidius' stern disapproval of Cleopatra's lavish plans for celebrating Antony's birthday. But it is also the firing of Antony's soul, and this is the aspect which is emphasized. To Ventidius the enemy is, of course, Cleopatra, but the worst of her effect on Antony is to have made him a "mute sacrifice" and "the blank of what he was". The state of mind which Ventidius has to combat directly is a paralysing remorse:

> You are too sensible already
> Of what y'have done, too conscious of your failings;
>   (I, 312-13)

> you sleep away your hours
> In desperate sloth, miscall'd philosophy.   (I, 336-7)

In fact, Antony is at this time in a state very similar to Samson's when Manoa comes, in the second episode of *Samson Agonistes*, to warn him against being "over-just" with himself. The maintaining of the inner fire is so important a part of Dryden's concept of the heroic that it is stressed even in the depiction of Cleomenes, the nearly perfect hero of Dryden's last tragedy. The words of Cleomenes' mother might be almost as well applied to Antony:

> This melancholy flatters, but unmans you.
> What is it else, but penury of soul,

> A lazy frost, a numbness of the mind,
> That locks up all the vigour to attempt,
> By barely crying,—'tis impossible!   (I, SS, VIII, 276)

Only when Cleomenes assures her that his is a grief of fury, not despair, is his mother satisfied. "Desperate sloth", "penury of soul", "a lazy frost"—by the heroic code these are the true sins, beside which other forms of moral deviation pale.

Cleopatra is first seen as the cause of Antony's unmanning. The theatrical strategy of this first unfavourable impression, established only to be radically altered later on, is almost the only similarity between Dryden's treatment of his heroine and Shakespeare's. After exposure to the charms of Shakespeare's Cleopatra, who manages to remain marvellously attractive even at her most hoydenish and deceitful ("holy priests bless her when she is riggish")' one is apt to find the Cleopatra of Dryden shockingly tame and stiff. While it is easy to picture Shakespeare's Cleopatra in anything from Egyptian dress to the bodice and farthingale she probably wore on the Elizabethan stage, Dryden's Cleopatra belongs in late seventeenth-century court dress, complete with train. Passion never quite robs her of dignity. There is no haling of messengers by the hair, no riggishness. To understand this Cleopatra is an essential preliminary to understanding the play.

She dominates the second act as Ventidius does the first. In her initial appearance with Iras and her eunuch, Alexas, she proclaims her love a "noble madness" and a "transcendent passion" which has carried her "quite out of reason's view" till she is "lost above it" (II, 17-22). Force and excessiveness combine here with nobility as they do in Ventidius' first description of Antony. The heroine is no mere temptress to lure the hero from the path of virtue.[34] She is herself carried away by a passion of heroic proportions like his. Serapion's description of the flood, already suggested as an analogue for Antony's love, may be associated even more properly with Cleopatra's:

> Our fruitful Nile
> Flow'd ere the wonted season, with a torrent
> So unexpected, and so wondrous fierce,
> That the wild deluge overtook the haste
> Ev'n of the hinds that watch'd it . . .   (I, 2-6)

N

Dryden has taken over Shakespeare's insistence on the resemblances between the lovers and added another in giving Cleopatra a heroic stature like Antony's. Grandeur and largeness of mind are hers as much as they are his. In fact it is her high-mindedness rather than her sensual attraction which persuades Antony not to leave her. The telling blow is her announcement that she refused a kingdom from Caesar because of her loyalty to Antony (in her noble contempt for wealth she resembles the Cleopatra of Fletcher and Massinger's *The False One*). By the end of the act these similar lovers have been brought together to the dismay of Ventidius, but it is to be noticed that Antony's conviction that Cleopatra is worth more than all the world does not alter his heroic determination to fight with Caesar. There is now the additional motive of revenge for Caesar's attempt to corrupt Cleopatra. Love for her is not entirely the effeminizing passion Ventidius thinks it to be, and despite her dignified bearing she is far from tame.

One sentence of self-description has exposed Cleopatra to a great deal of unfriendly laughter:

> Nature meant me
> A wife; a silly, harmless, household dove,
> Fond without art, and kind without deceit.   (IV, 91-3)

The comparison is not apt, and it is particularly unfortunate that the incongruity blocks the understanding of a crucial point —Cleopatra's attitude towards being a wife. In Shakespeare's play "Husband I come" owes its brilliance as much to its unexpectedness as to its rightness. It signals a transformation in Cleopatra matching the re-emergence of the heroic Antony. In Dryden's play the change is a much smaller one, and so thoroughly prepared that it is no shock to hear:

> I have not lov'd a Roman, not to know
> What should become his wife; his wife, my Charmion!
> For 'tis to that high title I aspire . . .   (V, 412-14)

Her first reference to marriage is contemptuous, as one might expect. Charmion has brought a message that, though Antony is leaving, he will always respect Cleopatra, and she picks up the word with obvious irritation:

Is that a word
For Antony to use to Cleopatra?
O that faint word, *respect*! how I disdain it!
Disdain myself, for loving after it!
He should have kept that word for cold Octavia.
Respect is for a wife: am I that thing,
That dull, insipid lump, without desires,
And without pow'r to give 'em?   (II, 77-84)

The speech not only expresses Cleopatra's pique but establishes an attitude towards the cold and the dull exactly like that of Antony (the speech precedes Antony's comments on Caesar by only thirty lines). Though Cleopatra in other moods and other circumstances speaks more favourably of being a wife, she retains to the end her scorn of a "dull, insipid lump". Immediately after vowing to follow the dead Antony as a dutiful wife, she adds:

Let dull Octavia
Survive, to mourn him dead: my nobler fate
Shall knit our spousals with a tie too strong
For Roman laws to break.   (V, 415-18)

The opposition between "spousals" and "Roman laws" provides the necessary clue here. Cleopatra considers her love above and beyond law as it is above and beyond reason, yet she borrows from marriage law the terms which distinguish this love from an infatuation of the senses. Her unfortunate self-comparison to a household dove (the context of which will have to be examined later) is part of this process of distinguishing her feelings both from the dullness of the routine and every-day and from the purely sensual and transient.

A glance back at *The Conquest of Granada* will make the distinction clear. Cleopatra's love (and Antony's too) is the sort that Queen Isabella defines[35]:

Love's a heroic passion which can find
No room in any base degenerate mind:
It kindles all the soul with honor's fire,
To make the lover worthy his desire.
(2 *Conquest*, I, 1, 145-8)

The fire and honour of such a love distinguish it from the "lethargy" to which Abdalla succumbs under Lyndaraxa's spell and also from the mere legality of Almahide's relationship to Boabdelin, "When all I knew of love, was to obey!" Almanzor at first takes love for a "lethargy", but by the time of his debate with Lyndaraxa he has learned that though it is not controlled by reason it is both constant and strong:

> 'Tis an enchantment where the reason's bound;
> But Paradise is in th'enchanted ground . . .
> My love's my soul; and that from fate is free;
> 'Tis that unchang'd and deathless part of me.
>   (2 *Conquest*, III, 3, 146-7, 179-80)

Similarly, Antony is lethargic at the opening of the play, seemingly unmanned by love. He is "fired" first by Ventidius, though still half unwilling to leave Cleopatra. When she has persuaded him of the nobility of her love, he identifies his passion with his heroism, much as Almanzor does, and prepares with a whole heart for his battle with Caesar. The spectacle of triumph with which the third act opens presents the momentarily successful fusion of warrior and lover.

When Cleopatra compares herself to a household dove she is explaining to Alexas why she does not want to adopt his plan of flirting with Dolabella to arouse Antony's jealousy: she is opposed to all deceit. Repeatedly during the play her plainness is brought out. Though she finally takes the advice of Alexas, she is unable to maintain the counterfeit. Later, when the false news of her death is carried to Antony, she, unlike Shakespeare's heroine, is unaware of the ruse. Antony, too, has a transparent nature, and both of them in this respect resemble Almanzor, who compares his heart to a crystal brook. Antony complains of his "plain, honest heart", and compares himself to "a shallow-forded stream" (IV, 432-40). Plainness is another heroic trait which Dryden has given to Cleopatra; his desire to emphasize it in the scene with Dolabella leads him to force the comparison of his heroine to a wife, who is further compared to a fond and artless dove. If Cleopatra lacks the dullness of a wife, she hopes to prove that she lacks the meretriciousness of a mistress.

The comparison of two kinds of love is best seen in Cleopatra's interview with Antony's legal wife, who is hardly more like a household dove than Cleopatra. Dryden was well aware that

the unhistorical introduction of Octavia in Act III was his most
daring innovation. I doubt whether it has the effect which
Dryden most feared, of dividing the audience's sympathies
(and he notes that no critic made this objection), but it has
other consequences, very likely unintentional, though by no
means damaging to the total effect of the play. Briefly stated,
they are the shift from the contrast between Cleopatra
and Caesar to the contrast between Cleopatra and Octavia
and the resulting transfer of heroic values to the realm of
love.

In Shakespeare's play Caesar remains throughout the chief
embodiment of the Roman point of view as Cleopatra of the
Egyptian. Caesar's ideal of heroic man is a Stoic concept of the
warrior, whereas Cleopatra's includes both warrior and lover.
The same might be said of the ideals of these two characters in
All for Love, but from the moment that Octavia appears, she
usurps her brother's antipodal position. The confrontation with
Cleopatra establishes her firmly as Antony's alternative choice.
Even Ventidius, who represents Roman values though qualified
by his admiration for Antony, relies on Octavia to make the
Roman ideal compelling. Thus, though the issue remains
Antony's choice of love or his responsibilities in the world, the
stage presents as the dramatic symbols of these alternatives two
women, Cleopatra and Octavia, and the choice at the centre of
the play becomes one between love and marriage. The turn of
the third act which determines Antony for the second time to
leave Cleopatra is not, as it was in the first act, the responsibility
to fight Caesar in order to show the world who is master, but
duty to a wife, through whom he may reach a peaceful understanding with Caesar. Octavia's weapons are her unrequited
love and her children. Cleopatra, who was portrayed in the
first act as a deterrent to heroic action, now appears as an
alternative to domestic love. When the two women meet, they
naturally quarrel over which one of them loves Antony more,
and Cleopatra stakes her claim on the very extravagance of her
love, which has made her give up her good name in order to
become Antony's mistress. The fourth act in effect tests the
truth of this love in the episode of Dolabella, showing that it is
too great to be concealed. Octavia's love, in this same act, is
overwhelmed by outrage. When she leaves in the midst of

angry (though justifiable) accusations, it is reduced to duty, its basic component all along.

In the fifth act Antony is separated from both women. Octavia has left and he has quarrelled with Cleopatra over her supposed liking for Dolabella. The problems of empire are raised again but only to be reabsorbed in the problems of love. Though the Egyptian fleet has deserted and Caesar is at the gates, Antony is primarily concerned with Cleopatra's feelings towards him. When he thinks that she has fled, his first thought is that she has "fled to her Dolabella"; the accusation that she has turned to Caesar comes second. The idea of a heroic last stand is banished in an instant by the false news of Cleopatra's death, which seems to prove her innocence. The only possible heroic action now is suicide, since

> I was but great for her; my pow'r, my empire,
> Were but my merchandise to buy her love . . .
> (V, 270-1)

The structure of the play has been called episodic. Noyes says that "like that of *The Conquest of Granada*, it deals with successive adventures in the life of one man, not with one central crisis" (p. xlix). Jean Hagstrum says the play "is not a closely concatenated action that unfolds moral justice. It is a gallery of related heroic poses intended to arouse our sympathy . . . and our admiration . . ." (*The Sister Arts*, p. 196). The second judgment is much the more acceptable, and surely the relatedness which Hagstrum recognizes is provided by the crisis in the love-relationship of Antony and Cleopatra, the concern of each act in the play. It is strange to complain of looseness of structure in a play whose strength resides in concentration upon one problem. In this respect the structure is a refinement upon that of *The Conquest of Granada* and *Aureng-Zebe*. The three plays constitute a series in progressive tightness and simplification.

In *All for Love* the Herculean hero's quest for unbounded power is replaced by a quest for unbounded love. In *The Conquest of Granada* a noble love modifies the masculine drive for power, redirecting it towards a goal acceptable to society. In *Aureng-Zebe* Indamora tries to exert a similar modifying and redirecting influence, but without achieving the same results as Almahide. Aureng-Zebe's love for her is his one unruly passion,

and Morat gives up his ambition for "unjust dominion" only
to replace it by a love which ignores marital bonds. We never
see Antony, as we do Almanzor and Morat, at a time when
military conquest is his chief aim. In spite of the efforts of
Ventidius, the problems of empire rapidly sink to a position of
secondary importance, hardly competing in Antony's mind
with his desire for Cleopatra. At the end of the play, instead of
the heroic image of him conjured up by Shakespeare's Cleopatra, we are presented with a stage picture of the bodies of the
two lovers, regally attired and seated next each other in throne-
like chairs. When Serapion finds them he says:

> See, see how the lovers sit in state together,
> As they were giving laws to half mankind!   (V, 507-9)[36]

Only in this paradoxical image is the idea of world-conquest
restated, and even here it is subordinated to the triumph of love.

It is a curious fact that this play, which is so thoroughly a
love-tragedy, is in one important respect closer to the pattern of
Herculean plays than either *The Conquest of Granada* or *Aureng-
Zebe*. In both of these plays the final emphasis is on a reconciliation of heroic energies with the laws of society. Almanzor
remains an invincible hero but in the service of Ferdinand and
Isabella. Morat's case is more ambiguous, but at the end death
has removed his irregular greatness, and the compelling image
of the hero lying at Indamora's feet gives way to tableaux of
orderly family relationships. Aureng-Zebe, after a quarrel, is
reconciled to Indamora. Melesinda marches in a religious
procession to her husband's funeral pyre, where she will commit
suttee. Nourmahal, the spirit of restless disorder, dies on the
stage. Aureng-Zebe, having succeeded in restoring his father to
power, receives the crown from his hands. In *All for Love* the
effort to tame or redirect the hero's energies is totally unsuccess-
ful. The love which the play celebrates soars beyond reason and
legality, leading the lovers to defiance of the world and a final
self-assertion in suicide. In his unrepentant commitment to a
highly individualistic ideal Antony is a logical successor to
Morat, but far more Herculean than Almanzor or Aureng-Zebe.

For different reasons, the play as a whole is more like the
other Herculean plays than is Shakespeare's *Antony and Cleopatra*.
There Antony's love is more clearly an alternative to heroic

action, however attractively that alternative is presented. In *All for Love* it is not merely that the world is well lost for such a love, but that Dryden, largely through his treatment of Cleopatra, has elevated the love and made its truth and strength unquestionable, though to attain it the world must be defied. Thus presented, it becomes a suitable enterprise for a hero.

In the preface Dryden makes it clear that the lovers are to be blamed for not controlling their passions and finds the attraction of the story in the "excellency of the moral", but he also states that he has drawn the characters of the hero and the heroine as favourably as his sources would permit him. His emphasis on the greatness and nobility of their love is obviously part of this process. The result is a powerful claim on the sympathy of the audience and perhaps less moral instruction than Dryden liked to think. In fact, the love of Antony and Cleopatra, elevated to the level of a "heroic passion", contains the very sort of contradictions which make a moral judgment of Tamburlaine or Bussy so difficult. The love itself is an extravagant, fiery force, knowing no obligations, and yet ennobling in spite of its extra-legality. It is a pattern of loyal commitment. One might say that the moral is not (as Dryden implies) the punishment of lovers who fail to control their passions, but the tragic limitations imposed by human existence on the infinite aspirations of heroic passion.

*   *   *   *

The Herculean hero seen on the English stage from Marlowe's time to Dryden's was essentially a Renaissance figure—a revival of a heroic concept already very old when it was presented by Sophocles and Euripides. Though firmly based in a morality of its own, it was a concept which challenged orthodox morality and was not widely accepted even in times which prized individualism highly. If it formed the root of the Western idea of heroism, it never became the standard form of the idea. In the Christian era it was a lion in constant danger of being thrown to the faithful. In England at the end of the seventeenth century, Jeremy Collier's famous and ludicrously misnamed "short view" of the stage created an atmosphere still more hostile to moral ambiguity. But Collier's attack was, of course, only one manifestation of a general "shift of sensibility", to use

Frederick Pottle's phrase. The growing sense of civic responsibility which found persuasive advocates in Addison and Steele
demanded unequivocal self-sacrifice of the hero. Cato, on these
grounds, was infinitely preferable to Hercules. Parallel to this
development and intimately related to it was the increasingly
high regard for pity, already described by Dryden in 1679 as
"the noblest and most god-like of moral virtues",[37] and associated by Rowe with "good-nature",[38] that civic virtue so much
discussed in the eighteenth century. The Herculean hero, not
conspicuously good-natured himself, does not appeal primarily
to the good-natured pity of the spectator.

Admiration for the uncompromisingly individual warrior
ceases for a time, to begin again in a somewhat different form
in the Romantic movement. Heathcliff and Captain Ahab,
different as they both are from Tamburlaine or Morat, are
loved and feared for somewhat similar reasons. Their shocking
infractions of the code of ordinary decency are similarly
accepted as integral parts of their heroism. That the most
obvious examples of the type occur in the novel rather than on
the stage is one of many indications of the absorption by the
novel of themes formerly sacred to epic and tragedy. If the
Herculean hero is to be found on the nineteenth-century stage,
it is in the drama of Germany and France or in the opera. The
drama of England and America has hardly seen his like since
the time of Dryden.

NOTES

INTRODUCTION

1. *Sophocles* (Cambridge, Mass., Harvard University Press, 1951 [p. 64], and London, Oxford University Press [p. 64]).
2. *Tragedy* (London, E. Arnold, 1924 [p. 219]).
3. *Hamlet, Father and Son* (Oxford, Clarendon Press, 1955). See also Albert Cook, *The Dark Voyage and the Golden Mean* (Cambridge, Mass., Harvard University Press, 1949 [pp. 31-51], and London, Oxford University Press [pp. 31-51]).
4. *The Vision of Tragedy* (New Haven, Yale University Press, 1959 [p. 106]).
5. *Ibid.*, p. 5.

CHAPTER I   DEMIGOD

1. *Paideia: the Ideals of Greek Culture*, I (4th ed., Oxford, Basil Blackwell, 1954 [5], and New York, Oxford University Press [5]).
2. *Ibid.*, p. 8.
3. Kenneth Clark, *The Nude* (New York, Pantheon Books, 1956 [p. 190], and London, John Murray [p. 178]). I am indebted to Sir Kenneth and to his publishers, Pantheon Books Inc., for allowing me to correct one misprint in quoting this passage. The sense in which the energy of Hercules is "moral" emerges from a consideration of his character.
4. *Sophocles*, V, *The Trachiniae* (Cambridge, Cambridge University Press, 1892 [p. xii], and Chicago, University of Chicago Press [p. xii]).
5. See Ulrich von Wilamowitz-Moellendorff, *Euripides Herakles* (Berlin, Weidmann, 1889 [I, 258-340]); Jebb, *Sophocles*, V, x-xx.
6. Xenophon, *Memorabilia*, II, I, 21-34. See also Erwin Panofsky's brilliant and informative study of the theme of the choice of Hercules in art: *Hercules am Scheidewege* (Leipzig, 1930).
7. *Euripides Herakles*, I, 284.
8. In discussing the Greek plays I shall use the Greek form of the hero's name. For Deianira I shall use the Latin form throughout, since it is spelled thus in the English translation of Sophocles which I am using, Michael Jameson's *The Women of Trachis*, in *Sophocles*, II (Chicago, University of Chicago Press, 1957, and Cambridge, Cambridge University Press). I shall also use the form of the title chosen by Jameson instead of the somewhat more common form, *The Trachiniae*.
9. *The Women of Trachis* is taken by some scholars to be a very late play of Sophocles, following Euripides' *Heracles* (usually dated *c.* 424-420); see Wilamowitz, I, 341 ff., 382 ff.; Jebb, *Sophocles*, V, xxiii; H. D. F. Kitto, *Greek Tragedy* (New York, Doubleday, 1955 [pp. 304 ff.], and Barnes & Noble [pp. 291 ff.], and London, Methuen [pp. 291 ff.]). For the view that it is an early play see Max Pohlenz, *Die Griechische Tragödie*, 2nd ed., (Göttingen, 1954 [I, 198, II, 85]); *Sophocle*, I, ed. Adolphe Dain, trans. Paul Mazon (Paris, 1955 [pp. 8-9]). The question of precedence has no importance for my discussion; since it is quite possible that the play by the elder dramatist was also performed first I shall discuss it first. The precedence of

Sophocles is supported by Léon Parmentier, *Euripide*, III (Paris, 1923 [pp. 15-19]); and by Jameson, *Sophocles*, II, 70.

10. *Sophocles*, II, 65.

11. See Whitman, *Sophocles*, pp. 103-21, 267, n. 55; Pohlenz, I, 206; for the view that it is the tragedy of Heracles see C. M. Bowra, *Sophoclean Tragedy* (Oxford, Clarendon Press, 1944 [pp. 116 ff.], and New York, Oxford University Press [pp. 116 ff.]); Jameson, *Sophocles*, II, 66-7.

12. About this there is a fair amount of agreement among the critics. See Pohlenz, p. 206; Kitto (New York, Doubleday [pp. 306-7], and Barnes & Noble [pp. 292-3], and London, Methuen [pp. 292-3); Bowra, pp. 148-9; Jameson, *Sophocles*, II, 67-8.

13. Several shades of unfavourable opinion are expressed by Whitman, *Sophocles*, p. 119; Pohlenz, p. 206; Kitto (New York, Doubleday [p. 308], and Barnes & Noble [p. 294], and London, Methuen [p. 294]); Mazon, *Sophocle*, I, 8.

14. The last four lines are sometimes assigned to the Chorus.

15. Bowra, pp. 159-60.

16. *The Iliad of Homer*, trans. Richmond Lattimore (Chicago, University of Chicago Press, 1951 [XVIII, 117-19], and London, Routledge & Kegan Paul [XVIII, 117-19]).

17. Bowra, p. 132. See also p. 135.

18. All quotations from *Heracles* are taken from the translation by William Arrowsmith in *Euripides*, II (Chicago, University of Chicago Press, 1956, and Cambridge, Cambridge University Press).

19. *Euripides*, II, 54-5.

20. *The Drama of Euripides* (London, Methuen, 1941 [pp. 255-6]).

21. See Arrowsmith, *Euripides*, II, p. 53.

22. *Euripides*, II, p. 53. I feel that Arrowsmith somewhat overstates his case, however, in insisting that the Heracles of the second part of the play "is not merely untraditional; he is almost inconceivable in traditional perspective . . ." (p. 49). Similarly Léon Parmentier: ". . . Euripide a traité les éléments traditionnels avec une telle liberté que sa version en arrive à contredire les donneés les plus essentielles de la légende mythique" (*Euripide*, III, p. 5).

23. In a stimulating article C. Garton points out the danger of approaching the characters of Greek tragedy as if they were independent persons, "drawn in the round" ("Characterization in Greek Tragedy", *Journal of Hellenic Studies*, 77 [1957], 247-54). Among the shaping influences which may control or even distort a character in a given scene he mentions the Athenian love of a debate carried on by various *personae*. Particularly in Euripides, he argues, the spectator's emotional response to a character may be set aside while his interest is focused upon the putting of a case. Doubtless this warning should be borne in mind in any such attempt as I have made to define the character of a hero, and it may apply especially to the interpretation of such scenes as the debate between Heracles and Theseus. The chief value of the warning may lie in forcing the interpreter to put the character together in a particular way. He will not expect the same traits to be manifested in each scene, since every new situation may be expected to provoke different responses. He must therefore look for a central core of character from which each of these might logically emerge. Both Sophocles and Euripides seem to have posed a series of problems about the character of the fabulous hero, Heracles, and both plays might almost be thought of as prolonged debates on the subject of his heroism. As my discussion of the

two plays has indicated, the core of the concept of heroism in both seems to me essentially one.

24. See Moses Hadas, *The Stoic Philosophy of Seneca* (New York, Doubleday, 1958 [pp. 19-22]).

25. Cicero, *De Finibus*, II, 118, Loeb Library, ed. and trans. H. Rackham, 2nd ed. (Cambridge, Mass., Harvard University Press, 1931, and London, William Heinemann).

26. *Moral Essays*, Loeb Library, ed. and trans. John W. Basore (Cambridge, Mass., Harvard University Press, 1928-35 [III], and London, William Heinemann [III]).

27. *Moral Essays*, I.

28. *Moral Essays*, II.

29. *De Beneficiis*, IV, VIII, 1; *Moral Essays*, III.

30. The authenticity of the second, *Hercules Oetaeus*, has been debated at length by scholars. For a review of the controversy up to 1924 see Léon Herrmann, *Le Théâtre de Sénèque* (Paris, 1924 [pp. 49-57]). Herrmann is convinced of the authenticity. Among disbelievers since that time Wolf H. Friedrich has made the most vigorous attack: "Sprache und Stil des Hercules Oetaeus", *Hermes*, 82 (1954), 51-84. Karl Büchner says that though the question is not settled, most scholars take the negative view (*Römische Literaturgeschichte* [Stuttgart, 1957, p. 429]). Recent defenders include Franz Stoessl, *Der Tod des Herakles* (Zürich, 1945 [p. 88]); Berthe Marti, "Place de l'Hercule sur l'Oeta dans le corpus des Tragédies de Sénèque", *Revue des Etudes Latines*, 27 (1949), 189-210; E. Paratore, "Note critiche ed esegetiche al testo dello Hercules Oetaeus", *Ut Pictura Poesis, Studia Latina P. J. Enk* (Leiden, 1955 [pp. 141-5]); Italo Lana, *Lucio Anneo Seneca* (Torino, 1955), who believes that no reasonable doubt can be sustained (p. 207). Some scholars hold the intermediate opinion that the play as we now have it is the result of considerable additions to Seneca's original text; see Moses Hadas, *A History of Latin Literature* (New York, Columbia University Press, 1952 [p. 246], and London, Oxford University Press [p. 246]). It is immaterial to my argument whether *Hercules Oetaeus* was written by Seneca or by an imitator. It was thought to be Senecan throughout the period I shall be discussing. To the extent that I am able to judge the merits of the arguments, it seems to me that the weight of the evidence is on the side of the defenders, and I shall assume Senecan authorship.

31. See for example, Clarence W. Mendell, *Our Seneca* (New Haven, Yale University Press, 1941 [p. 153], and London, Oxford University Press [p. 153]).

32. See Eugene M. Waith, *The Pattern of Tragicomedy in Beaumont and Fletcher* (New Haven, Yale University Press, 1952 [Ch. III]).

33. *Hercules Furens*, ll. 125 ff., 279-80, 423; *Seneca's Tragedies*, Loeb Library, ed. and trans. Frank Justus Miller (Cambridge, Mass., Harvard University Press, 1917, and London, William Heinemann). All references to Seneca's plays are to this edition.

34. In this account of the scene I follow the stage directions supplied by Miller in the Loeb edition, but the completion of the murders off-stage is only a hypothesis. A much larger question is involved here. Scholars disagree as to whether Seneca's plays were ever produced, or even written to be produced on the stage. That they were in any case often given public readings appears most likely. The changes I have referred to here suggest that Seneca had the stage in mind, but even if he did not, it remains true that an *effect* of immediacy is created. It is agreed that there is no external

evidence of the performance of any of the plays in a theatre. Herrmann (pp. 153-232) believes that they may have been intended for production. Mendell (pp. 88-90) is convinced that they were not, and he is followed by W. Beare (*The Roman Stage* [Cambridge, Mass., Harvard University Press, 1951, pp. 226-7, and London, Methuen, pp. 226-7]) and Michael Grant (*Roman Literature* [Cambridge University Press, 1954, p. 237]). Hadas (p. 248) sensibly concludes that they were probably not intended for presentation, but were written with the conditions of presentation in mind.

35. *Moral Epistles*, Loeb Library, ed. and trans. Richard M. Gummere (Cambridge, Mass., Harvard University Press, 1917 [XXXIX, 2-3], and London, William Heinemann [XXXIX, 2-3]).

36. Stoessl (p. 125) makes the interesting point that in this play Seneca reverses the direction in which depictions of Hercules seemed to be going. Where Sophocles and Euripides both emphasize what is humanly understandable in the hero, Seneca emphasizes what is god-like and mysterious. Furthermore, Seneca is more directly responsible than the Greek playwrights for the form which the myth takes in later European literature.

CHAPTER 2 HEROIC MAN

1. *The Survival of the Pagan Gods*, trans. Barbara F. Sessions (New York, Pantheon Books, 1953 [pp. 84 ff., 149 ff.]).

2. *Ibid.*, p. 211.

3. See Merritt Y. Hughes, "The Christ of *Paradise Regained* and the Renaissance Heroic Tradition", *Studies in Philology*, 35, (1938), 254-77; John Milton, *Paradise Regained, The Minor Poems and Samson Agonistes*, ed. Merritt Y. Hughes (Garden City, N.Y., Doubleday Doran, 1937 [pp. 407-409]); Hallett Smith, *Elizabethan Poetry* (Cambridge, Mass., Harvard University Press, 1952 [pp. 293 ff.]).

4. Coluccio Salutati, *De Laboribus Herculis*, ed. B. L. Ullman (Zürich, 1951 [p. vii]).

5. Page references are to the 1669 Venice edition.

6. *De Laboribus Herculis*, p. 176.

7. *Nichomachean Ethics*, VII, 1; see J. A. K. Thomson, *The Ethics of Aristotle* (London, Allen and Unwin, 1953 [p. 170], and New York, Macmillan [p. 170]).

8. *Ibid.*, IV, 3; Thomson, pp. 103-4. See also Jaeger, *Paideia*, I, 11.

9. Paul Oskar Kristeller and John Herman Randall, Jr., Introduction to *The Renaissance Philosophy of Man*, ed. Cassirer, Kristeller and Randall (Chicago, University of Chicago Press, 1948 [p. 4], and Cambridge, Cambridge University Press [p. 4]).

10. With regard to the newly developing civic outlook which stressed freedom and the active life see Hans Baron, *The Crisis of the Early Italian Renaissance* (Princeton, Princeton University Press, 1955 [pp. 284 ff.], and London, Oxford University Press [pp. 284 ff.]). Salutati, in spite of some sympathy with the new movement, remained a conservative (Baron, pp. 61, 88, 121 ff.) and did not make Hercules the representative of active and civic life, as did Landino, a later humanist.

11. André Chastel points out that the so-called "academy" was in reality a "réunion libre de beaux esprits", rather than a formally organized institution (*Marsile Ficin et l'Art* [Genève, 1954], p. 7). See his discussion (pp. 7-56) of the individuals comprising this group and of their ideas.

12. "The Philosophy of Man in the Italian Renaissance", *Italica*, 24 (1947), p. 100.

13. Plato, *Opera*, Latin trans. Janus Cornarius, with argumenta and commentaria by Marsilio Ficino (Basle, 1561 [p. 387]).

14. Giovanni Pico della Mirandola, "Oration on the Dignity of Man", trans. Elizabeth L. Forbes in *Renaissance Philosophy of Man*, p. 225.

15. Fuit sapiens Hercules. At non sibi sapiens; verum sua sapientia omnibus paene mortalibus profuit. Nam maximam orbis partem peragrans horrendas feras substulit, pernitiosa ac immania monstra perdomuit; crudelissimos tyrannos coercuit. . . . (*Testi Inediti e Rari di Cristoforo Landino e Francesco Filelfo*, ed. Eugenio Garin [Florence, 1949], p. 31). See also Cristoforo Landino, *Camaldolensische Gespräche*, ed. and trans. Eugen Wolf (Jena, 1927 [pp. 3-55]). I have shown elsewhere the close relationship of this passage and of several others in this dialogue to two *Dissertations* by Maximus of Tyre: "Landino and Maximus of Tyre", *Renaissance News*, 13 (1960), pp. 289-94.

16. *The Prince and Other Works*, ed. and trans. Allan H. Gilbert (New York, Hendricks House, 1941 [p. 141]).

17. *The Counter-Renaissance* (New York, Scribner's, 1950 [p. 441]). Several points in this paragraph are indebted to Haydn's discussion of Machiavelli and to Gilbert's in the introduction and notes to *The Prince*.

18. An educated person in the Renaissance was bound to be familiar with Virgil's major reference to Hercules in the *Aeneid*, an extended description in Book VIII of the fight with the monster Cacus, in which Virgil repeatedly refers to the hero's terrible anger—"furens animis" (l. 228), "dentibus infrendens" and "fervidus ira" (l. 230). The "anger of Hercules killing Cacus" is one of the sources of admiration mentioned by Ronsard in the posthumous preface to the *Franciade*. The anger ascribed to Hercules in such encounters as this is not the same thing as the mad rage in which he kills his wife and children, though the difference was not always borne in mind in the Renaissance. Thomas Heywood speaks of Julius Caesar playing "*Hercules Furens*", and becoming so carried away by the part that he actually killed the actor playing Lichas (*An Apology for Actors* [1612], intro. Richard H. Perkinson [New York, Scholars' Facsimiles & Reprints, 1941], sig. E3ᵛ). It is perfectly clear that Heywood is thinking of *Hercules Oetaeus* and applying the term "furens" to the hero's murderous rage in the later play. See Rolf Soellner, "The Madness of Hercules and the Elizabethans", *Comparative Literature*, X (1958), 309-24. What I have to say about the anger of Hercules in this section does not apply to his madness. The difference between these two kinds of anger could be illustrated in Renaissance literature by the rage of Ariosto's Orlando, comparable to the mad rage of Hercules, and the war-like anger of Tasso's Rinaldo, discussed at the conclusion of this chapter.

19. *Testi Inediti e Rari*, p. 24. Landino's interpretation has a great deal in common with Salutati's interpretation of this same labour. Both of them speak of two lions, one representing hasty and short-lived anger, the other lasting anger. Both interpret the lion-skin as righteous anger. See Salutati, *De Laboribus Herculis*, pp. 184-91. See Edgar Wind, *Pagan Mysteries in the Renaissance* (New Haven, Yale University Press, 1958 [p. 69], and London, Faber & Faber [p. 69]), for further references.

20. In the Authorized Version this verse of Psalms appears as "Stand in awe and sin not". Several other translations made directly from the Hebrew render it in a similar way. St Paul was presumably quoting from the Greek

of the Septuagint, from which St Jerome's Latin translation in the Vulgate was also made. Hence "Irascimini" appears in the Vulgate both in Psalms iv. 4 and Ephesians iv. 26.

21. "Nota duplex est ira. Ira quae sit per vitium: et illa extinguit oculum. Et ira quae sit per zelum: et haec illuminat oculum: sed ad tempus turbat ut collyrium: ut postea limpidiorem reddat" (Bible with *postillae* of Hugues de Saint-Cher, fl. 13th c. [Basel, Amerbach, Petri, Froben, 1504]). I have expanded contractions here and in the following transcription.

22. "Ira per zelum quae non est contra naturam: sed contra eius vitium: sed quam in hoc mensura rationis de facili exceditur. propter quod legitur de Platone qui servum suum peccantem tradidit alteri puniendum: ne ipsam mensuram rationis iratus excederet. ideo subditur" (Bible with *postillae* of Nicolaus de Lyra, 1270-1340 [Nuremberg, Koberger, 1493]).

23. *Summa Theologica*, II-II, 158, 1.

24. Chastel, p. 32.

25. See Kenneth Clark, *The Nude* (New York, Pantheon Books [pp. 193-195], and London, John Murray [p. 183]).

26. Since the disappearance in the Second World War of the two miniatures, the *Rape of Deianira* in the Yale Art Gallery is the only Hercules painting by Pollaiuolo known to be extant.

27. Charles Seymour has pointed out to me that although Hercules had been treated prior to 1400 in Italian art, he was neglected by the great artists of the first half of the fifteenth century. His sudden recrudescence in the work of Pollaiuolo is therefore an artistic phenomenon which seems to call for an explanation. Mr Seymour suggests that it may lie in Pollaiuolo's connection with the Medici and Ficino's circle.

28. Ludwig Goldscheider believes that this passage in Landino was later illustrated by Michelangelo in three drawings, which show the triumphs of Hercules over the Nemean lion, Antaeus, and the hydra; *Michelangelo Drawings* (London, Phaidon, 1951), Cat. #68.

29. *The Lives of the Painters, Sculptors and Architects by Giorgio Vasari* (Everyman's Library, London, J. M. Dent, 1927 [II, 82], and New York, E. P. Dutton & Co. [II, 82]).

30. Erwin Panofsky, *Albrecht Dürer* (Princeton, Princeton University Press, 1943 [I, 74], and London, Oxford University Press [I, 74]).

31. *Ibid.*, p. 75. See also, Erwin Panofsky, *Hercules am Scheidewege*, p. 172.

32. Panofsky, *Dürer*, I, 33, 73.

33. See J. V. Cunningham, *Woe or Wonder* (University of Denver Press, 1951); Allan H. Gilbert, *Literary Criticism, Plato to Dryden* (New York, American Book Co., 1940), Appendix on admiration, pp. 459-61; J. E. Gillet, "A Note on the Tragic 'Admiratio' ", *Modern Language Review*, 13 (1918), 233-8; Marvin T. Herrick, "Some Neglected Sources of *Admiratio*", *Modern Language Notes*, 62 (1947), 222-6; Gordon Worth O'Brien, *Renaissance Poetics and the Problem of Power* (Chicago, Institute of Elizabethan Studies, 1956).

34. *Early Lives of Dante*, trans. Philip H. Wicksteed (London, Moring, 1904 [p. 66], and New York, E. P. Dutton & Co. [p. 66]).

35. Book XIV, trans. Charles G. Osgood in *Boccaccio on Poetry* (Princeton, Princeton University Press, 1930 [p. 59], and London, Oxford University Press [p. 59]).

36. See Franck L. Schoell, *Etudes sur L'Humanisme Continental en Angleterre* (Paris, Champion, 1926 [p. 176]); Henri Franchet, *Le Poète et son Oeuvre* (Paris, Champion, 1923 [pp. 247 ff.]). This theory of poetry is discussed further in connection with the obscurity of Chapman in Chapter 4.

37. *Early Lives of Dante*, p. 65.
38. William K. Wimsatt, Jr., and Cleanth Brooks, *Literary Criticism* (New York, Alfred A. Knopf, 1957 [p. 156], and London, Routledge & Kegan Paul [p. 156]). See the remainder of Wimsatt's discussion.
39. Page references are to the 1559 Venice edition.
40. On the Renaissance preference for epic see J. E. Spingarn, *A History of Literary Criticism in the Renaissance* (New York, Columbia University Press, 1908 [pp. 107 ff.], and London, Oxford University Press [pp. 107 ff.]).
41. The selection of the first of these two episodes as especially productive of wonder comes directly from Aristotle (*Poetics*, XXIV). Cf. *De Poeta*, p. 154.
42. See especially *L'Arte Poetica* (Naples, 1725), p. 76. This later treatise (1st ed. 1564) in Italian follows the earlier *De Poeta* closely in many passages. Certain points are made more clearly in one version, certain ones in the other.
43. Sir Philip Sidney, "The Defense of Poesie", in Allan H. Gilbert, *Literary Criticism*, pp. 426, 432, 434.
44. Kathleen M. Burton, ed. (London, Chatto, 1948), p. 26.
45. *Gabriel Harvey's Marginalia*, ed. G. C. Moore Smith (Stratford, Shakespeare Head, 1913).
46. Published 1612; probably written 1607-8; see E. K. Chambers, *The Elizabethan Stage* (Oxford, Clarendon Press, 1923 [IV, 250], and New York, Oxford University Press [IV, 250]).
47. Scholars' Facsimiles edition, sigs. B3r&v, B4r. The Hercules Heywood had seen may have been his own creation in *The Silver Age* and *The Brazen Age* (*ibid.*, p. x; Chambers, III, 345), though his enumeration of Hercules' feats does not correspond exactly with the episodes of his plays. Henslowe refers to *1 and 2 Hercules*, performed in 1595, which may have been the Heywood plays (W. W. Greg, *Henslowe's Diary* [London, A. H. Bullen, 1904-8], II, 175), or some other plays which have not survived. The role of Hercules, whether in Heywood, or in lost plays, or in translations of Seneca, was obviously well known in England at the end of the sixteenth century. It was associated with extravagant language and hence became, like the role of Tamburlaine, the target of satire and parody. Robert Greene has an actor say, "The twelve labors of *Hercules* have I terribly thundred on the stage" (*Groatsworth of Wit* [1592] in Chambers, IV, 241) and Shakespeare's Bottom "could play Ercles rarely, or a part to tear a cat in".
48. See J. E. Spingarn, *Literary Criticism in the Renaissance*, pp. 112-24.
49. Giraldi Cinthio, "On the Composition of Romances", in Gilbert, *Literary Criticism*, p. 270.
50. Minturno, "L'Arte Poetica", in Gilbert, *Literary Criticism*, p. 277.
51. "un non so che di grande ed un eccesso (per così dire) della virtù." Torquato Tasso, *Opere* (Pisa, N. Capurro, 1823), XI.
52. Torquato Tasso, *Discourses on the Heroic Poem*, in Gilbert, *Literary Criticism*, p. 484.
53. See Spingarn, *Literary Criticism in the Renaissance*, pp. 122-4.
54. All quotations from the poem and the Allegory are from the translation by Edward Fairfax: *Godfrey of Bulloigne, or The Recoverie of Jerusalem* (1600).
55. Fairfax's "*Irefull* vertue" is not an exact equivalent of the Italian at this point. Tasso wrote: "Irascibile è quella la quale fra tutte l'altre potenze dell' anima men s'allontana dalla nobiltà della mente" (*Opere*, XXIV, p. xi). Later, however, where Fairfax translated, "This violent, fierce, and unbridled furie", Tasso had "Questa virtù impetuosa, veemente, ed

invitta" (p. xii), and still later in connection with Hugo's appearance to Rinaldo in a dream, came the "irascibile virtù" (p. xiii), which gave Fairfax his phrase.

56. Tasso's "quali sono nell' adunanza degli uomini i guerrieri" better preserves Plato's comparison of the function of *thymos* to the function of the soldier in the state. Just as the state needs the courage of its soldiers to fight for the principles established by its wise guardians, so the soul needs the active support of spirit for the dictates of reason. Referring back to an earlier stage of the discussion of the soul, Socrates reminds Glaucon:

> You remember that passion or spirit appeared at first sight to be a kind of desire, but now we should say quite the contrary; for in the conflict of the soul spirit is arrayed on the side of the rational principle . . . But a further question arises: Is passion different from reason also, or only a a kind of reason; in which latter case, instead of three principles in the soul, there will only be two, the rational and the concupiscent; or rather, as the State was composed of three classes, traders, auxiliaries, counsellors, so may there not be in the individual soul a third element which is passion or spirit, and when not corrupted by bad education is the natural auxiliary of reason?

(Plato, *Republic*, 441; *The Dialogues of Plato*, trans. B. Jowett [New York, Random House, 1937, I, 704, and London, Oxford University Press, I, 704].)

CHAPTER 3 MARLOWE

1. The criticism has often been reviewed in recent years, as by Roy W. Battenhouse in some detail in *Marlowe's Tamburlaine* (Nashville, Tenn., Vanderbilt University Press, 1941 [pp. 1-17]).

2. T. M. Pearce, "Christopher Marlowe, Figure of the Renaissance", *University of New Mexico Bulletin, English Language and Literature Series*, I, No. 1 (1934), pp. 31, 36. See also Paul H. Kocher, *Christopher Marlowe* (Chapel Hill, N.C., University of North Carolina Press, 1946, and London, Oxford University Press); Mario Praz, "Christopher Marlowe", *English Studies*, XIII (1931), 209-23; William Empson, "Two Proper Crimes", *The Nation*, 163 (1946), 444-5; Willard Thorp, "The Ethical Problem in Marlowe's *Tamburlaine*", *Journal of English and Germanic Philology*, 29 (1930), 385-9; Michel Poirier, *Christopher Marlowe* (London, Chatto & Windus, 1951).

3. Kocher, pp. 70-81.

4. *Ibid.*, pp. 275-6.

5. "The Plays of Christopher Marlowe", *The Age of Shakespeare*. ed. Boris Ford (London, Penguin Books, 1955 [p. 162]).

6. Leslie Spence, "Tamburlaine and Marlowe", *Publications of the Modern Language Association*, 42 (1927), 604-22.

7. Helen L. Gardner, "The Second Part of 'Tamburlaine the Great' ", *Modern Language Review*, 37 (1942), 18-24.

8. M. M. Mahood, *Poetry and Humanism* (London, Jonathan Cape, 1950 [pp. 54-6]).

9. Battenhouse, *Marlowe's Tamburlaine*, p. 258.

10. I have referred in Chapter 2 (pp. 52-53) to the fact that Hercules was well known on the English stage at this time. The lines of "Ercles' vein" which Shakespeare gives to Bottom in *A Midsummer Night's Dream* (c. 1595) seem to glance at Jasper Heywood's translation (1561) of Seneca's *Hercules*

O

Furens (see *New Cambridge Shakespeare*, 1924 [p. 109]), though it is unlikely that it was ever publicly acted (see H. B. Charlton, *The Senecan Tradition in Renaissance Tragedy* [Manchester University Press, 1946], pp. cliv-clv). To give the joke point there must have been some more popular stage version of Hercules such as the *1 and 2 Hercules* referred to by Henslowe as being staged in 1595 (Chambers, II, 143-4). It has not been determined whether Thomas Heywood's *Silver Age* and *Brazen Age* were written early enough to be the plays Henslowe refers to; they were certainly too late to have been known to Greene in 1592 when he was writing his *Groatsworth of Wit* and, *a fortiori*, to Marlowe in 1587-8. It is impossible to be sure what Hercules achieved such notoriety, but it seems likely that he was already familiar at the time that Marlowe was writing *Tamburlaine*. From Greene's and Shakespeare's allusions it is obvious that this Hercules was a speaker of extravagant tirades, and this characteristic may have strengthened the association in Marlowe's mind with the hero he was creating. Heywood's plays do not provide any valuable points of comparison with the plays I am treating because, although they give us the only extant major treatment of Hercules on the Elizabethan stage, they are spectacles rather than coherent dramatizations of heroic character, and they have no great literary merit.

11. Mario Praz, "Machiavelli and the Elizabethans", *Proceedings of the British Academy*, XIV (1928), 71 ff. See also Battenhouse, pp. 196 ff., where the parallel to Seneca's Hercules is used to show that Marlowe depicts Tamburlaine as the type of insatiable conqueror who falls victim to his own covetousness. Since my interpretation of Seneca is totally different from Battenhouse's, the parallel does not seem to me to show anything of the sort.

12. See Hallet Smith, "Tamburlaine and the Renaissance", *Elizabethan Studies, University of Colorado Studies*, Series B, II, 4 (Boulder, Colorado, 1945); Erich Voegelin, "Das Timurbild der Humanisten", *Zeitschrift für öffentliches Recht*, XVII (1937), 545-82.

13. All references to *Tamburlaine* are to the revised edition by Una Ellis-Fermor (London, Methuen, 1951). In the performance of Tamburlaine directed by Tyrone Guthrie in New York in 1956 a very large map was spread on the floor of the stage, making possible an extraordinarily effective theatrical image. Tamburlaine walked on the map as he pointed to his conquests, and at the end fell down on it, almost covering the world with his prone body.

14. Battenhouse has pointed to the Machiavellian combination of the fox image in this scene with that of the lion in the following scene (p. 209). See also Harry Levin, *The Overreacher* (Cambridge, Mass., Harvard University Press, 1952 [pp. 37-8], and London, Faber & Faber [p. 56]).

15. Passages describing action supposedly taking place onstage in Seneca's plays have been used to support the contention that the plays were never intended for the stage. It is interesting to see a technique so nearly approaching Seneca's here and later in Dryden. This obviously proves nothing about Seneca, but it shows that such an effect was accepted by certain audiences and conceivably might have been by Seneca's audience.

16. On the importance of this idea in *Tamburlaine*, see Battenhouse, pp. 99-113.

17. Early in Part I he promises Theridamas friendship "Until our bodies turn to elements, / And both our souls aspire celestial thrones" (I, 2, 235-6), but here the reference seems more conventional.

18. I cannot agree with Battenhouse (pp. 165 ff.), who believes that the comparison of her to Helen of Troy in Tamburlaine's lament for her death

shows her to be a "pattern of pagan, earthly beauty" and "devoid of religion or conscience". Her attitude towards her father and towards the deaths of Bajazeth and Zabina leads to an opposite conclusion.

19. "The Dramatic Structure of Marlowe's 'Tamburlaine the Great', Parts I and II", *English Studies (Essays and Studies*, New Series), I (1948), 101-26. I do not wholly agree as to the extent of the modification Duthie sees. I am not so sure as he is that the marriage of Tamburlaine and Zenocrate symbolizes the establishment of an ideal relationship between beauty and the warrior.

20. See Ellis-Fermor's note, V, 2, 115-27.

21. *Homer and the Heroic Tradition* (Cambridge, Mass., Harvard University Press, 1958 [p. 182], and London, Oxford University Press [p. 182]). See also C. M. Bowra, *The Greek Experience* (London, Weidenfeld & Nicolson, 1957 [Chap. II], and New York, World Publishing Co. [Chap. II]).

22. "The Dramatic Structure of Marlowe's 'Tamburlaine the Great' ", pp. 118, 124.

23. Helen L. Gardner has written about the importance of the theme of necessity in Part II in an excellent essay, "The Second Part of 'Tamburlaine the Great' ", *Modern Language Review*, 37 (1942), 18-24. I cannot agree with her that Marlowe's sympathies are much changed, however, nor that the moral of Part II is "the simple medieval one of the inevitability of death".

24. *The Complete Works of Shakespeare*, ed. G. L. Kittredge (Boston, Ginn & Co., 1936 [IV, 1, 58-60]).

25. *Gabriel Harvey's Marginalia*, pp. 134, 156.

26. *Anacrisis* (1634?), in *Critical Essays of the Seventeenth Century*, ed. J. E. Spingarn (Bloomington, Indiana University Press, 1957 [I, 182, 183], and London, Oxford University Press [I, 182, 183]).

27. Harry Levin has written brilliantly of this style in *The Overreacher* (Cambridge, Mass., Harvard University Press [especially pp. 10 ff.], and London, Faber & Faber [pp. 30 ff.]), where he comments on the superb appropriateness of the term of Puttenham's for hyperbole. As he says, "It could not have been more happily inspired to throw its illumination upon Marlowe—upon his style, which is so emphatically himself, and on his protagonists, overreachers all" (p. 23). See also M. P. McDiarmid, "The Influence of Robert Garnier on some Elizabethan Tragedies", *Etudes Anglaises*, XI (1958), 289-302; and Donald Peet, "The Rhetoric of Tamburlaine", *ELH*, 26 (1959), 137-55. Commenting on Marlowe's use of amplification, Peet remarks that "there can be little doubt that Marlowe wants us to *marvel* at Tamburlaine", whether or not he seeks approval (p. 151).

CHAPTER 4   CHAPMAN

1. A. S. Ferguson points out many allusions to Hercules Oetaeus in his "The Plays of George Chapman", *Modern Language Review*, 13 (1918), 1-24.

2. *Bussy D'Ambois* was probably performed for the first time in 1604. See *The Plays and Poems of George Chapman, The Tragedies*, ed. T. M. Parrott (London, Routledge & Kegan Paul, 1910 [p. 541]). All quotations from Chapman's tragedies are made from this edition. The play was first printed in 1607, was revised by Chapman, possibly in 1610, and published in this second edition in 1641. See Parrott, p. 541; Barbara Sturman, "The 1641 Edition of Chapman's *Bussy D'Ambois*", *Huntington Library Quarterly*, 14 (1951), 171-201; Peter Ure, "Chapman's 'Tragedy of Bussy d'Ambois':

Problems of the Revised Quarto", *Modern Language Review*, 48 (1953), 257-269. Parrott follows the 1641 quarto, printing passages which appear only in the first edition in his Text Notes. See Appendix.

3. See Parrott, *Tragedies*, pp. 542 ff.; Jean Jacquot, *George Chapman* (Paris, Les Belles Lettres, 1951 [pp. 123 ff.]).

4. See Franck L. Schoell, *Études sur l'Humanisme Continental en Angleterre* (Paris, Honoré Champion, 1926 [pp. 197-8]).

5. I do not believe that this speech can be disposed of by pointing out, as Ennis Rees does, that the King is "consistently characterized as a weakling and flatterer" (*The Tragedies of George Chapman* [Cambridge, Mass., Harvard University Press, 1954, p. 44]). It is only in *The Revenge of Bussy D'Ambois* that the King is obviously so characterized, and in any case his comments here fit with so many other estimates of Bussy given by both friends and enemies, that they cannot easily be brushed aside.

6. This part of the scene is omitted from the 1641 quarto. I quote from the Text Notes, p. 563.

7. The repetition of this idea undoubtedly explains the cut which was made in the revised edition.

8. In the revised quarto the order of the final speeches is changed, perhaps with a view to preparing better for the sequel, *The Revenge of Bussy D'Ambois*. Since Tamyra and Montsurry were to appear in the second scene of that play, it may have seemed better to end the first play with their speeches to each other. See Peter Ure, *Modern Language Review*, 48 (1953), 257-69.

9. See M. C. Bradbrook, *The School of Night* (Cambridge, Cambridge University Press, 1936, and New York, Macmillan); Paul Kocher, *Christopher Marlowe*, pp. 7-18; E. A. Strathmann, "The Textual Evidence for 'The School of Night' ", *Modern Language Notes*, 56 (1941), 176-86.

10. All quotations from Chapman's non-dramatic works are from *The Poems of George Chapman*, ed. Phyllis B. Bartlett (New York, Modern Language Association, 1941).

11. Following Landino, Conti, and others, Chapman often associates Hercules with learning. See for instance *The Tears of Peace*, l. 698, and "To M. Harriots", accompanying *Achilles Shield*, l. 70.

12. See Gordon Worth O'Brien, *Renaissance Poetics and the Problem of Power*, pp. xvii-xviii; Jacquot, *Chapman*, pp. 237-8; Marcello Pagnini, *Forme e Motivi nelle Poesie e nelle Tragedie di George Chapman* (Florence, 1957 [pp. 79-97]).

13. See Ficino's remarks on the *furor poeticus* in his commentary on Plato's *Ion* (*Opera*, 1561 [pp. 536-7]).

14. "Oration", trans. Forbes, *Renaissance Philosophy of Man*, p. 250. For the Latin see G. Pico della Mirandola, *De Hominis Dignitate*, ed. E. Garin (Florence, 1942 [p. 156]).

15. "Oration", p. 253; *De Hominis Dignitate*, p. 162.

16. *Pagan Mysteries in the Renaissance*, pp. 17, 18, 22.

17. See Schoell, pp. 179-97.

18. *Mythologiae* (Venice, 1581 [p. 1]).

19. See Henri Franchet, *Le Poète et son Oeuvre* (Paris, Champion, 1923 [pp. 247 ff.]).

20. I quote from the edition by F. S. Boas (London, Methuen, 1949).

21. *The Overreacher*, p. 116.

22. *Tragedies*, pp. 545-6.

23. John W. Wieler, *George Chapman—The Effect of Stoicism upon his*

Tragedies (New York, King's Crown Press, 1949 [pp. 35-6], and London, Oxford University Press [pp. 35-6]); Theodore Spencer, *Death and Elizabethan Tragedy* (Cambridge, Mass., Harvard University Press, 1936 [p. 243], and London, Oxford University Press [p. 243]).

24. *The Tragedies of George Chapman*, pp. 28, 30-1, 50.

25. For a most judicious discussion of Bussy and Achilles, see Elias Schwartz, "Seneca, Homer, and Chapman's *Bussy D'Ambois*", *Journal of English and Germanic Philology*, 56 (1957), 163-76.

26. Peter Ure, "The Main Outline of Chapman's Byron", *Studies in Philology*, 47 (1950), 581.

27. "The Ethical Bias of Chapman's *Homer*", *Studies in Philology*, 36 (1939), 174-82.

28. *Homeric Renaissance* (New Haven, Yale University Press, 1956 [p. 41], and London, Chatto & Windus [p. 41]).

29. Cf. Parrott: "Like Hercules, Chapman's Bussy has been the self-reliant hero who pitted his own strength and 'virtue' against a hostile world, and like Hercules he falls at last a victim to inevitable, because unsuspected, fate" (*Tragedies*, p. 546).

30. *Shakespeare and the Rival Traditions* (New York, Macmillan, 1952), p. 56. See Appendix.

CHAPTER 5   SHAKESPEARE

1. "The Metamorphosis of Violence in Titus Andronicus", *Shakespeare Survey*, 10 (1957), pp. 39-48; see esp. p. 48.

2. All references to Shakespeare's plays are to *The Complete Works of Shakespeare*, ed. G. L. Kittredge. I have discussed the conflict between Caesar's and Cleopatra's ideals in "Manhood and Valor in Two Shakespearean Tragedies", *ELH*, 17 (1950), 262-73. While my interpretation of *Antony and Cleopatra* remains essentially what I presented there, my brief comments on *Coriolanus* in that article do not exactly coincide with the interpretation presented in this chapter.

3. "It is rare spirits deeply tainted that Shakespeare places at the center of his last tragic world", as Willard Farnham says in his chapter, "Taints and Honors", *Shakespeare's Tragic Frontier* (Berkeley, University of California Press, 1950 [p. 1], and Cambridge, Cambridge University Press [p. 1]). Farnham's entire discussion of this subject is most illuminating. See also his chapter, "Antony and Cleopatra", pp. 139-205. In two articles J. Leeds Barroll has emphasized Antony's taints. In "Enobarbus' Description of Cleopatra" (*Texas Studies in English*, 37 [1958], 60-78) he compares Antony's rejection of Octavia to a Hercules who chooses Pleasure rather than Virtue at the crossroads. In "Antony and Pleasure" (*Journal of English and Germanic Philology*, 57 [1958], 708-20) he portrays Antony as an example of sloth and its concomitant sins of gluttony and lechery. My disagreement with Barroll's use of the Herculean analogy will be apparent in what follows.

4. *Shakespeare's Plutarch*, ed. C. F. Tucker Brook (New York, Duffield, 1909 [II, 105]).

5. It has often been noted that Shakespeare substituted Hercules for Plutarch's Bacchus in this episode. This change is perhaps the strongest indication of his deliberate use of the Herculean myth as a point of reference in his presentation of Antony.

6. I interpret her behaviour in the later scene with Caesar and her treasurer, Seleucus (V, 2, 112-90), as it is interpreted in Plutarch—a

stratagem to deceive Caesar by persuading him that she wishes to live. But critics who accept this interpretation sometimes object that her conversations with Proculeius and Dolabella show some wavering (see M. R. Ridley's introduction to the revised Arden edition [London, Methuen, 1956, pp. xlvi-xlviii, and Cambridge, Mass., Harvard University Press, pp. xlvi-xlviii]). To such objections it may be replied that although devotion to Antony is not the sole reason for her suicide, fear of disgrace in Rome is not so much an alternative reason as a supporting one. If she pauses to find out what would happen to her in Rome, she is no more disloyal to Antony than he is to her when he speaks to Eros about the shame of a Roman triumph after he has already vowed to follow Cleopatra. The combination of love and personal honour is another of the remarkable resemblances between the two.

7. John F. Danby is interesting on this aspect of the play in *Poets on Fortune's Hill* (London, Faber & Faber, 1952 [pp. 128 ff.]).

8. *Shakespeare* (New York, Doubleday, 1954 [p. 232]).

9. John Palmer, *Political Characters in Shakespeare* (London, Macmillan, 1945 [p. 297]); D. J. Enright, "*Coriolanus*: Tragedy or Debate?" *Essays in Criticism*, 4 (1954), 1-19.

10. R. Browning, "Coriolanus, Boy of Tears", *Ibid.*, 5 (1955), 18-31.

11. O. J. Campbell, *Shakespeare's Satire* (London, Oxford University Press, 1943 [pp. 213, 215]).

12. Notable among these are: G. Wilson Knight, "The Royal Occupation", *The Imperial Theme* (London, Methuen, 1951 [pp. 154-98]); Hardin Craig, *An Interpretation of Shakespeare* (New York, Dryden, 1948 [pp. 282-301]); Willard Farnham, *Shakespeare's Tragic Frontier*, pp. 207-64; Peter Alexander, *A Shakespeare Primer* (London, Nisbet, 1951 [pp. 103 ff.]); Hermann Heuer, "From Plutarch to Shakespeare: A Study of *Coriolanus*", *Shakespeare Survey*, 10 (1957) p. 50; Harry Levin, ed. *Coriolanus* (Baltimore, Penguin, 1956 [pp. 7-24]); H. J. Oliver, "Coriolanus as Tragic Hero", *Shakespeare Quarterly*, 10 (1959), 53-60.

13. D. J. Enright (*op. cit.*), noting this dialectical quality, considers the play more of a debate than a tragedy.

14. In Plutarch Coriolanus has "very few men"; Shakespeare gives him none.

15. There is no such reluctance in Plutarch. See M. W. MacCallum, *Shakespeare's Roman Plays and their Background* (London, Macmillan, 1910 [p. 508]).

16. MacCallum describes Shakespeare's opinion of the plebeian mass in this way: "Despite his sympathy with those of whom it is composed, it is to him a giant not yet in his teens, with formidable physical strength, with crude natural impulses to the good and the bad, kindly-natured and simple-minded, not incapable of fair-dealing and generosity; but rude, blundering, untaught, and therefore subject to spasms of fury, panic, and greed, fit for useful service only when it finds the right leader, but sure to go wrong if abandoned to its own or evil guidance" (p. 532). See also the rest of Mac-Callum's discussion, pp. 518-48.

17. Palmer finds no fault with this behaviour. "Only one course of action is politically possible," he writes. He calls it "good sound electioneering . . . admittedly dishonest, but . . ." (*Political Characters in Shakespeare*, p. 273). To attempt in this way to interpret the play in the light of contemporary British (or American) political practice, however, is to warp it beyond recognition. H. J. Oliver makes the telling point that "the blame for the banishment of

Coriolanus is clearly taken by Shakespeare from the shoulders of the hero and put on those of the tribunes" ("Coriolanus as Tragic Hero", *Shakespeare Quarterly*, 10, 57).

18. *Shakespeare's Plutarch*, II, 162. See Hermann Heuer, "From Plutarch to Shakespeare: A Study of *Coriolanus*", *Shakespeare Survey*, 10, 58.

19. *Shakespeare's Plutarch*, II, 176.

20. Alexandre Hardy introduces a similar scene in his *Coriolan*, which dates from about the same time as Shakespeare's play. Since it was not published until much later it is unlikely that Shakespeare knew the play, although there are one or two striking similarities. See MacCallum, p. 478. Hardy's Coriolan thinks of himself more explicitly as a scourge of God (see III, 2) than does Coriolanus, and Farnham has pointed out that he is portrayed as almost faultless (*Shakespeare's Tragic Frontier*, pp. 214-15).

21. *The Imperial Theme*, pp. 155 ff.

22. *Shakespeare Survey*, 10, 55. Heuer shows in this essay how the emphasis on "nature" is introduced into the story by North in his translation.

23. Hardy's Volomnie also makes a very personal appeal, but she has more to say about the central problem, the justice of her son's revenge as opposed to the mercy he might show (IV, 4). Hardy also makes her bitterly remorseful for having succeeded in her plea (V, 3).

24. It is particularly difficult to see the tragedy as does L. C. Knights, as a "failure of relationship between strongly asserted personal values and something very much greater than those values", *Some Shakespearean Themes* (London, Chatto & Windus, 1959 [p. 143], and Stanford, Stanford University Press [p. 143]). It is characteristic of Knights's view that he sees the city as the true protagonist of the play (p. 150). For him, Coriolanus remains a boy to the end, incapable of responding to the "ideal of creative mutuality hinted at by Menenius's fable of the belly" (p. 155). Though Rome might well represent such values, and very possibly did for Plutarch, I see very little indication that it does in Shakespeare's play.

25. MacCallum, p. 621.

26. James Thomson, *Works* (London, 1766), IV, 282.

27. J. P. Kemble, *Shakespeare's Coriolanus . . . adapted to the stage with additions from Thomson* (London, 1814 [pp. 59-63]); Variorum edition of *Coriolanus*, ed. H. H. Furness (Philadelphia, J. B. Lippincott Co., 1928 [pp. 730-1]).

28. H. J. Oliver challenges Farnham's theory that Shakespeare's later tragic heroes, such as Antony and Coriolanus, are more deeply flawed than the earlier ones (*Shakespeare Quarterly*, 10, 60). I believe that what is important in the case of these two heroes is not whether they are morally better or worse than their predecessors but that moral judgment on them is less emphasized in the plays and what Farnham calls their "rare spirits" emphasized more.

INTERCHAPTER SHAKESPEARE TO DRYDEN

1. As in the Restoration period, discussed in the next chapter, the romance was largely responsible for this emphasis on love. For a thorough discussion of the main developments of Caroline drama see Alfred Harbage, *Cavalier Drama* (New York, *Modern Language Association*, 1936 [esp. Chapter III], and London, Oxford University Press).

2. References are to Vol. I of the edition of Wm. Gifford (London, 1805). In this passage Malefort even compares himself to Hercules in the

shirt of Nessus, but the poisoned blood is the blood of Malefort's son, for whose murder he feels pangs of guilt. Only in degree of suffering is he comparable to Hercules. He is unequivocally portrayed as corrupt.

3. Allan Gilbert's translation, *Literary Criticism*, p. 293.

4. *The Prince and The Discourses*, trans. Christian E. Detmold (New York, Modern Library, 1940 [p. 186]).

5. References are to Vol. III of the Scott-Saintsbury edition (Edinburgh, 1883).

6. Gilbert, *Literary Criticism*, p. 293.

7. Among the many discussions of this aspect of Corneille see Georges May, *Tragédie Cornélienne et Racinienne* (Urbana, Illinois, University of Illinois Press, 1948), pp. 23-4; Jean Boorsch, "Remarques sur la Technique Dramatique de Corneille", *Studies by Members of the French Department of Yale University*, ed. Albert Feuillerat (New Haven, Yale University Press, 1941 [pp. 101-62, esp. pp. 140-1], and London, Oxford University Press [pp. 101-162, esp. pp. 140-1]); Paul Bénichou, *Morales du Grand Siècle* (Paris, Gallimard, 1948 [chapter on "Le Héros Cornélien"]).

8. The influence of Corneille is discussed at length by Cecil V. Deane, *Dramatic Theory and the Rhymed Heroic Play* (Oxford, Oxford University Press, 1931), esp. pp. 15-27, 154-5. With particular regard to critical theory see John M. Aden, "Dryden, Corneille, and the *Essay of Dramatic Poesy*", *Review of English Studies*, n.s. VI (1955), 147-56.

9. Pierre Corneille, *Œuvres*, ed. Ch. Marty-Laveaux (Paris, Hachette, 1862 [I, 32]).

10. *Morales du Grand Siècle*, p. 28.

11. *Œuvres*, V, 508.

12. *Paideia*, I, 8-14.

13. See Jacques Debu-Bridel, "La Préciosité: Conception Héroique de la Vie", *Revue de France*, 18 (1938), V, 195-216; J.-E. Fidao-Justiniani, *L'Esprit Classique et la Préciosité* (Paris, 1914).

14. *Cavalier Drama*, pp. 41, 55 ff.

CHAPTER 6   DRYDEN

1. All quotations from *The Conquest of Granada* and *All for Love* are from *Selected Dramas of John Dryden*, ed. G. R. Noyes (Chicago, Scott, Foresman, 1910). Noyes's text is more reliable than that of Montague Summers and is preferable to that of Scott-Saintsbury, since it is based on the first quartos. On the superiority of these first editions see Noyes's preface and George Nettleton, "Author's Changes in Dryden's *Conquest of Granada*", *Modern Language Notes*, 50 (1935), 360-4. "1" or "2" prefixed to "*Conquest*" refers to Part I or Part II. Quotations from *Aureng-Zebe*, not included in Noyes's selection, are taken from the first quarto (1676—I have used the copy in the Yale Library), but for convenience of reference I give the page in Volume V of the Scott-Saintsbury edition (Edinburgh, 1883), referred to as SS.

2. *Essays of John Dryden*, ed. W. P. Ker (Oxford, Clarendon Press, 1926 [II, 137-8]). All quotations from Dryden's critical writing are taken from this edition unless otherwise indicated.

3. The reasons for including Morat in my discussion will be found below in the treatment of *Aureng-Zebe*.

4. The influence of Renaissance theory and practice of heroic poetry upon Dryden's plays is discussed by B. J. Pendlebury, *Dryden's Heroic Plays*

(London, Selwyn & Blount, 1923 [pp. 9-23]), and most recently by William K. Wimsatt in his chapter on Dryden in *Literary Criticism*, pp. 196 ff.

5. The general question of the degree of influence exercised by the French seventeenth-century romances on the heroic play has been much written about and hotly debated. See, for example, W. S. Clark, "The Sources of the Restoration Heroic Play", *Review of English Studies*, 4 (1928), 49-63; the reply of Kathleen M. Lynch, "Conventions of Platonic Drama in the Heroic Plays of Orrery and Dryden," *Publications of the Modern Language Association*, 44 (1929), 456-71; Clark again in *Publications of the Modern Language Association*, 45 (1930), 623-4; and Lynch, *ibid.*, pp. 625-6. Montague Summers writes with his customary verve: "He who has not read at least his *Polexandre, Cassandre, Cléopâtre* and *Faramond*, his *Ibrahim, Artamène, Clélie*, and *Almahide*, whether in the original or in the English translations, to which the dramatists so frequently turned, is simply neither equipped nor competent to write upon the Restoration theatre." (Introduction to *Dryden: The Dramatic Works* [London, Nonesuch Press, 1931, I, xl, and New York, Random House, I, xl]).

6. See Scott C. Osborn's distinction between two kinds of love in Dryden's plays and his remarks on the effects of ideal love: "Heroical Love in Dryden's Heroic Drama", *Publications of the Modern Language Association*, 73 (1958), 480-90; also John Winterbottom's analysis of the effect of Almahide upon Almanzor: "The Development of the Hero in Dryden's Tragedies", *Journal of English and Germanic Philology*, 52 (1953), 161-73, and "The Place of Hobbesian Ideas in Dryden's Tragedies", *Journal of English and Germanic Philology*, 57 (1958), 665-83.

7. See A. E. Parsons, "The English Heroic Play", *Modern Language Review*, 33 (1938), 1-14.

8. Werner Bleuler points out the marked conflict in Dryden's heroes between the elements of self-conquest (*Selbstüberwindung*) and what he aptly calls the *Achilleische* (*Das Heroische Drama John Drydens als Experiment dekorativer Formkunst* [Bern, Francke, 1957], pp. 59-95; see also his summary of these points, pp. 111-12). While this observation seems to me exactly right, the fact that Almanzor, for instance, ultimately learns to submit himself to certain obligations appears to invalidate one of Bleuler's chief contentions, that there can be no development in heroic drama (p. 106). Recognition of the static quality of many scenes need not lead to the conclusion that there is no movement in the plays as wholes. The development is precisely the readjustment of these opposing forces in the hero.

9. Arthur O. Lovejoy and George Boas, *Primitivism and Related Ideas in Antiquity* (*A Documentary History of Primitivism and Related Ideas, I*) (Baltimore, Johns Hopkins, 1935 [pp. 9-11], and London, Oxford University Press [pp. 9-11]).

10. See Robert Loveday's translation, *Hymen's Praeludia* (1674), Division I, pp. 72 ff., 363 ff.

11. The contrast with Machiavelli's interpretation of the education of the training of Achilles is striking. "To have as teacher one who is half beast and half man means nothing else than that a prince needs to know how to use the qualities of both creatures. The one without the other will not last long" (*The Prince*, trans. Allan Gilbert, p. 148).

12. See the articles by John Winterbottom already referred to: *Journal of English and Germanic Philology*, 52 (1953), 161-73, and 57 (1958), 665-83. It is a well-made point that Almanzor is shown to accept in addition to his personal honour, Platonic love, family duty, and patriotic duty. As I hope

to make clear, I do not agree that Dryden asserts an unequivocal disapproval of ambition in his portrayal of Almanzor and the other heroes.

13. Scott-Saintsbury, V, 188-9. In transcribing from the 1676 quarto I have changed italic to roman.

14. *Ibid.*, p. 192.

15. *Essay on Criticism*, I, 153, 159-60.

16. Bleuler sees the structure of the heroic plays as very loose, held together by no necessary progression (p. 106). While it may be granted that the ordering of the scenes is not always the only possible one, the connection between them is firmly rooted in the theme.

17. The very accusation Dryden had made of himself and his contemporaries as compared to Shakespeare, in the preface to *Troilus and Cressida* (Ker, I, 227).

18. The engravings printed with Settle's *Empress of Morocco* (1673) and the later illustrations to Rowe's Shakespeare (1709) give some idea of scenery and costume. See Allardyce Nicoll, *History of English Drama 1660-1900*, I, Restoration Drama, 4th ed. (Cambridge, Cambridge University Press, 1955 [25-83]), and A. M. Nagler, *Sources of Theatrical History* (New York, Theatre Annual, 1952 [pp. 203-53, especially the quotation from Addison, pp. 244-5]).

19. See the opening of the essay "Of Heroic Plays".

20. On Dryden's artifice see Bonamy Dobrée's chapter, "John Dryden and Artificial Tragedy", in his *Restoration Tragedy* (Oxford, Clarendon Press, 1929), pp. 91-109; Moody Prior, *The Language of Tragedy* (New York, Columbia University Press, 1947 [pp. 164 ff.], and London, Oxford University Press [pp. 164 ff.]).

21. Mark Van Doren cites several as illustrations of the inferiority of Dryden's verse in the heroic plays; *The Poetry of John Dryden*, 2nd. ed. (Cambridge, W. Heffer & Sons, 1931 [pp. 40-1]).

22. *Restoration Tragedy*, p. 91.

23. *Dryden: The Dramatic Works*, I, xlviii.

24. In the interim, Dryden had written his opera, *The State of Innocence*, based on *Paradise Lost*. See E. S. Le Conte, "*Samson Agonistes* and *Aureng-Zebe*", *Etudes Anglaises*, 11 (1958), 18-22. See Appendix.

25. See the preface to *Tyrannic Love*.

26. *The Works of Thomas Otway*, ed. J. C. Ghosh, (Oxford, Clarendon Press, 1932 [I, 245]).

27. In "A Parallel of Poetry and Painting" Dryden explains that the characters of comedy and tragedy are "never to be made perfect", but that "there is scarce a frailty to be left" in the heroes of epic, though "Homer's Achilles is a kind of exception to this rule" (Ker, II, 125-7). To the extent that Aureng-Zebe and later Cleomenes approach faultlessness they presumably reflect Dryden's effort to make his heroic plays imitate heroic poems, though on many occasions he stated his preference for a dramatic hero with faults, and for the faulty Achilles as a model.

28. *An Apology for the Life of Mr Colley Cibber*, ed. Robert W. Lowe (London, 1889 [I, 121]).

29. *Ibid.*, p. 122.

30. Cibber's opinion was supported by his son, Theophilus Cibber, in his life of Booth, but was opposed by Thomas Davies in his *Dramatic Miscellanies* (1st ed. 1783; I have used the 1785 ed. [III, 164-5]).

31. F. Hannmann, *Dryden's Tragödie "All for Love" und ihr Verhältnis zu Shakespeare's "Antony and Cleopatra"* (Rostock, 1903).

32. Preface to *All for Love* (Ker, I, 200).
33. Winterbottom, *Journal of English and Germanic Philology*, 52, 162.
34. Largely for this reason I cannot accept in its entirety the interesting parallel between the play and Carracci's "Choice of Hercules" proposed by Jean Hagstrum, *The Sister Arts* (University of Chicago Press, 1958 [pp. 184 ff.]).
35. See Scott C. Osborn's article already referred to, *Publications of the Modern Language Association*, 73, 480-90.
36. Noyes, departing from the quarto, prints the first "See" as a separate line.
37. Preface to *Troilus and Cressida* (Ker, I, 210).
38. Epistle Dedicatory to *The Ambitious Stepmother* (1700).

APPENDIX

First Performances and Editions

I. TAMBURLAINE

First performance: Part I probably winter 1587; in the epistle "to the gentlemen readers" prefixed to his *Perimides the Blacksmith* (1588) Greene speaks of "daring God out of heaven with that Atheist Tamburlan". Part II shortly after, before November 16th, 1587, the date of a letter which seems to refer to it. First recorded performance, August 1594. The title-page of the first edition shows that the play was performed by the Admiral's Men. From Heywood's prologue to a revival of *The Jew of Malta* it is known that Edward Alleyn, Henslowe's son-in-law, was famous in the part of Tamburlaine.

First edition: 1590 (Octavo).

See *Tamburlaine*, edited by Una Ellis-Fermor, pp. 1-17; Chambers, *Elizabethan Stage*, III, 418-22.

2. BUSSY D'AMBOIS

First performance: probably 1604, though possibly as early as 1597; the evidence is partly internal, partly derived from information about the actors. The title-page of the first edition shows that the play was performed by the Children of Paul's. If it was staged in 1597 it was probably in a somewhat different version from either of those preserved in the existing texts and performed by the Admiral's Men. Such an early performance remains conjectural. From the prologue to a revival of the play it is known that Nathan Field was a very successful Bussy, but this must have been either when he was with the Queen's Revels Children at Whitefriars, *c.* 1610, or after he had joined the King's Men, *c.* 1615, who certainly performed the play later.

First edition: 1607 (Quarto). The Second Quarto (1641) is a revision, possibly made for a revival *c.* 1610.

See *Bussy D'Ambois*, edited by F. S. Boas, p. xii; T. M. Parrott, "The Date of Chapman's 'Bussy D'Ambois' ", *Modern Language Review*, 3 (1907-8), 126-40; Parrott, *Tragedies*, p. 541; Chambers, *Elizabethan Stage*, II, 317, 340, III, 249, 253-4; Ennis Rees, *The Tragedies of George Chapman*, pp. 197-8; Elias Schwartz, "The Dates and Order of Chapman's Tragedies", *Modern Philology*, 57 (1959), 80-2.

3. ANTONY AND CLEOPATRA

First performance: probably early 1607; during that year Daniel made revisions in his *Cleopatra* which seem to show familiarity with Shakespeare's play. Acted by the King's Men.
First edition: Shakespeare Folio of 1623.
See Chambers, *William Shakespeare*, I, 477-8.

4. CORIOLANUS

First performance: probably 1608, judging from internal evidence.
First edition: Shakespeare Folio of 1623.
See Chambers, *William Shakespeare*, I, 479-80.

5. THE CONQUEST OF GRANADA

First performance: Part I December 1670; Part II January 1670 or 1671. Both parts performed by the King's Men at the Theatre Royal in Bridges Street. Information about the performances of Dryden's plays is given on title-pages and in contemporary letters and newspapers. Casts are recorded in the early quartos. Some of the chief players were:

Almanzor	Hart
Boabdelin	Kynaston
Abdelmelech	Mohun
Almahide	Mrs Ellen Gwyn
Lyndaraxa	Mrs Marshall
Benzayda	Mrs Boutell

First edition: 1672 (Quarto).
See Allardyce Nicoll, *A History of English Drama, 1660-1900*, I, *Restoration Drama*, 4th edition, 404.

6. AURENG-ZEBE

First performance: November 1675 by the King's Men at Drury Lane. Some of the chief players were:

Aureng-Zebe	Hart
Morat	Kynaston
Old Emperor	Mohun
Nourmahal	Mrs Marshall
Indamora	Mrs Cox

First edition: 1676 (Quarto).
See Nicoll, *History*, I, 405.

7. ALL FOR LOVE

First performance: December 1677 by the King's Men at Drury Lane. Some of the chief players were:

Antony	Hart
Ventidius	Mohun
Cleopatra	Mrs Boutell

First edition: 1678 (Quarto).
See Nicoll, *History*, I, 406.

INDEX

Editors and translators have not normally been indexed except when their opinions have been cited. Figures in italic type refer to an extended discussion of a topic.